D1598468

Members Only

⌐⌐⌐ D⸱

Members Only

Elite Clubs and the Process of Exclusion

Diana Kendall

ROWMAN & LITTLEFIELD PUBLISHERS, INC.
Lanham • Boulder • New York • Toronto • Plymouth, UK

ROWMAN & LITTLEFIELD PUBLISHERS, INC.

Published in the United States of America
by Rowman & Littlefield Publishers, Inc.
A wholly owned subsidiary of The Rowman & Littlefield Publishing Group, Inc.
4501 Forbes Boulevard, Suite 200, Lanham, Maryland 20706
www.rowmanlittlefield.com

Estover Road
Plymouth PL6 7PY
United Kingdom

British Library Cataloguing in Publication Information Available

Library of Congress Cataloging-in-Publication Data:

Kendall, Diana Elizabeth
  Members only : elite clubs and the process of exclusion / Diana Kendall.
    p. cm.
  Includes bibliographical references and index.
  ISBN 13: 978-0-7425-4555-7 (cloth : alk. paper)
  ISBN 10: 0-7425-4555-5 (cloth : alk. paper)
  ISBN 13: 978-0-7425-4556-4 (pbk. : alk. paper)
  ISBN 10: 0-7425-4556-3 (pbk. : alk. paper)
  1. Clubs—United States. 2. Elite (Social sciences)—Social networks—United States.
3. Social capital (Sociology)—United States. 4. Marginality, Social—United States. I.
Title.
  HS2723.K46 2008
  366—dc22   2008001572

Printed in the United States of America

⊗™ The paper used in this publication meets the minimum requirements of
American National Standard for Information Sciences—Permanence of Paper
for Printed Library Materials, ANSI/NISO Z39.48-1992.

Contents

The World of Exclusive Clubs

A popular *New Yorker* cartoon shows two men standing outside an imposing multistory building with high arched windows in Manhattan as one man says to the other, "This is my private club, and you can't come in." This cartoon demonstrates a defining feature of elite clubs: members can—and do—exclude outsiders. Therein lies an important sociological story that must be told in regard to how social stratification and inequality work in the United States. Although some people are like the late comedian Groucho Marx, who played down the importance of private clubs when he said, "I would not join any club that would have someone like me for a member," at a deep psychological level many of us are either pleased that we are members of an exclusive club or alienated by the fact that we will remain outside the walls of such organizations throughout our life.

WHY IS *MEMBERS ONLY* IMPORTANT?

The purpose of *Members Only* is to investigate how elites use the world of exclusive clubs as their private domain to entertain, to conduct business, and to further enhance their social capital. Key topics of sociological interest and concern in this research include how and why club members engage in the process of exclusion and what kinds of social capital members accrue in these clubs that is unavailable to outsiders. The larger concern addressed in this study is how elite organizations such as exclusive clubs serve to maintain and perpetuate class-based privilege and how patterns of social exclusion contribute to the increasing levels of social inequality that we see in the United States and other high-income nations in the twenty-first century.

The Issue of Exclusionary Practices

What is unique about elite clubs? Elite clubs operate on the assumption that their members are "insiders," that everyone else is an "outsider," and that club members have the right to determine who shall or shall not be allowed in their midst. As Phil,[1] a white male respondent, prominent attorney, and member of six exclusive Texas clubs, stated, "In this country we have a God-given right to associate with whomever we please. And, frankly, this includes my right to *not* associate with people I don't want to. If I don't want to be around somebody, why should I have to let them in my club? Let them go start their own club." Phil's perspective on club membership is in keeping with the classical sociologist Max Weber's description of a *closed relationship*—a setting in which the "participation of certain persons is excluded, limited, or subjected to conditions" (Gerth and Mills 1946:139).

For almost three centuries, elite clubs around the world have thrived on closed relationships. The earliest English clubs, such as White's (established in 1736), Boodle's (1762), and Brooks's (1764), all of which still exist today, started as eateries or drinking halls that were open to the general public (meaning men), but before long, a select group of men decided they wanted to privatize the clubs and exclude from membership those individuals with whom they did not wish to associate (see chapter 2). Why did the men decide to turn these open spaces into private clubs? If we apply Weber's idea of open versus closed relationships, the men had a greater expectation that their resources would be enhanced through the use of monopolistic exclusionary tactics in a closed relationship as compared to the greater inclusion of outsiders in an open relationship. In *open relationships* such as voluntary community service organizations, anyone is welcome to join as long as they desire to participate in "mutually-oriented social action" (see Gerth and Mills 1946:139). Although the rewards for participating in an open relationship may be significant in terms of personal fulfillment or community recognition, open organizations do not afford the same level of exclusivity and social capital as that found in many by-invitation-only, elite organizations.

What are the distinguishing characteristics of clubs with closed relationships? One of the first indicators of the closed relationship is found on the outside of the club where "Members Only" signs are prominently posted on the premises. Clubs across the United States have elaborate fences and ornate gates, imposing architectural facades, and well-polished—but brusk—door attendants who discourage the uninitiated from seeking entry. Consider, for example, one journalist's description of the fortification surrounding the Bohemian Grove, a campground set in 2,700 acres of giant redwoods sixty-five miles north of San Francisco, where members and high-profile guests of the prestigious Bohemian Club gather for their annual summer retreat: "Signs abound: No Thru Traffic. No Trespassing. Members and Guests Only. No Turn Around. Sentries scan the paths from above with binoculars, helped out by infrared sensors" (Lara 2004:A1). This level of security and exclusion first caught the attention of the sociologist G. William Domhoff (1974), one of the few sociologists to systematically investigate how elite clubs contribute to ruling-class cohesiveness. My interest in elite clubs grew out of Domhoff's research and my own interest in how social capital and cultural capital are accumulated by women and men in the upper classes and how these forms of capital provide them with social power that money alone cannot purchase.

Social Capital and Cultural Capital in Elite Clubs

Let's look first at the issue of social capital and how it relates to membership in elite clubs. *Social capital* refers to the groups and organizations to which a person belongs and the social networks (who people know) that arise as a result (Kendall 2002). Elite club membership provides individuals a chance to get to know other people over a period of time, to learn which persons are most trustworthy, and to develop networks that can be drawn on as needed. In the words of one respondent in my study, "Other club members are money in the bank when you need to draw out a favor."

Club members typically expect that if they cooperate with other members, they will have reciprocal benefits and will not be exploited or defrauded by other members. Trust is not only a key component of social capital but also one of the most important resources that people expect to gain from social networks such as membership in an elite club (based on Coleman 1994; Putnam 2000; Woolcock 2001). Some elite clubs function very smoothly because they serve as high-trust networks that offer members more rewarding social relations than they usually would find in low-trust networks formed with outsiders (Field 2003). A high value is placed on trust by the privileged in our society. For example, media commentators often focus on President George W. Bush's tendency to rely on people from his long-term inner circle rather than so-called outsiders: "I think Bush is comfortable with him; he's a known commodity; he's trusted," is a statement made by a Republican strategist about a person chosen to be one of Bush's closest advisers (quoted in Stolberg 2007:A22). The emphasis on being "comfortable" with a person who is a "known commodity" and who is "trusted" is in keeping with the Old Boy, Old School approach that typically is found among members of elite clubs.

Most new members join exclusive clubs based on their *bridging social capital*—such as being known to each other for their distinguished reputations in business, industry, finance, education, government, medicine, or the arts. Bridging social capital helps people who are distant acquaintances, moving in somewhat different circles, to become linked to each other through shared interests in club activities and social events. Over time, club members who were originally held together by *bridging* social capital may become united with one another through *bonding* social capital whereby they come to think of other members as very close friends and associates or even become their kin through the marriage of their children. Bonding capital binds together people from similar sociological niches and reinforces their privileged identity as "insiders," whereas everyone else is an "outsider." In studies spanning nearly three decades, the sociologists Mark Granovetter (1973) and Nan Lin (2001) made distinctions in their research between strong ties and weak ties. *Strong ties* connect individuals who consider themselves to be good friends or close professional contacts who are around each other on a fairly regular basis and are more likely to be motivated to be of assistance to each other (Granovetter 1983). Strong ties are based on the *principle of homophily*, which means "love of the same" or "similarity breeds connection" (McPherson, Smith-Lovin, and Cook 2001:415), which suggests that individuals who share such ties tend to enjoy the same things and like being around each other because they share similar interests. By contrast, *weak ties* provide people with access to information and resources beyond those available to them in their own social circle, and these benefits typically come from individuals with whom they do not share much in common with the exception of knowing a mutual friend or professional acquaintance. The term *weak ties* is often used by social scientists to refer to a situation in which a "friend of a friend" is called on to help an individual perform a specific task such as finding a new job. Weak ties may offer people, such as job seekers, a wider range of information about a more diverse set of opportunities than they otherwise might know exists, particularly if they relied only on their strong ties (see Granovetter 1973). Strong ties may be based on *status homophily*, which is rooted in individuals' formal, informal, and ascribed statuses, such as race and gender, or on *value homophily*, which is rooted in individuals' similarities in values, attitudes, and beliefs (Lazarsfeld and Merton 1954; McPherson et al. 2001). In elite private clubs, both status homophily and value homophily are important because they are related to the reasons why people are either included or excluded from these organizations.

When we shift our attention to the issue of cultural capital, we see that this is another important factor in explaining why people join exclusive clubs and why some members wish to exclude outsiders who do not share their cultural attitudes, preferences, and behaviors. In the broadest use of the term, *cultural capital* refers to attitudes, preferences, formal knowledge, behaviors, and goods and credentials. Most analysts using this term also suggest strong class-based linkages between this form of capital and the social class of its possessor (see Lamont and Lareau 1988). Cultural capital is a class-specific concept because the amounts and kinds of cultural capital that an individual possesses are indelibly linked to the person's family background and life experiences. According to the late French social theorist Pierre Bourdieu (1984), cultural capital is both an indicator and a basis of class position. By this statement, Bourdieu means that individuals born into high-income families typically have accumulated the kinds of cultural capital that are most useful to adults and children for getting ahead or staying ahead as compared to the cultural capital that usually accrues to people from lower-income families: the upper classes typically have better educational backgrounds, more experience with "high culture," and extensive world travel, for example. Bourdieu refers to a person's cultural attitudes, preferences, and behaviors as "tastes," and he further points out that tastes are class specific but might be modified by giving young people from the lower classes appropriate schooling and greater exposure to the cultural preferences of the upper classes. In chapters 3 and 4, I look more closely at how social capital and cultural capital relate to the membership selection process and the privileges of members in elite clubs. As I will show, the issue of why "birds of a feather flock together" is related not only to people's feelings of comfort with the familiar—or, in sociological terms, "consciousness of kind"—but also to a distinct feeling on the part of many elite club members that "birds of a different feather" should be sent away to find their own flocks where they supposedly will be more comfortable. Social capital and cultural capital are important concepts in our study of exclusive private clubs because they help us delve inside issues such as how social inclusion and exclusion occur and what effect this process has on larger sociological issues pertaining to growing economic and social inequality.

The Issue of Growing Economic and Social Inequality

Elite social clubs are both a reflection and a perpetrator of larger social inequalities in the United States. As I noted in *The Power of Good Deeds* (Kendall 2002), inequality is perpetuated in many ways in a class-based society, and one of these is through the social organizations of the upper classes.

Most people in the United States are aware of the economic inequality that continues to grow as increasing numbers of households in our country are worth from $10 million to more than $1 billion. Today, the richest 1 percent in the United States earn more than $1.35 trillion a year (Frank 2007). According to Robert Frank (2007), a *Wall Street Journal* writer who has extensively analyzed the New Rich, there are so many new millionaires and billionaires that they have virtually created a self-contained world (which he refers to as *Richistan*) full of expensive cars and private jets, megayachts, world travel, homes in the United States that are like hotels, and three or more additional luxury residences located throughout the world. However, as the richest 1 percent of Americans have gained control of more than one-third of the total wealth in this country, the median incomes for other American households have continue to fall. Not only has this income gap affected the core institutions in our society, including education and the health-care system, but it has also contributed to rampant consumerism, even among those who can least afford to purchase unnecessary "luxury" items (Frank 2007; Kendall 2002).

Unlike economic inequality, which has been the focus of more media reports and public scrutiny in recent years, social inequality rooted in people's networks, levels of prestige, and presence or absence of social and cultural capital has received far less attention. It is true that both Old Rich (those that have had great wealth for several generations) and New Rich families are able to pass on vast economic advantages to their children that are not available to other people. However, in many cases, the Old Guard is able to maintain its top-tier position in the social hierarchy because these families have the ability to control the process of *sponsored mobility*—the process through which individuals come to be accepted in the inner circles of the existing upper social society in a city, state, or nation. Newcomers, regardless of their wealth, must show their compatibility with those who are already in those circles, and the newcomers must be deferential to and supportive of those practices that are held dear by the Old Guard and that serve to maintain elite privilege (Kendall 2002). These clubs are upper-class institutions that protect long-term elites from the New Rich social climbers while also preserving a way of life across generations that gives members a wide variety of opportunities and advantages that nonmembers do not possess. Elite clubs may help some members forget—at least temporarily—the problems that people in other classes face and what is going on in the rest of the world, such as war, environmental pollution, homeless people, and crime. Private clubs offer their members a place to get away from it all and enjoy the leisure and luxury that their money will buy. As one male respondent in his forties stated, "My kids have Disney-World; I have my golf club."

CONDUCTING RESEARCH FOR *MEMBERS ONLY*

The initial research for *Members Only* started with the data I gathered for *The Power of Good Deeds: Privileged Women and the Social Reproduction of the Upper Class* (Kendall 2002), which examines how upper-class women are able to pass on class-based advantages to their children and contribute to the larger societal process of legitimization (maintaining an ideology of class-based and race-based segregation) through their philanthropic activities as members of by-invitation-only elite women's volunteer organizations. During this earlier study based on personal interviews and participant observation, I collected data not only on the women's activities and organizations but also on their husbands' memberships and leadership roles in high-status men's clubs. My ethnographic research started in Austin, Texas, and was made possible by positions I held at that time on the board of directors of the Austin Symphony Orchestra, the board of trustees of the Austin Lyric Opera, and other prestigious social and women's organizations in that city. Several of these organizations held their trustees' meetings and social occasions in exclusive private clubs. My participant observation took place at board meetings, debutante balls, invitational dinner parties, and other social gatherings organized for the purpose of announcing each year's new leadership or "royalty" for these clubs.

For *Members Only*, I interviewed more than 100 male club members, ranging in age from twenty-four to eighty-six. Ninety-five of these members were white (non-Hispanic) while only three were black and two were Latino. I also sifted through my research notes from previous interviews with more than 100 women (many of whom are the wives, daughters, or other relatives of the respondents for this study) to find information regarding these predominantly male-only organizations. I must admit that I sometimes found myself in an awkward position in discussing issues with the male respondents because they typically were more defensive and showed more suspicion about my intentions than the women in my previous study. Some men were particularly unwilling to answer questions about the composition of their club's membership, especially after widespread media coverage of the alleged exclusion of women and/or minorities at exclusive golf clubs such as Augusta National in Georgia. In addition to interviews with club members, I also talked with a number of current or former club employees, most of whom were African American or Latino. I found that even the former club employees are not willing to divulge what happens inside the clubs because the former staff members are often employed by local caterers or other fine restaurants that cater parties thrown by club members.

To round out my research, I conducted a systematic analysis of media accounts and written documents of more than thirty elite men's organization in Texas; in major U.S. cities such as San Francisco, Chicago, New York, and Boston; and in London, England. From content analysis of a variety of media reports—including wedding and death notices of club members and articles about high-society social events—as well as official documents and websites produced by the clubs, I gained a wealth of information about *patterns* of social behavior found in exclusive clubs, including membership practices, social events, and other club activities, and the influence these organizations have on the outside world. The media analysis in *Members Only* was informed by my previous research, published in *Framing Class: Media Representations of Wealth and Poverty in America* (Kendall 2005), which examined how media outlets report on social class in America, particularly the divergent ways in which stories about the upper and upper-middle classes are framed as compared to those involving the middle class, working class, and poor in this country.

Overall, I believe that *Members Only* offers readers new insights on the workings of elite clubs, one of the oldest social institutions of the privileged in the United States, western Europe, and other high-income nations. Although my data were collected primarily in Austin and other Texas cities, I believe that my findings can be generalized to cities throughout the United States where the kinds of clubs I discuss are all found. These include (1) exclusive social clubs "without walls" that are high in prestige and long on tradition but have no need for permanent club facilities, (2) country clubs with manicured lawns and high walls, and (3) city clubs with a view of the members' world.

EXCLUSIVE SOCIAL CLUBS WITHOUT WALLS

Although some elite clubs in my study are highly visible to outsiders because they have elaborate buildings and a high profile in the cities or communities where they are located, other clubs are largely invisible or "wall-less" because they do not have brick-and-mortar locations but rather are comprised of an elite membership network that meets in members' luxurious homes or exclusive city or country clubs for parties and other gatherings. Some of these by-invitation-only clubs are among the most prestigious of men's organizations because they are made up of individuals of high social standing in the community. They are the "Good Old Boy Networks" in the true sense of the phrase, and in states such as Texas, this powerful social connection remains a central way of doing business, participating in politics, and gaining social power for one's family.

In some of the highly exclusive, wall-less men's clubs, it is made very clear to prospective members that club membership belongs only to the man and not to his wife or other family members. James, the top officer in one of the most prestigious men's clubs in Texas, explained how his club handles this situation:

> When we take a prospective member and his wife out for lunch [at an exclusive city club] before deciding whether or not to invite him to membership, it's my job to say to him, "Your membership is not community property. If you die or get a divorce, the membership *does not* pass to your wife. And, the membership isn't hereditary either, so it doesn't pass to your kids. In other words, the membership is yours and yours alone! Are you okay with this?"

This approach is consistent across many elite clubs in Texas and other states because organizational leaders do not want there to be any misunderstanding about who possesses membership in clubs such as the Idlewild Club in Dallas.

As one of the oldest and most prestigious wall-less clubs in the southwestern United States, the Idlewild Club (founded in Dallas in 1884) has been referred to as "THE symbol of high society" (Dallas Historical Society 2006). Idlewild conducts the state's premier debutante ball each year, one in which privileged young women are presented to society and get to meet some of the state's most eligible bachelors. Although changes have been made in the club's structure over time, the prevailing goal of its current members remains to uphold the club's tradition and to continue its rituals. As one journalist stated, "In a town where every charity courts the new rich and the ephemerally famous, Dallas' tradition-bound Idlewild men's club marches discreetly on as it has since 1884" (Peppard 2003). Idlewild members typically are very discreet in providing information about themselves, their organization, or the young women whom they present as debutantes. However, obituaries of members typically list their affiliation with this club as a defining accomplishment in the person's life. For example, the death notice of John Rauscher Jr., who built the well-known investment firm of Rauscher, Pierce and Company, lists the following among his many accomplishments: "He was a past member and past president of Brook Hollow Golf Club. He had been a member of the Dallas Country Club, the Idlewild Club and Terpsichorean Club in Dallas" (Simnacher 2006). In listing these four clubs, this death notice calls attention to the fact that Rauscher, like many other prominent Dallasites, held membership in the most exclusive and most prestigious clubs in that city. As one respondent in my study stated, "Although some of them would surely deny it, the next generation of movers and shakers would give their eye teeth to join Brook Hollow, DCC, Idlewild, and Terpsichorean."

Despite the fact that Idlewild is a men's-only club, the women who are presented as debutantes throughout the years are also proud of their selection by members of this club. This fact is evident to the general public when the women are presented, when they marry, and when they die because their wedding and death notices often indicate that they were "Idlewild debutantes." Consider, for example, the death notice of one ninety-six-year-old Dallas woman: "Hanna Frank Howell: '32 debutante gave time to arts charities. . . . Hanna Frank Howell was an active member of the Dallas social scene for more than 70 years after her debut in 1932. . . . She made her debut in the fall and winter after her graduation from Smith. She attended the Idlewild Club debutante function last fall, her daughter said. 'She certainly was one of the most senior debs still going,' Mrs. Henry said" (Simnacher 2007). Among members of the Old Guard, weddings and death notices are among the only proper places for indicating that one was presented as a debutante by an exclusive club such as the Idlewild of Dallas.

In other Texas cities, many wall-less elite clubs are similar in regard to membership practices, customs, traditions, and club events. The Order of the Alamo (founded in San Antonio in 1909), for example, was originally created for the purpose of selecting a Queen (debutante) to be crowned in an elaborate coronation associated with Fiesta San Antonio, a ten-day, citywide event (Maguire 1990). Throughout the history of the Order of the Alamo, the club's leadership and royalty have been primarily from Old Money or Old Name families (see Haynes 1998). By definition, Old Money families have possessed significant wealth for three or more generations, whereas Old Name families may (or may not) have as much wealth as Old Money families but are known primarily for their well-known family name (Kendall 2002). Sometimes Old Name families are better known for their civic or political involvement than for possessing great wealth. Originally, the Order of the Alamo (1925) was comprised of "some one hundred selected men of recognized social position" and led by its founder, John Carrington, who modeled the club and its coronation on an English model (Haynes 1998). In the 2000s, the Order of the Alamo continues to select King Antonio and other royalty for the annual Fiesta celebration.

Like the Order of the Alamo, the Bachelors Club of Austin (founded in 1933) is an elite group of men who want to promote fellowship and the social season. The first Bachelors Club debutantes were presented in 1951, beginning a lengthy tradition that continues today. The Bachelors Club has active members (single men who are less than forty years of age) and associate members (married men who were active members when they were single and those who are fathers of past or present debutantes).

Although the Bachelors Club is considered to be among the most prestigious clubs for younger men in Austin, older privileged men typically are members of the Admirals Club and/or the Knights of the Symphony. The Admirals Club (founded in 1962) is comprised of married men thirty years of age or older who have shown an interest in socializing with each other, having a good time, and seeing their friends' children or their own daughters presented at the club's annual Coronation Ball, which features themes such as "An Evening in Monte Carlo." The club's hierarchy is organized along the lines of admiralty with some members serving in positions such as Fleet Admiral, Chief of Naval Operations, or Admiral of Finance. Members of the Admirals Club are referred to as "Admiral" (as in Admiral John Doe) in all the club's correspondence and publications. According to one journalist, the Admirals Club roster of members represents the "old Austin" economic elite, and the club's Coronation Ball is nothing short of "the mother of all debutante gigs" (Clark-Madison 1998). For the Coronation Ball and other high-society club events, members wear their club regalia—pale blue nautical coats with tuxedo pants—while nonmembers who attend the ball are easily identified by their traditional black tuxedos.

Another elite wall-less men's club in Austin, the Knights of the Symphony (founded in 1966), is included in my study. Like the "Admirals," members of the Knights of the Symphony are referred to as "Knight So-and-So" in club activities and publications. Club members participate in the annual Jewel Ball, a debutante presentation sponsored by the Women's Symphony League of Austin. Knights typically are husbands of League members or are major contributors to the Austin Symphony Orchestra. During the week of festivities prior to the Jewel Ball, the Knights throw their own party and crown "King Brio," a well-respected club member who is chosen by the Privy Council, a group made up of all past King Brios. At the Jewel Ball, King Brio wears an elaborate crown, robe, and scepter, and he serves as the official escort of the Diamond (queen), who is presented along with her Princesses and the Visiting Jewel Court (college-aged young women who represent other Texas symphony organizations). Although King Brio serves as the Knights' titular head, routine club operations (such as selecting new members or planning parties) is controlled by the Chancery, which includes officers with titles such as Lord Chancellor, Chancellor of the Ceremonies, Chancellor of State, and Vice Chancellor. According to "The Legend of the Knights," this club is "an exclusive organization of Austin business and professional men [that] limits membership to those included by invitation only. The group was determined to be Austin's most prestigious men's group in a survey conducted by an Austin bank" (Knights of the Symphony 2006).

The elite men's clubs without walls that I have described here are only a few of the many prestigious organizations that exist among social elites in Texas cities and throughout the United States. Many of the groups remain exclusively male organizations, but a few have opened their membership on a limited basis to women designated as "Honorary Members," which typically means that they are widows of deceased members. We now turn our attention to two kinds of closed-membership clubs that provide lavish facilities for members: country clubs and city clubs. We will look first at country clubs because, in many Texas cities, the country clubs were established prior to the city clubs.

COUNTRY CLUBS WITH MANICURED LAWNS AND HIGH WALLS

Although wall-less elite clubs have maintained and perpetuated themselves for many years on the basis of strong membership ties, country clubs not only offer members "in-group social capital but they also give them access to luxurious facilities often located on prized real estate in their city" (Mayo 1998). Consider, for example, the physical setting and lush green fairways of clubs such as the Dallas Country Club, Austin Country Club, Houston Country Club, and River Oaks Country Club. Let's take a brief look at each of these clubs because they will be mentioned again later in the book.

Among the apex of elite Texas country clubs is the Dallas Country Club, located in the heart of Highland Park, Texas (an affluent residential community four miles north of downtown Dallas). Part of this club's appeal is the difficulty people have in gaining membership in the club. Another part is the club's physical setting and facilities. A final part is the membership roster, which includes some of the most wealthy and influential Dallasites. If the real estate on which the club is located were sold today, the sale would produce billions of dollars in instant revenue, being located, as it is, in one of the most expensive areas for residential and commercial development in the state. The Dallas Country Club originally was located near downtown Dallas by two English businessmen who decided in 1895 to set up a six-hole golf course and create a hangout for local businessmen and other power players (Miller 1987). In 1912, members moved the Dallas Country Club to Highland Park and built a "magnificent three-story clubhouse" that provided members with a view of lovely, meandering Turtle Creek, which runs through the property (Galloway 1996). Early on, Dallas Country Club became *the* society location for elite events in the city. In 1915, *Dallas Society News* featured the club in its premier edition, and shortly thereafter, the club had become the site of the most fashionable debutante parties, wedding receptions, and dinner dances (Galloway 1996). In the twenty-first century, membership is very difficult to come by, a relatively low membership cap is strictly enforced, and the few who are "lucky enough" (in the words of one respondent) to be invited to membership are required to pay a large initiation fee and monthly dues that do not include other expenses that members may incur for various goods and services, such as meals, spa treatments, and lessons with golf and tennis pros (*D Magazine* 2005).

Exclusive clubs—such as the Dallas Country Club, the Galveston Country Club, and the Artillery Club of Galveston—are often referred to as "Old Guard" clubs because of the history and rich tradition of the clubs and the power and influence that club members wield in the world beyond club walls. Terms such as "Old Guard," "Old Boy," and "Old School" are also used as shorthand for praising the stature of a club and the length of time the club has been in existence. For tradition-bound elites, longevity is a crucial issue in determining the value of anything, ranging from an antique's age or the number of generations that a family has resided in a city or state (such as a seventh-

generation Texan) or, in this case, how long a club has been in continuous operation and how many elite families have been on the membership roster
throughout the club's history. For this reason, members of clubs such as the
Galveston Country Club and the Artillery Club of Galveston sometimes debate which club is the "oldest" and the "best." Galveston Country Club (chartered in 1898) claims to be the oldest country club in *continuous* operation in
Texas. As the club's website indicates, Galveston Country Club was chartered
when Galveston was an important economic center with a flourishing port, a
bustling business district, and a large tourism industry. However, members of
the Galveston Artillery Club believe that the "oldest" distinction belongs to
their club, being founded as it was during the Civil War. Artillery Club members also believe that their club is more exclusive than the Galveston Country
Club because the Artillery Club strictly limits its membership to 100 privileged men, who must live in the Galveston area. The club also sponsors the
prestigious Artillery Club Anniversary Ball, where debutantes have been presented for more than 160 years. An excerpt from a reporter's description of the
ball highlights the intergenerational nature of this social tradition:

> The haute event of the [Galveston social] season is always the prestigious Ar-
> tillery Club Anniversary Ball. Trumpet blasts heralded the beginning of the
> ceremony of the 164th ball [where] tenting over the pool and the dancing wa-
> ters provided a regal background, and crystal chandeliers glowed in the tent
> as copper torches shimmered in the gardens of the club. Tables were gowned
> in champagne crushed silk and accented with candelabra adorned with Os-
> iana roses, Casa Blanca lilies, white tulips, and hydrangea. . . . Debutante Jen-
> nifer Worsham was glorious in diamond white silk satin. . . . She wore pearls
> worn by her mother during [her] own presentation in 1972. . . . The lovely
> Katherine Anne Hughes wore a strapless candlelight gown of Italian cream
> silk and a diamond and pearl necklace worn by her sister during her presen-
> tation in 2002. (Powell 2004)

Tradition, legacy, and staying power are all crucial in the determination
of the "top" clubs in various cities. In addition to country clubs in Dallas and
Galveston, other Old Guard clubs included in my study are located in San
Antonio, Austin, and Houston, where country clubs were established early in
the twentieth century.

Today, the membership rosters of the San Antonio Country Club
(founded in 1904), the Austin Country Club (1904), and the Houston Country Club (1908) list many members who represent Old Money or Old Family
Names. Some of these clubs accept new members with newly minted money
or movers and shakers (often investors or entrepreneurs) who have recently re-
located to the city; however, the majority of club memberships remain in the

hands of the older inner circle because the total number of available member-ships is limited by restrictive caps and exclusionary practices that tend to dis-courage individuals from applying for membership. As one club member in my study stated, "Somebody's got to die, move away, or get kicked out before we have an opening in our membership." Because this attitude is typical of many club members, outsiders tend to view the country club lifestyle as something that is not only beyond their grasp but something they do not want or need. As one respondent who is not a club member stated, "If they don't want me, I certainly don't want them!"

Media reports on club life often report on the snobbery of club members and the exclusionary practices of these organizations, giving nonmembers even more of a feeling that they are not wanted. In an article about country clubs in the Houston area, for example, one journalist stated, "There are three things in Houston money *alone* can't buy: membership in the Houston Coun-try Club, the River Oaks Country Club and the Bayou Club. . . . Collectively, these three clubs form an inviolable social fortress that carefully preserves Houston society" (Miller 1987:123–24).

The Houston Country Club (founded 1908) is described as a "Power House" club because of its rich and famous members, including a number of state and national political elites, high-profile physicians at the Texas Medical Center, billionaire attorneys well known for winning high-profile legal cases, and other extremely wealthy and influential individuals (Seal 1987). By con-trast, River Oaks Country Club (founded in 1922) is known for its impres-sive golf course, 4,000-seat tennis stadium and eighteen courts, and a club-house that resembles a grand southern colonial mansion with a French portico running the length of the second floor. The club is located on a cul-de-sac at the end of River Oaks Boulevard, where it is surrounded by other River Oaks mansions (Miller 1987). "Inside the River Oaks Country Club," one journalist reported, "members admit that the Houston Country Club has more prestige, but for outsiders, River Oaks represents Arrival" (Seal 1987:44). Similar to the setting of the River Oaks Country Club, Houston's Bayou Club has a Louisiana plantation–style clubhouse with a large, well-manicured lawn located in the middle of a magnolia-studded clearing. This club has a very limited membership comprised of "ultrarich, ultrainfluential" people who enjoy polo, fine dining, and rubbing shoulders with older elites such as former President George Herbert Walker Bush (Kleiner 2002).

In the twenty-first century, an overlap exists in Texas between what we might consider to be country clubs and city clubs because, as the population of various cities has grown dramatically, a club that started as a country club in a suburb or outlying area (such as a horse farm) is now located well within what most people consider to be the city proper. What is distinct about most country clubs, as compared to city clubs, is the emphasis on recreational and leisure activities, family-centered events, and a more informal atmosphere overall (except at black-tie events) than is characteristic of most city clubs, where the daytime focus is on elaborate luncheon buffets and members' business and social networking, while the nighttime focus is on fine dining, wine tasting, and special holiday events (such as an annual club Christmas party or a Fourth of July celebration where members and their families dine at the club, are entertained, and watch fireworks from high above the crowds gathered below).

CITY CLUBS WITH A VIEW OF THE (MEMBERS') WORLD

Most city clubs in Texas are located on the top floors of high-rise downtown buildings. Clubs such as the Petroleum Club of Dallas and the Headliners Club of Austin boast of panoramic views of the cities in which they are located. As social analysts have pointed out, clubs "high in the sky" offer a *vista*, a symbolic *topos*, or place of social identity for members (see Brook 1985; Herman 1999). Club members literally and figuratively are able to "look down" on other people and on the city that the members (or their ancestors) helped to create. Referring to this phenomenon as the *power of view*, sociologist Andrew Herman (1999:11) describes how one wealthy entrepreneur looked out at the panoramic city view from his seventy-sixth-floor club:

> The world below is his community, not simply in terms of the community being a *space* of involvement but, more importantly, in terms of it being a topos or place of sovereignty and moral identity. It is a space that he can claim as his own, upon which he is able to inscribe his desire, values, and priorities. Thus, his gesture to the world below is not simply a gesture of inclusion ("I am part of what I see"); it is also a gesture of appropriation and possession ("what I see is part of me").

This man's claim to "ownership" is not unusual for members of city clubs, particularly those who have been actively involved in politics, business, and investment: they tend to "appropriate" and "possess" certain aspects of the vista as their own. For example, members of the Headliners Club of Austin (founded in 1954) who graduated from the University of Texas and have given large sums of money to the school or who merely have attended the football games there may mentally claim ownership of the university when they see school's glowing tower and extensive campus on the horizon beyond the windows of their twenty-first-floor club. Other Headliners members claim ownership of the state capitol if they have served in the state government or been elected to the legislature because the dome of the capitol is also visible from some of the club's floor-to-ceiling windows.

Most of the city clubs in my study were founded between 1930 and 1950, when the Texas economy was growing rapidly because of vast expansions in the oil, banking, and insurance industries. The Dallas Petroleum Club (founded in 1934), for example, claims to have "evolved from a fraternity of prominent oil men into one of the finest private city clubs in the country." According to club literature, the Dallas Petroleum Club (2005) provides "a spirit of pride and tradition" because some of its members were able to become rich by making "something out of what appeared to be nothing" in the oil business. Although Petroleum Clubs located throughout the state were for members in the oil business, some other city clubs focused on different membership populations, including businessmen, politicians, or journalists. The Headliners Club of Austin, for example, was created "to foster communication and camaraderie between those who are *in the news* and those who *report the news*" (Headliners Club 1992). The founders of this club sought to bring together politicians, journalists, and outstanding citizens so that they could interact with each other, give awards for excellence in journalism, and provide scholarships for students pursuing a career in journalism. Across the decades, well-known print and television journalists, including Walter Cronkite, Dan Rather, and Tom Brokaw, have been club members, as have many individuals who are frequently "in the news" because of their roles as business leaders, politicians, or socialites. In the 2000s, the Headliners Club Foundation continues to raise money for college scholarships for young people interested in pursuing a career in the media. Overall, however, the Headliners Club—like other influential city clubs—is known first and foremost for its influential membership. An article reporting the sale of the building in which the club is located, for example, included this statement: "The building is best known for its Headliners Club, a private club that is frequented by powerhouses, including politicians, business leaders and others" (Novak 2006:D2).

City clubs typically are owned by the membership and guided by an active board of directors or a board of trustees that is made up of well-respected club members who are elected to maintain and perpetuate the club's viability and to protect the club's membership ranks. However, as more corporations moved their business operations from the central city and more upper-middle- and upper-class Texas families bought residences away from what they perceived to be the "inner city" and its problems, the leaders of some city club leaders found that they were going to have to be more open in their membership requirements to bolster the club's membership roster. An example is the City Club in Dallas (founded in 1918, closed during the Great Depression, and officially chartered in 1941), which offers incentives for existing members to bring in new members. Information received by members about the Annual City Club Holiday Party, for example, included the following statement: "Bring a Prospective Member to the Holiday Party and It's Free." Members were informed that if their prospective member joined the club before the beginning of the next year, the member would receive a credit (up to a $200 value for a couple) against the cost of the ticket to the Holiday Party (City Club of Dallas 2007).

Actively seeking new members obviously does not mean that a club's social standing in the community is diminished. In many exclusive city clubs, the Old Guard maintains control of the leadership structure. Membership applications typically require that two or more members serve as sponsors for a prospective member, and hefty initiation fees and monthly dues discourage the less affluent from considering club membership. However, some clubs are more lenient in how they enforce membership requirements, such as this statement on the website of the City Club of Dallas:

> All applications for membership shall be made to the Board of Directors in writing. Two Sponsors are required at the time the application is submitted. *If for any reason said applicant does not currently know two members, arrangements can be made for said applicant to be introduced to members of the Membership Committee.* [emphasis added]

This concession that a person who does not know club members might actually be considered for membership certainly would not be found among many of the most prestigious city, country, and wall-less social clubs in my study, where being well known and liked by other members is a crucial factor considered by the membership committee.

The most exclusive clubs typically do not have to seek out new members because the membership ranks are refreshed by legacy members. It is not unusual for three or four generations of family members to participate in club events, and the newsletters of these organizations often show several generations gathered for a wedding reception or anniversary party at the club. For example, San Antonio's Argyle Club (founded in the 1850s) has a strictly controlled membership cap of about 1,000 members, and some social analysts believe that nearly half the current membership is made up of legacy members. Located in a former mansion in Alamo Heights, an incorporated area of San Antonio known for Old Money and Old Name families, the Argyle Club has long been associated with elite families not only in that city but throughout the state as well. As one journalist stated, "This membership *means* something to people" (Seal 1987:44).

LOOKING AHEAD

In *Members Only*, I will show how club membership is important to individuals and families in the top tiers of the U.S. economic and social hierarchies. Although some members have vast and ever-growing amounts of economic and sometimes political capital, elite private clubs uniquely provide them with a source of identity, vast amounts of easily accessible social and cultural capital, and the ability to exclude those whom they do not want in their inner circle of friends and acquaintances. But are elite clubs still relevant in the outside world of the twenty-first century? This issue is further addressed in other chapters of *Members Only*.

In chapter 2, I describe how elite U.S. clubs were patterned on the gentlemen's clubs of London, including the *material cultural dimensions* of club life—the physical or tangible (visible) creations of a club's members—and the *nonmaterial cultural dimensions*—the abstract or intangible (largely invisible) creations of club members. The chapter shows how members of contemporary city, country, and wall-less men's clubs in the United States have found justification for their exclusionary membership practices and sometimes snobbish behavior in the gentlemen's clubs of London.

Chapter 3 examines the formal membership processes of elite city and country clubs and compares this approach with the more informal (but even more exclusionary) manner in which wall-less elite men's clubs typically select new members. This chapter focuses on specific patterns of exclusion based on class, race, ethnicity, religion, gender, and sexual orientation that greatly limit diversity in contemporary elite clubs.

In chapter 4, I describe the privileges and benefits that people gain when they join an exclusive club and show how new members learn about their club privileges and responsibilities. I explain the methods by which new and established members enhance their social and cultural capital through participation in the club's programs, social events, and rituals. Finally, chapter 4 addresses an underlying sociological question regarding privilege in elite clubs: if members ("insiders") have much to gain from their clubs, what—if anything—do nonmembers ("outsiders") lose by not being members?

Chapter 5 explains how exclusive clubs help members and their guests make the right political connections and build careers in (or that are aided by) the local, state, and/or federal government. The chapter describes how club-member lobbyists are a crucial linkage between other club members, major campaign contributors, and current and future politicians who need their support. It also examines how national and international networks of private clubs enable members to enjoy reciprocal membership benefits throughout the United States whereby they are able to further enhance these important political and economic linkages.

In chapter 6, I describe why individual and organized efforts to change the practices of elite clubs in the United States and the United Kingdom have succeeded in some areas but not in others. The chapter discusses lawsuits that have been filed, laws that have been passed regarding discrimination in private clubs, and the responses of clubs to these efforts to bring about changes in their exclusionary practices. Chapter 6 also describes why some New Rich individuals prefer clubs where their money is always welcome regardless of their own pedigrees.

Chapter 7 returns to the basic question of why the exclusionary practices of elite clubs should matter to people when there are so many other pressing social problems to consider. In this chapter, I raise the larger question about exclusionary practices in all areas of social life, including other social organizations and institutions, that may affect an individual's life chances and opportunities. I hope that as we learn more about the practices of elite clubs, we will also consider the many other areas of social life where people are categorically excluded and how these practices tarnish the principles of democracy and equality on which the United States of America was founded.

NOTE

1. The names of all of the respondents in my study are pseudonyms. To protect the privacy of each respondent and his or her family, I have not revealed anyone's true identity. As is true of all sociological research, it is the responsibility of the researcher to protect the identity of those who agree to participate in a study as those who are the "subjects" in observational research.

· 2 ·

Exclusion and Snobbery Take a Trip
from London to America

$\mathcal{A}$s discussed in chapter 1, elite private clubs in the United States operate on the assumption that their members are "insiders," that everyone else is an "outsider," and that club members have the right to determine who shall and who shall not be allowed in their midst. How did this come about? According to social historians Charles Graves and James Mayo, London was the birthplace of the exclusive gentlemen's club, and privileged men in America wanted to model all aspects of U.S. club life, including the membership process, on the British model:

> Clubland is a purely English invention. The Travellers' in Paris, the Oglethorpe in Savannah, the Knickerbocker in New York, the St. James's in Montreal, the Rand in Johannesburg would never have seen the light of day if Francesco Bianco [aka Francis White] had not started White's and if two Coldstream Guards officers had not invented the first members' club in St. James. (Graves 1963:xv)

> No committee received more attention than the admissions committee. Its procedures were explicit, because it selected the candidates who received club membership and a concomitant gain in social status. The rules governing entry into the American club were clearly British in origin, and the social consequences were significant. (Mayo 1998:13)

Based on the English model, U.S. elites built clubhouses in this country that looked (and many of which still look) very much like those in London, and by the same token they also adopted written (and unwritten) rules, policies, and procedures similar to those of the British clubs to fit their own clubs. Privileged men in the United States embraced the English notion of the unwritten "gentlemen's agreement" regarding membership from London's finest clubs and incorporated this idea into their own elite organizations: they were entitled to exclude anyone they wanted from membership or from visiting the club as a guest on the basis of whatever criteria the members desired to utilize—criteria that today might not be legal outside the private club environment.

Although—as discussed later in this book—many elite "members only" clubs in the United States may have relaxed (somewhat) the rigid formal or informal rules they once had regarding exclusion of individuals from membership based on race, ethnicity, sex, religion, or sexual orientation, vestiges of those rules remain in their membership practices, and it is therefore important to understand how elite clubs in the United States found moral and social justification for their elitism and snobbery from the gentlemen's clubs of London.

THE EXCLUSIVE CLUB AND THE
PRIVATE CLUBHOUSE COME TO AMERICA

Throughout modern history, U.S. elites have been strongly influenced by the lifestyles and possessions of the British royalty and other privileged citizens of the United Kingdom, and the development of exclusive social clubs is no exception. As one of the founders of New York's Union Club stated, "If [the Union Club] can be gotten up like the English clubs, it may succeed; little short of that will meet the views of the members" (Porzelt 1982:4). In the United States, many elite clubs were founded by affluent men of Anglo-Saxon descent who had a strong desire to emulate the British way of life in their homes, churches, and clubs. We particularly see the English influence on elite U.S. clubs in two important ways: (1) the establishment of clubs that were highly exclusive and exclusionary and (2) the shift from holding the clubs' social gatherings in public places—where members had no choice but to interact with "outsiders" and were subject to community scrutiny—to meeting in their own clubhouses, which were closed to nonmembers and were outside of public view.

Exclusivity and Exclusion: From Public Accommodations to Private Sanctuaries

In England and the United States, the earliest gentlemen's clubs were founded in local coffeehouses or taverns; however, it soon became apparent to privileged men, first in London and then in the United States, that they should create an exclusive membership club with a fixed clubhouse rather than relying on public accommodations for their social gatherings. An examination of the histories of a number of gentlemen's clubs shows that a fairly rapid transition occurred from club members meeting in public to conducting all official club activities in private settings.

White's is the oldest and still one of the most prestigious London clubs and is a good example of this transition. Its existence began at White's Chocolate House, and within this public coffeehouse, members of the British aristocracy and other wealthy and influential men formed an "inner club" that they referred to as the "Old Club." Not too long after the Old Club was founded, it became known as White's and moved to its own clubhouse, which, even today, is one the most impressive buildings in London's West End. Boodle's, the second-oldest London club, was founded in Almack's Tavern (where a man named "Boodles" was head waiter). Shortly thereafter, Almack acquired the building adjoining his tavern and set it up as a clubhouse "for the sole use of a society founded upon certain rules" (Graves 1963:6).

The same process occurred in the United States. The Philadelphia Club, one of the country's oldest, originated in Mrs. Rubicam's Coffee House, but the club soon moved to the Adelphi Building and later to the former mansion of one of the city's wealthiest families. Truly following the British model, the Old Colony Club of Plymouth, Massachusetts, originally held its gatherings in a local tavern but then established a "proper" clubhouse that received praise from the local newspaper: "The Old Colony Club has in these new quarters as elegantly appointed rooms as can be found outside the Hub, and the fitting is highly creditable to the taste and good judgment of those having it in charge" (Old Colony Club 2007).

Perhaps one of the seven founders of the Old Colony Club put into words what many elite club members were thinking when they decided to stop meeting in local taverns and coffeehouses and instead to rent a club building or buy their own clubhouse: He stated that Old Colony Club members wanted their own club facilities so that they could "avoid the many disadvantages and inconveniences that arise from intermixing with the company at the taverns in this town of Plymouth" (Old Colony Club, 2007). Rather than having to jostle with the "company" that frequented the local tavern, elite club members wanted to hobnob with their peers ("our kind of people") but not deal with individuals they considered to be beneath them ("not our kind of people"). Starting a permanent, by-invitation-only club and establishing a fixed clubhouse that was open to "members only" was the ideal solution to this problem: the clubhouse provided members with a sanctuary away from their homes and offices where they could visit with acquaintances, eat, drink, gamble, sleep, read, and enjoy themselves with like-minded men (Rogers 1988).

If we shift our focus from earlier centuries to the late twentieth and early twenty-first centuries, we find that exclusive clubs and the privacy that their clubhouses provide to members continue to have great appeal for many people, as reflected in this quotation from a popular business publication:

> Belonging to the right club still confers a measure of prestige and status on members. It allows entree to the most powerful and connected in a community—great for contact-hungry lawyers, bankers, or job-hunters—and it provides a way to impress out-of-town visitors and clients. Just as important, private clubs remain a comfy retreat from the day's pressures, a place to meet friends, enjoy a superior meal, or just read—often without the inconveniences of today's crowded and service-less culture. Clubs offer exclusivity, dress codes, and, more often than not, Old World ambience. (*BusinessWeek* 1997)

As this statement suggests, people who are members of the "right club" are able to enhance their social capital through their associations with individuals who are influential and well connected in the community. "Old World ambience" or its modern-world equivalent is part of the cachet that many elite private clubs offer to their members in order to enhance the club experience. Here, again, we see a strong and continuing British influence on elite American clubs.

The Clubhouse: Adopting the English Model of Stately Segregation

From the gentlemen's clubs of London, American club members learned that stately segregation of the upper class from the rest of humanity could be accomplished by the location of the clubhouse and its architectural styling. Having the "right address" in the midst of the wealthy and powerful but away from the poorer masses was essential for the most prestigious clubs: club buildings should be located on valuable real estate in a wealthy area of the city. For London's gentlemen's clubs, this exclusive location was the city's West End, where, at one time, so many stately clubs lined the streets of St. James and Pall Mall that the area became known as "clubland" (Porzelt 1982). Elite American men who visited the London clubs realized that their own clubhouses in this country should be located in or near wealthy neighborhoods, such as Fifth Avenue in New York, Beacon Street and Commonwealth Avenue in Boston, and the areas known as Union Square and Nob Hill in San Francisco. Looking more closely at San Francisco, for example, the Bohemian Club and the Olympus Club have been located for many years on adjoining blocks only a short distance from the world-famous Union Square. These clubs, along with their rural retreats, such as the Bohemian Grove, seventy-five miles northwest of San Francisco, have had the "right address" across multiple generations of club members. Similarly, since its inception in 1852, the Pacific-Union Club has stood at the crest of Nob Hill, high above the city proper, in a Second Empire chateau-style, sandstone mansion that serves as its clubhouse. The club building and its surrounding manicured grounds occupy an entire city block in an area that is known for its wealthy residents, stately old hotels, a "blue-blood" Episcopal church, and the highest point in the city to which the historic cable cars travel.

In addition to its prestigious location, the clubhouse of the Pacific-Union Club exemplifies another important influence of British club life on American clubs: former townhouses and mansions of the wealthy can easily be transformed into outstanding clubhouses, and these locations add prestige to the club and its members. A number of London's gentlemen's clubs are located in the former townhouses of the aristocracy, providing even those club members who are not royalty with the ability to enjoy the trappings of royalty. Even the mansions of the New Rich provided an excellent location and facilities for members of clubs such as San Francisco's Pacific-Union, where the clubhouse was the former mansion of the Gilded Age "Bonanza King" James C. Flood, who originally operated a saloon but made his fortune in the stock exchange and Nevada's silver mines. Flood spent lavishly on his mansion, including the Connecticut brownstone he had imported for the mansion's facade and its ornamental fence constructed of bronze and thick slabs of the brownstone, which created an attractive but visible barrier to his property—the same visible barrier that today keeps nonmembers at a distance from the clubhouse.

Locating elite clubs in the former residences of the wealthy and powerful provided club members with lavish buildings that often contained elaborate, curving staircases and large, ornate, high-ceilinged rooms with massive crystal chandeliers. Although the clubhouses varied, many included large reading or sitting rooms, dining rooms with snowy white tablecloths, libraries with heavy wooden paneling, billiards rooms, smoking rooms, and coffee rooms in which, according to historians, coffee was the one thing not usually consumed (Lejeune and Lewis 1984).

Privileged men in the United States easily adopted the British idea of locating their clubs in former townhouses or mansions because a number of these residences became available in such cities as New York and Chicago when rich families in the nineteenth century moved to outlying areas where they could build even larger residences and remove themselves from their city's growing social problems (Cable 1984).

In Texas, where my research was conducted, a similar pattern exists of elite club members often either establishing club facilities in former mansions or building new clubhouses as replicas of older estate homes. San Antonio's Argyle Club is located in a stately southern mansion, a Louisiana plantation-style clubhouse is home to Houston's Bayou Club, and the clubhouse for the

River Oaks Country Club emulates in impressive architectural styling (and in its large, carefully manicured grounds) the multi-million-dollar residential properties that surround it. An exception to this practice is found in many of the downtown city clubs, which do not occupy a separate building like the elite city clubs of London, New York, Boston, Chicago, and San Francisco but rather are usually located on the top floors of high-rise office buildings or in historic buildings in the downtown area. The explanation for this difference may be attributed to the fact that elite Texas clubs typically were founded later than those in the northeastern and western United States because Texas has been a state for slightly more than 150 years and, for many years, the economy in this state was dominated by agriculture, with two-thirds of the populace living in rural areas. Early in the twentieth century, however, the rapid growth of businesses such as banking and finance; the wide-scale urban expansion of cities such as Houston, Dallas, and San Antonio; and the Texas oil boom led to the development of elite city and country clubs. For example, petroleum clubs were founded throughout the state by prominent oilmen, but these clubs evolved into distinguished city clubs with members in business, finance, education, government, medicine, and the arts as well as oil and gas executives. Today, although these clubs are located on the top floors of prestigious downtown buildings, their interiors include many of the same treasured features—such as antiques, oil paintings, massive libraries, and elaborate dining facilities and sitting areas—that are found in the gentlemen's clubs of London and in Old Guard private clubs in New York City.

One of the prestigious downtown clubs in Texas is the Headliners Club of Austin. The club's official history describes the influence of an exclusive California club—the Bohemian Club—on Charles E. Green, who founded the Headliners in 1954:

> During his service with the Navy in World War II, Green had occasion to visit a number of gentlemen's clubs, including the renowned Bohemia [*sic*] Club of San Francisco. After returning to Austin, Green envisioned a similar club for the Capital City—an ambient setting for the exchange of thoughts and ideas between those involved with the arts and sciences, business and politics, and those in the news media. With his good friends, Robert and Pearle Ragsdale, who owned a flying service in Austin, Green made frequent trips in those post-war years to visit clubs all over the country. (Powers 1992:3)

Although city clubs such as the Headliners Club have remained in downtown locations, country clubs have had a wider variety of locations and a number of specific issues to deal with in regard to exactly where the clubs should be located within an array of suburban or sometimes semirural areas that are available for purchase. For some Texas country clubs, the debate among club members over where to locate the clubhouse and its accompanying facilities has been intricately intertwined with issues of race and class. The debate over the location of the Austin Country Club (ACC) is one example of many that might show how and why such issues arise in elite clubs.

The Most Desirable Club Locations in Texas: Racism and Classism?

Because of the extensive residential and social segregation—based on race and class—that exists in many cities in Texas (and in other states as well), social elites have had definite ideas about what constitutes an acceptable (or an unacceptable) location for everything, particularly their residences and their private clubs. Although many privileged people seldom talk about such concerns in public, they have extensive discussions in private about the best neighborhoods, problems with race in their city, and how to protect their children from individuals (such as the homeless) who might harm them. As one respondent in my study concisely stated, "We want to stay on the right side of the tracks."

In some Texas cities, a major highway or a river that runs through town is the equivalent of the railroad tracks that might divide a city socially and economically. In Austin, for example, Interstate 35 divides the historically "white" (non-Hispanic) west side of the city from the historically "black" (African American) and "brown" (Hispanic/Mexican American/Latino) east side. In the past—but to a lesser degree today—wealthy and powerful white residents of Austin almost universally lived, worked, and played on the west side, whereas people of color and recent immigrants resided on the east side. When ACC was founded in 1899, its initial membership list contained many early pioneer families of Austin and read like "Who's Who" in Texas (Austin Country Club 2007), and the club was located in a prestigious residential and commercial area near the University of Texas campus—west of Interstate 35. In the late 1940s, when more space was needed for club facilities, ACC moved to a southeast Austin location on Riverside Drive. For more than thirty years, the club was located east of Interstate 35 in a somewhat underdeveloped, mixed-land-use area that provided ACC with relatively inexpensive property for its large clubhouse, golf course, swimming pool, tennis courts, and other club facilities. However, within several miles from the country club, most of the population was made up of a community of African Americans who had lived in the area for many years, an increasing number of Mexican Americans and lower-income white (non-Hispanic) Americans, and a growing population of college students who could find cheaper apartments in the area than were available near the University of Texas campus. As Austin continued to grow in population and the diversity of its racial and ethnic composition, ACC members frequently held discussions and sometimes engaged in bitter arguments over where the club should be located. One segment of the membership wanted to move the club to a more desirable location in a prestigious new subdivision being built in far west Austin that would be closer to members' homes. Another segment wanted the club facilities to remain where they were because of the club's relatively close proximity to the state capitol and downtown office buildings where many members had their offices. Other factors such as the safety of club members and their families were considered as well: in the words of one club member, "I wanted the club located where my wife and kids could feel safe coming and going, even in the evening." Eventually, ACC was moved to the exclusive Davenport Ranch subdivision, located off Highway 360 in far west Austin, in a setting about as far removed geographically as the club could get at that time from east Austin but still be near the most affluent residential neighborhoods. Ironically, one of the sticking points about moving the club facilities to Davenport Ranch was the fact that the club was going to have to make a concession to the developer of the area in order to get the land they wanted for the price they wanted to pay. The developer wanted the purchase price of some homesites to include a membership in the country club; however, this was not agreeable to club members who wanted their club to be more, not less, exclusive as a result of relocating the club's facilities. Eventually, a compromise was reached between the club and the land developer whereby only a limited number of properties in early stages of the subdivision's development would offer a membership in the country club, and home owners who chose the club membership option would be required to pay the same initiation and monthly fees as all other members.

It is important to note that many factors other than race and class are involved in the selection of a site for elite clubs such as ACC. Country clubs often need larger facilities to accommodate a growing membership, and relocation of the residences of wealthy and influential club members makes it necessary for some clubs to move from one area of a city to another to ensure the club's survival. Obviously, the old adage that the most important thing in real estate is "location, location, location" applies to the placement of exclusive clubs. In addition to the club's location, the appearance and quality of the clubhouse and other club facilities are important in maintaining members and attracting desirable new ones.

Designing Clubhouses as Bastions of Privilege:
Importing English and Italian Architecture

Privileged American men who traveled to London and visited the most prestigious gentlemen's clubs were impressed with (and, for their own clubhouses, emulated) the architectural styling of the English clubhouses. The stately architecture of many of London's gentlemen's clubs inspired U.S. elites to build elaborate clubhouses that reflected the best of Georgian or Regency style. For example, Stanford White and Charles McKim, who became New York's foremost clubhouse architects, derived many of their designs from the English clubs. New York City's Metropolitan Club, designed by the firm of McKim, Mead and White, was modeled on the Italian Renaissance Palazzo style of London's Reform Club, where Sir Charles Berry had introduced this style of architecture to England after his extensive travels in Italy (Porzelt 1982).

Georgian-style clubhouses typically have reddish brick walls, with courses and cornices of white stone and trimmings of white painted woodwork. The Regency style of architecture found in other British clubhouses is similar to neoclassical Georgian style, including the bow window on the ground floor, but these clubs often have a white stucco facade and an entryway to the main front door (usually painted black) that is framed by two columns. Some clubs have wrought-iron fences at the ground level and wrought-iron railings on upper-level balconies. According to one social historian, stately Georgian and Regency clubhouses not only spell grandeur for their members but, through their architecture, also send a visual message to outsiders: "Members Only: All Others Stay Out!" (Graves 1963).

The bow window is a classic example of an architectural feature in clubs that sends such a "go away" message and reflects elite club members' attitudes toward outsiders. At London's Boodle's club, for example, the table of honor was situated in front of the bow window. When Sir Winston Churchill sat there to smoke his cigar, a crowd of onlookers typically watched him in admiration: "I like this club," Churchill is reported to have said (Lejeune and Lewis 1984:62). Over the years, other club members in England and America have shown their assumed superiority over the masses outside their bow windows while looking out at the world from the comfort of their club. An anecdotal story is told of one duke who was fond of sitting near Boodle's bow window on a rainy day because he could enjoy "watching the damned people get wet" (Lejeune and Lewis 1984:62). From this club tale, it is apparent that some club members liked to think of themselves as physically separated from outsiders and socially superior to them.

Whether in England or in the United States, the architectural design of an elite clubhouse does more than provide members with a grand backdrop for their social interactions: the physical appearance of these clubs may also intimidate and discourage "the masses" from attempting to enter the premises. If the physical structure alone does not have this effect on people, clubs often have other reminders such as "Members Only" signs, fences and gates, doormen and other security personnel, and cameras and other surveillance equipment to control access to the club facility and keep intruders away.

The symbolic value of an elite clubhouse is as great, if not greater, than its actual use value: for centuries, the British clubhouse has been a male bastion of privilege that serves as a visible reminder of the members' prestige. Privileged men in the United States accepted this belief and created their own clubs in a similar manner in order to gain esteem for themselves and their clubs. According to social theorist Thorstein Veblen (1953:42), "In order to gain and to hold the esteem of men it is not sufficient merely to *possess* wealth or power. The wealth or power must be *put in evidence*, for esteem is awarded only in evidence." The clubhouses of the privileged in England and the United States were built in such a way as to "put in evidence" the power and wealth of club members and help them gain higher levels of social esteem. The written (and sometimes unwritten) rules governing membership practices in elite clubs bolstered their exclusivity and privilege.

BRITISH CLUBABILITY AND
BLACKBALLING COME TO AMERICA

One of the major contributions of elite London clubs to those in the United States was the establishment of elaborate criteria for membership that made it possible to reject any person who was not deemed to be a social equal of current members. The clubs' constitutions provided for a board of governors to create club rules and to establish various committees, including one of the most important—the membership committee. The benefits and costs of seeking membership in early elite clubs was particularly great: to become a member of a highly prestigious club was to increase one's social capital and prestige; however, to be rejected for membership was to be devalued not only in the eyes of club members but also in the community at large.

The Gentlemen's Club and the "Clubable Disposition"

In the early gentlemen's clubs of London, having a "clubable disposition" was the most important criteria for membership. Having a clubable disposition meant that a person was sociable and congenial and that he would be able to interact well with other club members. The most exclusive U.S. men's clubs embraced the British idea of the clubable disposition but, finding that terminology cumbersome, based their own membership criteria on the idea that an individual must be considered a "gentleman" by all who know him. In the words of John Bradley, a member of the Admissions Committee for New York's Knickerbocker Club in the 1980s, "The chief criterion for selection

really is that the candidate be a gentleman—a fair-minded, open and dis-
passionate man, of good sense and good taste" (Masello 1989:272). The key
word in this statement is *gentleman*: in both England and the United States,
male club members did not believe that women were clubable and they believed that many men were not "gentlemen" enough in the true sense of the
word to merit an invitation to join the club.[1]

Blackballing and Exclusion

The rules of most early British gentlemen's clubs gave every member an opportunity to decide who the new members would (and would not) be by casting his
ballot on each candidate who was proposed. The founders of these clubs typically believed that a club should be self-perpetuating: in other words, the existing members should be the ones who chose the new members because some day
these individuals would be the replacements of existing members when they re-
signed from the membership or died. One of the earliest methods of casting bal-
lots was through the use of a wooden box into which each member placed either
a small white or a black ball to cast his vote. A white ball indicated a vote of "yes"
for admitting a particular candidate; a black ball signified "no," that this individual should be rejected for membership. In many clubs, only one or two blackballs
were required to reject a candidate for membership. Individuals who received a
sufficient number of "no" votes to be excluded were said to have been "blackballed" by the members. Balloting with white and black balls was an effective
way for members to decide whom they wanted or did not want in their club;
however, some disgruntled members voted against virtually all proposed new
members and nearly wrecked their clubs because it became impossible to replace
members who no longer paid their dues or participated in club life. The attitude
of members who were quick to blackball most candidates is revealed in this 1870
statement by a Garrick Club member: "It would be better . . . that ten unobjec-
tionable men should be excluded than that one terrible bore should be admitted"
(Lejeune and Lewis 1984:14). Clearly, this club member believed that if a candidate for membership was a "bore," he was not "clubable." Gradually, elite clubs
in London created more specific rules about how many blackballs must be cast
by members for a candidate to be rejected. For example, the Travellers Club of
London rules stated that "the members elect by ballot. When 12 and under 18
members ballot, one black ball, if repeated, shall exclude; if 18 and upwards ballot, two black balls exclude, and the ballot cannot be repeated. The presence of
12 members is necessary for a ballot" (Dickens 1888).

English membership rules, including blackballing as a method of voting
for candidates, were adopted by many U.S. clubs where members were adamant

about maintaining their club's exclusivity. As an example, consider this report on membership at New York's Union Club:

> Of course, social struggles and bickerings of the bitterest sort have been engendered by this exclusiveness and occasionally contemptuous snubbing by the representatives of the first families, of applicants and candidates of wealth, *though of undemonstrated pedigree*: it being a canon and proverb of *habitués* that a man is to be black-balled, unless he has not only a father but a grandfather, and is a hidalgo in the old Castilian sense. Some few deficient in grandfathers have been admitted, but only with great misgivings as to precedent. (Fairfield 1975:63)

Although it was unlikely in the early years of elite U.S. clubs that a candidate for membership would have a father or grandfather previously in the club, members of the most prestigious clubs instead chose factors such as the country of origin of a proposed member's family, his religion, and whether he might have Old Money or an Old Family Name. Similar to the British clubs, a number of U.S. clubs had difficulty replacing departed members because of the blackballing process. At New York's Knickerbocker Club, according to an 1897 newspaper account, nearly every person proposed for membership that year was blackballed: "The result was that the club house was nearly always empty. It was a standing joke for some years that there was an agreement among certain of the younger members that they would take turns in sitting at the front windows so as to prove to the world at large that there was at least one solitary soul in the precincts" (Dunn 1971:41). Although this statement probably exaggerated the problems experienced by the Knickerbocker Club, club members apparently were sufficiently concerned about the effects of the blackballing process that they changed their club's bylaws to give the board of governors authority over membership decisions. Members were allowed to nominate or second candidates for membership, but only the board of governors participated in the final decision-making process.

To determine the extent to which blackballing is now or ever was an issue in elite Texas clubs, one of my research questions asked respondents about blackballing and other methods of voting on new members. I was informed by all the city and country club members and officers I interviewed that no such practice exists today and, in most cases, that none had ever existed in their club. However, members of several wall-less elite men's clubs recall how older members referred to a ballot box with black and white balls that was used for voting "in their day." Current club members still speak of "blackballing" a proposed member, but they are speaking figuratively about the act of rejecting a membership candidate, not of actually dropping a blackball into a ballot box. The following statement by one respondent, Eric, explains how his wall-less men's club shifted from blackballing candidates to what he referred to as a more civilized process:

> I think [club] did use black balls at one time. My great uncle mentioned something about that to me, as a joke ("Ha-ha!"), when I was up for membership. But we use a more civilized process now: at our annual membership meeting we've already received information about the candidates, and we candidly discuss the merits of each person and decide among ourselves who to invite to join us. But sometimes you'll get a guy who puts up one of his pals and he isn't going to back down real easy, like when some other member says he won't fit in, you know? Then we have a standoff, and we may have to actually vote. Paper ballots are laid out on the table, and everybody marks theirs and puts in a box. The officers get off by themselves and decide who got the most votes and how many openings there are for new members. After one meeting like that, I heard somebody say, "I'm glad we blackballed him. I don't know why [the sponsor] thinks [the candidate] is such a big deal." After that, I do know that stuff like blackballing is still on some people's mind even if we don't do it that way . . . maybe it goes back to their college fraternity.

As this individual suggests, club members may speak of excluding prospective members in the traditional terminology of exclusion (such as "blackballing") regardless of the selection method employed.

Up to this point, we have seen how the material cultural dimensions of club life, including the physical environment of the clubhouse and the club's written rules and procedures, create a club atmosphere in which it is possible to justify the exclusion of outsiders and the snobbery of insiders. Several nonmaterial cultural dimensions of club life also serve to maintain and perpetuate clubs' exclusionary practices and members' notions of superiority.

IMPORTING THE "PROPER" VALUES, BELIEFS, AND ATTITUDES

British club members have had a strong influence on American clubs in regard to what constitutes the "proper" attitudes, beliefs, and values for elite club members. Transmission of certain ideologies has served to legitimate exclusionary practices and some forms of deviant behavior at some of these clubs, such as excessive drinking and amassing heavy gambling debts. I focus on three separate but closely interrelated ideologies that have been used to justify the behavior of club members. The first ideology is the *value of privacy and secrecy*: it is assumed that members share many things in common that they do not wish to reveal to outsiders, and the ultimate form of disloyalty is to violate other members' privacy by revealing information about them to outsiders. The second, related ideology is a *belief in the primacy of men over women, of white people over people of color, and of the upper classes over the lower classes*. By viewing their own kind of people as being first and foremost, club members believe that they have no choice but to exclude individuals who are "not our kind" and thereby protect their privacy and secrecy. The third ideology is an *attitude of self-righteousness and snobbishness* that can be traced to London's early gentlemen's clubs and may be a result of members' embracing the ideologies of privacy, secrecy, and primacy within the club's environment.

The Club Atmosphere: Privacy and Secrecy in the Company of Our Kind of People

Elite clubs offer their members privacy and secrecy within a "club atmosphere." In the early gentlemen's clubs of London, the club atmosphere referred to a comfortable haven in which members could relax and enjoy themselves in a safe environment where members were physically secluded from everyone else (Rogers 1988). In contemporary times, elite clubs in England and the United States still pride themselves on the wall of privacy and secrecy these institutions provide for their members. One of the primary ways in which the clubs protect their members is by giving no information to outsiders about how the club operates or who the members are. Elite clubs generally do not allow reporters or photographers (unless they are club members) in the club building, and boards of directors typically are publicity shy when it comes to a public discussion of their position at the club. According to one British journalist who extensively studied London's gentlemen's clubs in the 1980s,

> For an institution which is well known to be central to the whole British Establishment, the men's clubs are striking for their absence from any of the normal sources of information; books by independent observers, analyses of their influence and how they work. Some have their own, highly favorable official histories publishing the glories of a bygone age when Victorian novelists wrote their books in the club, hardly the basis for understanding the real role of the club today. (Rogers 1988:167)

As this journalist states, the most prestigious clubs zealously guard the privacy of their members by providing few, if any, details about their facilities or membership roster. The value of privacy continues to be honored in contemporary U.S. clubs, as the general manager of one top-ranked golf club stated, "If you want to be private, you have to act private" (*BusinessWeek* 1997).

How does a club "act private"? In order to act private, elite clubs typically try to appear invisible or impenetrable to outsiders. When some of the oldest and most prestigious U.S. clubs were being formed, the founders were impressed that British clubs left so few tracks that could be followed by outsiders. By adapting the idea of the "club atmosphere" from the British, U.S. clubs focused on Old Guard, "blue-blooded" members who could engage in frank and open exchanges with each other but keep what goes on inside the club to themselves. In the words of one journalist, "The men's club is a prime emblem of male bonding, a tree house with more comfortable seating" (Lacayo 1988:43). In their so-called tree house, members could share valuable information from the marketplace, discuss the latest gossip, and reveal personal secrets in the strictest of confidence, knowing that the sacred trust that they placed in other members would not be violated. The members believed that male bonding would be easier for men if the only other people present were men from the upper class who shared their race or ethnicity, religion, and sexual orientation. Consider, for example, the history of New York's Union Club: the founders of this club wanted to cater to old, wealthy families that traced their roots to English and Dutch ancestry. After the outbreak of the Civil War, however, some members had strong political differences and left the Union Club to create their own Union League Club. In turn, the Union League Club created its own exclusionary policies and procedures, and club members' general sentiment toward diversity was found in the club's unwritten motto "No women, no dogs, no reporters, and no Democrats" (Porzelt 1982). By the late 1860s, some members of the original Union Club believed that too many "outsiders" had become members, and these individuals seceded from the Union Club to form the Knickerbocker Club, where they once again restricted membership to a few carefully chosen people of English or Dutch descent. As was the case in this example, members of many elite clubs thrive on similarity but are easily threatened by diversity and will be quick to exclude anyone they perceive to be a threat to the club's stability.

Why do club members place such a high value on secrecy? Secrecy contributes to a group's mystique, and it also serves to protect insider goings-on, such as decisions about new members or the reprimand or expulsion of an errant member. According to sociologist Georg Simmel, secrecy serves not only to exclude outsiders but also provides a "correspondingly strong feeling of possession for insiders" (Wolff 1964:332). Traditionally, elite club members have placed a high value on privacy and secrecy because they could bond with each other not only through their conversations but also by participating in controversial and sometimes illegal activities, such as gambling and drinking.

Elite social clubs have served many functions for their members over the years, but one of the most continuous has been serving alcoholic beverages ("intoxicating liquors") to club members and their invited guests. As you will recall, a number of the earliest elite clubs in Britain and the United States started as drinking clubs that were founded in taverns. After members built their own clubhouses, they still wanted to drink with other members and not necessarily be held accountable for their actions by wives and law enforcement officials. The longevity of the relationship between elite clubs and the consumption of alcoholic beverages is evident in the widely repeated anecdote about White's club in London: a new member asked Wheeler, the club's longtime bartender, "Is the bar open?" Wheeler replied, "Bless my soul, sir. It has been open for 200 years" (Lejeune and Lewis 1984:295). Since the private club was a "home away from home" for many club members, the amount of alcohol consumed at White's and in similar club settings over the centuries would no doubt be amazing. In the past, privileged men often spent as much or more time at their club as they did at home. Consider, for example, this diary entry written by the wife of an early Brooks's member: "We have now been married exactly a year, in which time my husband has dined with me but once. Every other night he dined at Mr. Brooks's Club" (Lejeune and Lewis 1984:14).

Although alcohol was never legally banned in Britain (as it was during the Prohibition era in the United States), club members in both nations have always been able to enjoy a drink in the privacy of their club, where they were treated with the respect they believed they so richly deserved and where they were served only vintage wines and excellent brandy and port at clubs such as White's. If a member consumed an excessive amount of alcohol, he was given a room at the club overnight, or he was safely delivered to his home by club personnel so that the member would have no unpleasant encounters with so-called street people or law enforcement officials.

During the era of U.S. Prohibition, elite clubs became a refuge for members because they could enjoy their intoxicating liquors without going to the local speakeasy or having to deal with the bootleggers who sold these contraband beverages. When Congress passed the 1919 Volstead Act to enable federal enforcement of the Eighteenth Amendment to the U.S. Constitution, which banned the manufacture, sale, or transportation of intoxicating liquors, elite club members across the United States decided that they must protect their own interests if they wanted to continue drinking alcoholic beverages. As a result, clubs ranging from the Knickerbocker in New York to the Dallas Country Club had special rooms fitted with lockers that any interested member could rent and use as he so desired. The official stance of elite clubs was that no liquor was allowed on club property and that alcohol could not be consumed anywhere on the premises; however, members merely rented a locker or a room at the club where they felt free to do what they wanted. Most clubs were unwilling to search the men's lockers or private bedrooms because these areas were considered to be a man's private space within the large club facility.

Being able to drink in exclusive city and country clubs had great appeal to wealthy and influential Texans even prior to Prohibition: alcohol consumption in Texas was already controlled by local election "dry" votes. Prohibition brought even greater loyalty to private clubs because it eliminated the legal purchase of alcoholic beverages throughout the nation. But club members in Texas typically found a way to get around these so-called blue laws and to enjoy themselves, even if on a more limited basis than in the past. For example, the official stance of the Dallas Country Club's board of directors was that "no person shall be permitted to have or to drink any intoxicating liquors on the grounds or in the buildings of this Club"; however, members who had lockers or resided at the club simply went there to have a drink whenever they wanted, and some also served drinks to other members as well (Galloway 1996:71). For many years, an African American locker room attendant, Flanagan, sold members alcoholic beverages that they could stow in their locker or take to their room for private consumption: "[Pat would] sell liquor at any hour to those that were of age, and sometimes to those that weren't" (Galloway 1996:255). When the Dallas Country Club's board of directors heard that a number of members were serving and consuming alcoholic beverages on the club premises, the board dutifully voted that any resident who possessed or served liquor in his room would be expelled from the club; however, no record exists that shows a member was ever expelled from the club for possessing or serving liquor (Galloway 1996).

Like alcohol consumption, gambling was another activity protected by the value of privacy and secrecy within the club atmosphere. In nineteenth-century London, gambling was a problem for wealthy men because public gaming houses were regularly raided by the police. Members of the gentlemen's clubs, however, could enjoy their wagers, large and small, within the privacy of their club. Many London clubs kept a betting book in which all the members' wagers were recorded. At White's, the earliest betting book is dated 1743, and when these books were made public many years later, it was apparent that the men made large wagers on virtually anything imaginable:

> The wagers were frequently heavy and, still more frequently, morbid. Members would bet on which of two duchesses or fellow members would die first, or that a particular baronet would go bankrupt within three months, or that some notorious character would be hanged. (Graves 1963:1)

Other wagers seemed equally ridiculous, but club members became quite caught up in betting on whether a man could live twelve hours underwater, the number of cats that would walk down opposite sides of the street during a specific period of time, and how long it would be before a certain young woman would get married.

Like members of the British clubs, U.S. club members enjoyed gambling and often passed time making wagers of all amounts on seemingly inconsequential matters. When New York's Union Club was located on Fifth Avenue, for example, a favorite sport among members was to bet on the total number of African Americans (although different terminology was used) who would pass the Club's windows during a specified period of time. To show how seriously members took these wagers, the story is told of one member who had lost a number of these bets and decided to do something about it. One day, when the member was leaving his office, he saw a large parade of African American delegates starting to walk far down on Fifth Avenue, so he quickly took a taxi to the club and made as many bets as he could that 500 people of color would pass by the club building within the next half hour. Most of the members present thought this was a safe bet; however, much to their surprise, this member won his wager and really cleaned up on the other members (Wecter 1937). As this oft-repeated anecdote shows, elite club members often placed bets on the actions of outsiders whom club members looked down on, such as African Americans, Jews, Catholics, poor people, women, and other marginalized groups. Taking bets about the behavior of subordinate-group members, along with making unflattering jokes about their appearance and actions, gave club members a feeling of self-importance and superiority over others.

In contemporary London clubs, members now bet on such things as horse races, cricket matches, and other sporting events. However, we are not sure about other wagers because, as social historian Charles Graves (1963:5) explains, "The betting book is kept in a room to which non-members have no access."

In most contemporary U.S. clubs, an official stance has been taken against gambling because of its illegality in many communities. However, many games permitted on club premises, such as whist, all fours, cribbage, billiards, and poker, can informally be used for wagering. In some city clubs, for example, members have turned draw poker into a high-stakes game, and they have insisted that anyone who attempts to stop them is infringing on their rights and privileges as members of a *private* club (Dunn 1971). In Texas clubs, pseudogambling is a popular pastime. Members and their guests are invited to "Casino Night" parties where participants are given chips that they can wager at gaming tables set up for blackjack, roulette, craps, poker (including Texas hold 'em and five-card stud), and baccarat. Party services are hired to put on these events, attendants dress like upscale Las Vegas casino employees, and partygoers wear costumes that make them look like "high rollers." Although many of these parties only involve pseudogambling, it is possible for winners to go home with free international holidays, new cars, spa services, and other expensive "gifts." The early model of wagers in British clubs and in clubs in the northeastern United States is still found in modified form in elite clubs throughout the nation. According to Henry, a white male in his late thirties, "You can still feel like a stud when you win big at Casino night, even though you don't walk out with tons of money. The prizes are fun, and seeing other people impressed with your 'good luck' is even more exciting."

This comment brings us to the third ideology found in British clubs that has been readily accepted by members of exclusive clubs in the United States—an attitude of self righteousness and snobbishness.

Passing On Individual Self-Importance and Snobbery

A prevailing attitude among elite club members is self-importance, and this often translates into what some people might view as snobbish behavior. Looking back to London's gentlemen's clubs, the British lived among royalty in a well-defined and relatively rigid class structure, and many so-called commoners were fascinated with the aristocracy even as they were deeply frustrated with them. In the United States, rich Americans wanted to imitate the British way of life, which they saw as superior to their own (Cable 1984). Between 1870 and 1930, an era known in the United States as the period from Gilded Age through the Roaring Twenties, many newly wealthy families were particularly interested not only in having the best of everything, including exclusive club memberships, but also in enhancing their social and cultural capital through the people they met and the things they learned. In their opinion, what better place was there to learn about the finest things in life than in western Europe? Along with the French, who strongly influenced Americans in regard to "women's fashions, ladies' maids, chefs, governesses, hairdos, fabrics, perfumes, and poodles, to say nothing of splendid things to eat," the English were admired not only for their gentlemen's clubs but also for the British "accent, tweeds, butlers, manners, gardens, old silver, and very thin watercress sandwiches" (Cable 1984:124). As a result, privileged men and women in the United States felt more self-confident and increasingly self-important when they followed the model of western Europe in organizing their own lifestyle. In keeping with the English model of the gentlemen's club, for example, U.S. club members came to refer to themselves as "true gentlemen," on the assumption that individuals with this description were held in the highest regard by others. Many U.S. men began to judge other men by their club affiliation: "What is your club? "Who holds membership in the *best* club?" and "Who has no club membership at all?" were popular questions among privileged men in the late nineteenth and early twentieth centuries (Lejeune and Lewis 1984). According to social analyst Joseph Epstein (2002:133–34), who has written extensively about snobbery, it is inevitable that feelings of individual self-importance and displays of snobbish behavior are found in club life:

> Clubs are as much about keeping people out as joining them together, which is why they have always had a central place in the history of snobbery. . . . One joins a club for fellowship, but one of its perks is, inevitably, the quiet pleasure of knowing—or at least hoping—that not only can't everyone join, but one's own club is just a touch better than others of its kind. Even with the best intentions and histories of good works behind them, clubs are snobbery organized.

Since most definitions of a *snob* refer to a person with exaggerated respect for social position and wealth as well as a disposition to be ashamed of socially inferior connections, the picture that Epstein paints is not a particularly flattering image of the typical elite club member. However, it is perhaps true that snobbery is an essential feature of club life. As we have seen, elite clubs in this country have deep roots in the English gentlemen's club where imitation of British royalty was often condoned and even emulated. In the United States, elite men's clubs in the Gilded Age frequently required members to wear high hats to lunch at clubs such as the Temple Club (later renamed the Somerset Club) in Boston (Porzelt 1982). Other clubs required full evening dress—including a black tailcoat with silk facings, sharply cut away at the front; a white stiff-fronted shirt and wing collar; a white bow tie; and black patent leather pumps—for "routine" evening meals. Today, the general public usually sees men dressed in full formal attire at televised receptions and state dinners when the president of the United States is hosting a visiting head of state, such as the 2007 visit of Britain's Queen Elizabeth II and Prince Phillip with U.S. President George W. Bush and Laura Bush.

In contemporary city, country, and wall-less men's clubs, somewhat less formal attire is often required on special occasions when male members are asked to wear black tie (a standard black-tie tuxedo) or full evening dress. Elegant social occasions such as formal balls and debutante cotillions, weddings, and other exclusive parties often reveal British formality in attire, names of events, participants, and groups involved: popular terms include "coronation," "royalty," "robes and crowns," "King and Queen," and "Lords and Ladies." The names of elite clubs such as the "Order of the Alamo," the "Knights of the Symphony," and the "Knights of the Vine" also are patterned on British designations. Individuals who are members of the "Royal Order of Something-or-Another" and who are referred to as "King," "Queen," "Princess," "Lord Chancellor," or a similar regal title may be down-to-earth individuals in all other aspects of their life, but it may be easy to feel an elevated sense of self-importance when other club members routinely bow to the person and refer to him or her by their lofty (if temporary since it is passed on each year) title borrowed from the British aristocracy, past or present.

Apart from playing the part of royalty, some elite U.S. club members demonstrate an air of superiority because they believe that they possess vast amounts of cultural capital that other individuals do not have. Self-importance and snobbish behavior may be linked to the knowledge that a person has on a *particular subject of importance to the upper classes* (such as kinds of rare china, recent purchases of high-priced contemporary art, esoteric symphony composers, or an insider's information on world finance or real estate) or the *discerning taste of an upper-class connoisseur* regarding luxury items such as racing horses, yachts, private jets, and imported cigars or brandy. Over the past two centuries, elite clubs have been slow to change their customs and social rituals because these organizations may lose their social cache if they change too much or too quickly. In the words of one historian describing the gentlemen's clubs of London, if the best clubs change very much, they may lose their reason for being, and this reason is *exclusivity*, which comes close on the heels of self-importance and snobbish behavior:

> Clubs must provide at least a semblance of exclusivity. A club, after all, is a place where a man goes to be among his own kind. A good club should be a refuge from the vulgarity of the outside world, a reassuringly fixed point, the echo of a more civilized way of living, a place where . . . people still prefer a silver salt-cellar which doesn't pour to a plastic one which does. (Lejeune and Lewis 1984:19)

One of the grounds for snobbish behavior among club members in both England and America is the limited number of exclusive clubs that exist and the even more limited number of open slots that exist for membership in those clubs. Scarcity often leads to snobbish behavior among those who possess a resource that is in high demand but low supply. In elite clubs, a climate of scarcity exists in which members see their club as a rare commodity (perhaps without a price) that is attainable to only a few well-chosen individuals, including themselves. In Texas, scarcity is a strong factor in both the snobbery of club members and feelings of exclusion by outsiders. As the population of this state has increased dramatically over the past decade, many of the newer arrivals have been individuals with as much or much more wealth than native or long-term Texas residents. For the rich newcomers, it is a shock to find long waiting lists for clubs that they might want to join. Although many newcomers in high-tech industries and finance contend that they are not interested in joining locally prestigious city, country, and wall-less men's clubs, their actions often speak otherwise: they seek out current members to propose them for membership, realizing that important social and business connections may not be made without club membership. Wealthy and influential newcomers are particularly concerned about their children making the "right connections" when they move to a state such as Texas: the private club offers the safest and most prestigious place for their children to swim, play tennis and golf, dine, and meet other children from the "right families" in their community. As a result, current club members feel self-important because they already possess this valuable asset and can, if the waiting list is not too long, dole out new memberships in exchange for advantages—such as a large donation to an Old Guard member's favorite arts organization, hospital, or other charity—to the rich newcomers.

A snobbish attitude among members may be based not only on the limited number of memberships that are available but also on how costly the memberships are and how much expense is involved in participating in sports such as golf. The relationship between golfing and club-related snobbery was explored by one journalist who wrote, "Snobbery and exclusion have long been inseparable from golf. Playing even one round requires the use of expensive equipment, access to landscaped acres of greensward and, for most people, expensive lessons in technique. A caddy is a sort of walk-along valet" (Henry 1991). When William Henry III wrote the article containing this quotation in 1991, one club he mentioned, Baltusrol Golf Club, was charging new members an initiation fee of $25,000, plus a $5,250 bond, and $3,900 per year in dues; however, by 2005, these costs had risen to $75,000 for the initiation fee, and all other annual dues had more than doubled (Futterman 2005). According to a more recent journalist's account, members of golf clubs such as Baltusrol revere tradition and money, but anyone interested in joining such a club must remember, "If you talk about that crass second reason [money], you don't have a chance of getting in" (Futterman 2005).

Attitudes found in U.S. golf clubs about issues such as class, gender, and race clearly can be traced to England and western Europe: in 2007, for example, female golfers in the Women's British Open were allowed for the first time in history to play the historic Old Course at St. Andrews in Scotland shortly after a sign reading "No dogs or women allowed" was removed from outside the clubhouse behind the eighteenth green (Crouse 2007:SP1, 10).

In the few studies that have been conducted regarding contemporary city or country clubs in the United States, members firmly state that no snobs are allowed in their organization. For club members, snobbery is—like racism, sexism, classism, and anti-Semitism—a politically incorrect topic and a thing of the past, if it ever existed. Members who are asked about snobbish behavior typically indicate that they know some people (usually blue-blood or Old

Guard family members) in the larger community whom they consider to be "snobs" and that a few of these individuals might also be members of their club; however, the members firmly deny that there is any involvement between club membership and snobbery. This response from one elite club member is typical of what many others in my study stated: "You ask me if there are people who act snobbish in my club? Sure, there are always going to be snobs, and some snobs are going to be members of clubs. But that doesn't mean there's any relationship between club membership and being a snob." Most U.S. club members are staunchly opposed to (publicly) thinking of themselves as better than anyone else or as showing signs of superiority to nonmembers and other outsiders who are definitely "not our kind of people."

In this chapter, I have described how elite U.S. clubs were patterned on the gentlemen's clubs of London, including the *material cultural dimensions*, such clubhouses and written rules regarding the membership process, and the *nonmaterial cultural dimensions*, such as members' attitudes, beliefs, and values. I have shown that although many contemporary city, country, and wall-less men's clubs in the United States may have members today who represent greater diversity in regard to race/ethnicity, gender, and religion than in the past, the clubs still engage in exclusionary practices and justify their elitism and snobbery based on the traditional beliefs and practices of exclusive clubs over the past two centuries. In chapter 3, I look more closely at the membership process in contemporary clubs and show how patterns of exclusion based on class, race, ethnicity, religion, gender, and sexual orientation that remain today often are justified by some of the factors we have examined in this chapter.

NOTE

1. As discussed in chapter 6, external forces over the past four decades have mandated that some clubs in both the United States and the United Kingdom change their membership policies (such as automatically blackballing candidates for membership who are women and/or people of color) and club participation practices (such as who is allowed to use the club's golf course).

• 3 •

How the "Chosen Few" Are Chosen

Membership is by invitation only. In order to be considered for membership, a person must be sponsored by at least two members in good standing. The sponsors shall write the Chairman or Secretary of the Board stating the name, residence, and qualifications of the person proposed for membership. The person must submit a written application for membership on a form prescribed by the Board of Trustees. The application shall be first considered by the Membership Committee. On a two-thirds favorable vote by the Membership Committee, the name of the proposed new member shall be submitted to the Board of Trustees. The Trustees shall vote by signed ballot, and, on favorable approval by a majority of the entire Board of Trustees, the person shall be approved for membership and invitation tendered. Unless the invitation is accepted and initiation fees and initial dues tendered within thirty days after the date the invitation is extended, the invitation may be withdrawn.

Although elite clubs' rules for proposing new members typically are set forth in a straightforward manner (such as those stated in the previous paragraph) in members' handbooks or other in-house club materials, the actual membership process in most clubs is more covert—and sometimes more exclusionary—than it might appear. All the clubs in my study require that prospective members be sponsored by current members in good standing who place their social reputations on the line with other members by vouching that the candidate will be a good, congenial member if invited to join the club. However, individuals who might wish to become club members but are not part of their city's powerful and influential social circles—including some women without "old boy" ties; members of some racial, ethnic, or religious minority groups; and individuals from middle- and working-class backgrounds— often do not have the right connections to be nominated for membership. By

contrast, white upper-class and upper-middle-class men (along with a few affluent women or influential people of color) have a much easier time finding
established members who will serve as their sponsors. In the case of the wall-
less gentlemen's clubs in this study, for example, nearly all current members
are—and for the foreseeable future will probably remain—affluent, white, heterosexual males. Some club membership rosters include one or two well-
chosen, wealthy gay men or a smattering of Latinos and male African American members who are well known for their accomplishments in politics, business, or higher education, but these individuals remain few when compared to
the overall membership. As discussed in this chapter, the purpose of the membership process in exclusive clubs is to distinguish between who is "us" and
who is "not us," and this issue falls not only along lines of money and class but
also along lines of race/ethnicity, religion, gender, and sexual orientation. More
than anything else, the stringent membership process gives members a sense
of pride that they, rather than others, have been chosen for membership. As
one journalist stated about San Francisco's Pacific-Union Club, an Old Guard
establishment located in a mansion that covers a city block on the crest of Nob
Hill, "Belonging to a club like this says a lot about who you are. Tell someone
you're a member of the Pacific-Union Club, and you are saying you made it
through a rigorous vetting to filter out the 'not us'" (Lara 2004).

This chapter examines the formal and informal aspects of city, country,
and wall-less club memberships, including how the membership process
works. Next, the chapter discusses patterns of exclusion based on class, race,
ethnicity, religion, gender, and sexual orientation. Finally, the chapter briefly
examines the pretensions and realities of change in membership policies—are
these barriers really coming down?

THE FORMAL MEMBERSHIP PROCESS

Although some wall-less men's clubs leave the process of selecting new members
up to a small clique of longtime, highly respected members who make these decisions behind a cloak of secrecy, city and country clubs typically operate as formal organizations with set membership rules and procedures. This does not
mean that cliques and informal camaraderie do not play a part in how members
are selected in these clubs, but it does suggest that the guidelines of these clubs
are more likely to be followed when it comes to membership decisions.

Club Bureaucracy

In both city clubs and country clubs, a bureaucratic organizational structure
(as originally described by the early sociologist Max Weber) helps to create

and maintain club barriers, thus protecting the club from unacceptable outsiders. Like any other bureaucracy, an elite club has a division of labor and a hierarchy of authority. *Division of labor* refers to the process of dividing up tasks so that they are performed by different people and thus are performed in the most optimal manner. The division of labor in an elite club includes both the voluntary (nonpaid) efforts of club members who serve in various leadership capacities and the paid staff that is employed at the pleasure of the club's board of trustees or directors. *Hierarchy of authority* means that each lower position in an organization is under the control and supervision of a higher one. For a hierarchical pattern to work, everyone in the chain of command must recognize the necessity and legitimacy of the higher positions (Kendall 2002). The hierarchy of authority is visible in elite clubs, starting at the top with an elected board of trustees (or board of directors) and then having two tracks: (1) the unpaid club officers and committee chairs and (2) the paid staff, including the club's general manager, who is the highest-ranking employee. Members of the board of trustees typically are elected by the general membership from a slate of candidates proposed by the nominating committee. Although the trustees formulate the club's rules and policies, they usually leave day-to-day operations up to the general manager, who is hired by the board and is responsible for all other club personnel.

Club trustees also appoint members to various committees to handle specific tasks in accordance with the *rules and procedures* set forth in the by-laws. The membership committee is one of the most influential committees appointed by the trustees. Being asked to serve as chair of the membership committee is considered to be an honor because other members recognize that the membership chair is "the head gatekeeper who controls the lifeblood of the club" (in the words of one respondent).

Not only do trustees appoint the membership committee, but they also establish (and from time to time amend) the club's membership rules and procedures.

Membership Caps, Categories, and "Good-Bye Clauses"

In many clubs, the bylaws establish a membership cap, set up categories of membership, and have "good-bye clauses" for when a member dies, divorces, has extreme financial problems, or seriously misbehaves. Some of these criteria have both objective and subjective dimensions. For example, trustees may determine a club's membership cap (the maximum number of members) based on objective criteria—such as the capacity of the club's facilities—or on subjective criteria, such as the number of members needed to keep the club financially viable while also maintaining the club's exclusivity and reputation for being "very difficult, if not impossible, to join." According to one Dallas club member, "As odd as it may seem, the longer our waiting list is and the more time people think it may take to be considered for membership, the more they clamor to be nominated by their friends." As in other areas of life, scarcity may make a club membership more desirable to outsiders and more valuable to insiders. However, in some clubs, the primary rationale for membership caps appears to be the desire of long-term members to maintain control of the organizations because they have seen what change has done to other institutions in their city. In the words of one country club trustee, "We want just enough new blood to keep the club pumped up and runnin' smoothly. Some of us have been through years of ups and downs at the club and in this city, but some newcomers who got here 'yesterday' don't listen very well."

The formal membership process in most elite clubs also includes specific classifications of membership. Typically, a candidate will apply for "active" or "resident" membership status; however, some clubs have categories for people who do not live in the city where the club is located or who will be residing in the city for only a specific period of time. Robert, a trustee of one of the city clubs in my study, described the membership classifications in that club as follows:

> All new members come in as "resident" members unless they live somewhere else, and that's a different situation. Overall, we have ten membership classifications: resident, nonresident, interim, honorary, senior, surviving spouse, senior surviving spouse, leave of absence, transferable, and legacy. Only resident members get to vote and hold office. The nonresident members don't live here and usually come in for drinks and dinner or a party ever-now-and-then, when they're in from New York, LA, or wherever.

When Robert was asked about the difference in the resident and legacy membership classifications, he replied, "We added the legacy membership so that the adult children of our longtime members could join without having to pay a large initiation fee. Now we can bring in younger members who we know will appreciate what we have to offer because they grew up enjoying club activities with their parents."

Setting membership caps and identifying specific categories of membership helps trustees and rank-and-file members control their club; however, members are also interested in protecting the status of an existing membership if the person dies, gets a divorce, or fails to meet club obligations. Club bylaws typically cover such situations. Consider, for example, this statement from the bylaws of one Texas club: "Membership is non-transferable and except for the rights of surviving spouses, terminates upon the death of a Member." As this statement indicates, individuals who join this club are informed that their membership belongs to them alone (with the exception of a surviving spouse in the case of the member's death) and that their membership cannot be transferred to any other person. This statement holds true if the member gets a divorce. According to the club's bylaws, "In the case of divorce, no membership rights are transferable to the spouse because membership is individual and personal."

Club bylaws also state the conditions under which a member may be expelled from the club. These typically include nonpayment of dues, assessments, or other monies owed to the club as well as expulsion "for cause" (when a complaint filed against the member is not satisfactorily resolved). Money is a crucial factor in determining the acceptability of a potential member. It is essential that a candidate have sufficient resources to pay required initiation fees, monthly dues, and other club expenses incurred on a regular basis. Equally important, a potential member must have sufficient resources to maintain the "right" lifestyle (including having the appropriate clothing, jewelry, motor vehicles, and residences) to fit in with other members. Sometimes members are expelled for financial reasons; other times they lose all right to membership because their behavior violates club rules. Of course, issues such as these are of little concern to individuals seeking to join the club because they often believe they will never have such problems. Instead, candidates for membership are more concerned about how the process works and how the membership committee functions.

Gatekeepers: The Membership Committee and Board of Trustees

In many clubs, a potential member must be nominated by a specific number of regular members who vouch for the person and describe his or her qualifications for membership. In letters of recommendation, it is particularly important that sponsors state that the candidate will make a good club member and that he or she fit in well with other members. Along with their letters of recommendation, sponsors obtain an application form that the prospect must fill out. This application requests some of the same kinds of information that a person would provide when applying for a credit card or a license. The applications may also ask for information that makes the membership committee aware of the person's family and social ties, such as the wife's maiden name, relatives who are club members, college fraternities or sororities, other club memberships, and business or professional connections. Some application forms ask the potential member to explain why he or she is interested in joining the club.

Although most membership committees do not invite sponsors to meet with them when they deliberate on their candidate's application, a few committees allow sponsors to come to one of their meetings, particularly if committee members have unanswered questions or concerns about a prospect. An example of this process was described by William, a single man in his late twenties, who had been the president of a prominent wall-less men's club:

> When you want to put up somebody for membership, you write a letter of recommendation as the sponsoring club member. Then, you get signatures from other members, or better yet, letters of recommendation from well-liked members who support your man's nomination. At the membership committee meeting, the candidates' names are brought up one at a time, and sponsors and other people who know them talk about them. The sponsors vouch for their guy by saying stuff like, "I know some of you don't know him, but he's one of us." After that we leave the room, the committee votes them either "in" or "out." We don't find out who was invited to join until [the candidate] gets a call from the committee chair inviting him to come have a drink.

As this statement suggests, if a prospective member is described by a current member as "being one of us," that candidate has a distinct advantage. Based on the principle of homophily, individuals serving on the membership committee typically are more comfortable inviting a person to membership who is already "one of us" rather than an individual who is unknown or who is perceived to be "not one of us."

Interviews with membership chairs and committee members reaffirmed the fact that the principle of homophily applies to how new club members are selected. Consider, for example, the factors that one membership chairman—Steve, a married entrepreneur in his late sixties—considered to be important when looking at potential members:

> First, we want to know how well this candidate is known by the members. Is he related to a current member? Second, we want to know if he is well liked by other members, especially if they know him well. Has anybody had a bad experience with him in business or otherwise? After we cross these bridges, we look to see what he might contribute to the club. Since we have club activities for the entire family, we want to know if his wife and kids will fit in. Does his wife work? What does she do? Where do the kids go to school? Do our kids know his kids? We want him and his family to fit in with the rest of us.

In this club and a number of others, a two-thirds favorable vote of the membership committee is required for the proposed new member's name to be forwarded to the board of trustees for consideration. The trustees then make the final decision on new club members. However, in other clubs, the membership committee may circulate a list of candidates for membership or call a meeting in which the general membership can look over the applications and recommendations for the proposed new members. Any club member who wishes to offer an opinion to the committee may so do, but the final decision still rests with the committee or the club's board.

Social politics often play an important part in the collective decision-making process of membership committees. As in other aspects of elite social life, members of private clubs frequently "owe" other members a *favor of reciprocity*, which means that one member "returns" the favor of a second member—who previously helped the first member by introducing him or her to an important new social contact, for example—by doing the second member a favor that is equally advantageous to him or her. Consider, for instance, how club members take turns sponsoring other club members for membership in other elite clubs or how they nominate each other to serve on the governing boards of corporations, universities, hospitals, and prestigious nonprofit arts organizations.

In sum, most of the clubs I studied were top heavy in regard to membership decisions: the clubs' board of trustees or directors and/or the membership committee played key roles in determining who would be invited to membership, and, although the general membership was involved in the process, the officers and membership committee members served as the club's gatekeepers in regard to who would be included or excluded from their organization.

In addition to the formal membership process as described previously, I found that a number of informal activities may take place in the membership selection process. In some clubs, for example, members have a number of informal discussions before they recommend a new member and ask him or her to fill out an application form. These discussions were referred to as putting up a "trial balloon" by George, an influential member of several of the clubs in my research:

> If you want to propose a new member, I think it's better to see what the others think of him before asking if he wants to join or putting his name up [for membership]. I don't want to be left hanging out on a limb, if you know what I mean. So, I talk to members who know the guy . . . put up a trial balloon, so to speak, and see what reaction I get. If they're lukewarm to the idea or know somebody who's had a scrape with him, I will probably forget about it.

As George suggests, it is not unusual for some members to have informal discussions about prospective members before they take any of the formal steps involved in putting the individuals up for membership. Similarly, another respondent stated that, if he was thinking about proposing a new member, he sought out the chair of the membership committee for a "casual chat" in which he hoped to learn the number of openings that would be available for new members that year. According to George, "If I know how many slots the [membership] chairman has to fill, I have a much better way of knowing whether my man will get in or not. In the years where there are very few open slots, [the membership committee and board] usually go to candidates whose sponsors are club 'big wigs.'"

In comparing the formal and the informal aspects of the membership process in elite clubs, I have found that some clubs operate with a great deal openness and transparency, while others are highly secretive about the process. In all cases, however, the key operative word among club members is *tradition:* officers and rank-and-file members expect that tradition will be followed in the process and that the club will come out stronger because of the new members who are chosen. Individuals who may produce strife or demand significant changes in how the club operates are generally considered to be "liabilities that should be avoided at all costs," as one member stated. This individual, who is a thirty-year member of a wall-less men's social club, as well as two city clubs and five country clubs (located in four cities), continued, "I enjoy watching the wheels turn each year to see who gets invited to join. If somebody complains, he's usually told, 'Hey, this is how we've always done it. It's tradition.'"

Club traditions support certain patterns of inclusion, such as the ready acceptance of legacy members. These traditions may also support patterns of exclusion, such as greater hesitancy by the clubs to accept individuals who represent diverse religions, racial or ethnic backgrounds, or any other characteristic or attribute not widely found among the club's general membership. Elite club members believe that they have the right to choose new members on the basis of the legal principle of *freedom of association,* which states that adults should be able to mutually choose their associates for whatever purpose they see fit. Freedom of association is important to club members because it supports the reason why they joined the club in the first place: they want to be around "people like us" who are perceived to be similar to themselves and who are thought to possess comparable amounts of economic, political, social, and cultural capital. Sociologists suggest that individuals feel a "consciousness of kind" when they are around others who are similar to them in family background, education, wealth and income, professional status, and social power. Members may also feel a consciousness of kind when they associate with people who share their appreciation for the "finer things in life," such as outstanding wine and gourmet food, music, art, or other "high-culture" endeavors. Consequently, some club members may feel that they are outside their "comfort zone" when they interact with people who differ significantly from them in these attributes.

EXCLUSION BASED ON CLASS

The cost of membership prohibits the majority of people in the United States from even considering the possibility of joining an elite club, much less actually applying for such a membership if they so desired. Along with the perceived secrecy and snobbishness of club members, a key exclusionary factor in prestigious clubs is how much money it takes to become a member and participate in the club's activities. Consequently, the most obvious class-based exclusionary practice of elite clubs is the amount of income and/or wealth a family must have to be able to comfortably afford an exclusive club membership. *Income* is the economic gain that a person derives from wages, salaries, income transfers (governmental aid), and ownership of property. Although a large number of club members have high annual incomes, many rely primarily on their wealth to support this and other components of their upper-class lifestyle. *Wealth* is the value of all of a person's or family's economic assets, including income, personal property, and income-producing property. These economic assets may be earned during a person's lifetime; however, Old Money or Old Family Name club members typically have inherited most of their wealth and may use it to pay for their routine living expenses, including club memberships. According to a sixty-year-old "self-made-multimillionaire" male club member, "We used to call them 'coupon clippers,' but now they don't even have to cut coupons: they can play golf all day or work out [in the club's fitness center] while the interest keeps pouring in from their [deceased] daddies and granddaddies' wise investments." The "coupon clippers" this respondent referred to are people who purchase or inherit bonds: until recently, each bond had a number of coupons attached, and the holder of the bond sent in a coupon at fixed intervals to obtain the agreed-on payments of principal and/or interest on the bond. Individuals who hold a sufficient number of lucrative bonds are able to live extremely well by "clipping coupons," a meaning that is vastly different from the one most people associate with saving store coupons to get a small reduction in the price of an item.

Economic Capital

Living the club lifestyle has its price, particularly at some of the nation's most expensive country clubs. The expense of initiation fees, monthly dues, golf and tennis fees, dining and drinking tabs, and other costs associated with membership (such as having the "right" residential address, late-model luxury vehicles, high-end golf and tennis gear, and designer clothing for a wide array of club events, ranging from black-tie soirees to casual luau parties by the pool) is prohibitive for people who are not in the upper income and/or inheritance brackets. For example, Old Guard clubs such as the Dallas Country Club and Brook Hollow Golf Club (Dallas) have initiation fees ranging from $100,000 to $150,000, monthly dues of $500 to $800, and many other expenses associated with dining and drinking at the club or participating in other club-sponsored activities or special events. Some newer, less prestigious clubs have more elaborate facilities than the Old Guard clubs and typically charge higher initiation fees and monthly dues. Examples include the $250,000 membership fee at Westmoor, a club established at the old Vanderbilt estate in Nantucket, and the $400,000 initiation fee at Nantucket Golf Club (Frank 2007). Clubs with considerably lower initiation fees and monthly dues than these Nantucket clubs still require a major financial commitment from members that is far beyond the economic resources of the typical middle-income family in the United States. As the general manager of the Atlanta Athletic Club succinctly stated, "You have to have a good bit of money to enjoy a private club" (*BusinessWeek* 1997).

Social Capital

If sociological ideas regarding the importance of social capital are accurate, many middle- and working-class individuals, particularly children, might benefit from having routine interactions with financially successful and sometimes politically powerful members of elite clubs. As discussed in chapter 1, social capital is an *actual* or *potential* resource that is linked to the "possession of a durable network of more or less institutionalized relationships of mutual acquaintance or recognition" (Bourdieu and Wacquant 1992:119). As this definition suggests, social capital is embedded in group memberships, social relationships, and networks of influence and support. From this perspective, social capital is instrumental: individuals who possess social capital have an advantage that others do not have, and many people participate in activities that constitute a "deliberate construction of sociability for the purpose of creating this resource" (Portes 1998:3). Social capital involves two key elements: (1) the social relationship itself, through which an individual can claim access to resources possessed by his or her associates, and (2) the amount and quality of these resources (Portes 1998). Social capital is an asset that varies based on *whom* a person's associates are, *how much* social capital those individuals possess, and the overall *quality* of that social capital. Across the centuries, elite men and a few privileged women have maintained and enhanced their social capital through memberships in exclusive clubs and organizations. These affiliations provided them with "strong links"—ready access to their associates' resources—as well as "weak links"—access to their associates' acquaintances (individuals whom they, at least initially, do not personally know). Using the resources (social capital) of other club members may produce significant results for the recipient of these resources. Journalists and social scientists have found that elite club memberships have helped individuals accomplish such desirable outcomes as getting one's child admitted to an exclusive private school (despite a long waiting list), participating in a lucrative business deal or a financial investment, being invited to the "right" parties or other gatherings of the inner circle of social elites, and gaining support for one's political campaign. Individuals who cannot afford to join elite clubs may be limited in both the quantity and the quality of the social capital they might derive from interactions with people "who can make things happen" unless nonmembers are able to find other means to economic and social mobility, such as starting their own company and selling it and then creating their own luxury club from which they exclude outsiders who are unable to pay (see Frank 2007).

Cultural Capital

Enhanced social capital is not the only resource that elite clubs offer their members: a person's cultural capital—the ideas, knowledge, and cultural style that individuals draw on when they participate in social life—is enriched by association with other persons who are well acquainted with the attitudes, beliefs, and behaviors of the dominant class. For purposes of this study, I have adopted a definition of cultural capital that was set forth by sociologists Michele Lamont and Annette Lareau (1988): *cultural capital* refers to widely shared, high-status cultural signals (attitudes, preferences, formal knowledge, behaviors, goods, and credentials) used in direct or indirect social and cultural exclusion. As this definition suggests, people from marginal or subordinate groups typically have a harder time competing successfully without the so-called social skills, knowledge, and cultural style that elites expect from those in high-status positions in society. Across the generations, members of the upper classes have not only biologically but also socially reproduced themselves by endowing their children (and sometimes nonrelatives who are their closest, most trusted associates) with forms of cultural capital that make them successful, well-accepted members of an elite inner circle.

Exclusive social clubs, city clubs, and country clubs are three venues in which elites maintain and enhance their cultural capital. Many clubs also offer activities and services that socialize members' children in the appropriate ways of the upper classes, including having the "right" attitudes, preferences, formal knowledge, behaviors, goods, and credentials for the upper-class lifestyle. At some exclusive country clubs, for example, members' children may learn to play polo, golf, tennis, and other sports historically associated with the Old Guard. They also learn good manners for social occasions, foreign languages and travel skills so that they can accompany their parents on international trips at an early age, and the history of their city, including the contributions of their ancestors (or other social elites) in the building of that city's institutions.

For adult members, some elite city and country clubs offer speakers and short courses that enhance their cultural capital by providing information that is considered to be valuable by social elites. Examples include presentations by wine experts on the best new wines or by opera aficionados on why a current opera has important historical significance. By possessing these kinds of information, club members may show that they are culturally savvy and thus people of high social status. Lamont and Lareau (1988) use the wine connoisseur as an example of how cultural capital serves as a high-status cultural signal: wine connoisseurs believe that it is important to know what a good wine is (attitude), they know how to consume and evaluate wine (formal knowledge), they have the confidence to recognize that a wine is good even if it has not yet been identified by experts as a "good wine" (attitude and preferences), they know how to tastefully consume wine (behaviors), and they possesses a wine cellar full of the best wines (goods and credentials). Although there are other approaches an individual might take to becoming a wine connoisseur, many elite clubs make it easy for members to enhance their knowledge about wines, to associate with other members and experts who share similar interests, and to demonstrate how savvy they are when it comes to an activity (in this case, enjoying fine wines) that is widely associated with the privileged class. Just as the wine connoisseur and other "high-culture" experts send signals to elites about their competence and social acceptability based on what they know, how they behave, and what they possess, individuals who are "outsiders" to the privileged lifestyle soon reveal their own lack of competence or social unacceptability because they are unable to demonstrate that they have the exquisite taste, insider's knowledge, or "good manners" of the upper classes. Consider, for example, the multitude of novels and films that have focused, at least briefly, on the discomforts experienced by individuals in the lower classes when they have tried to associate with or emulate the behavior of the "upper crust" in society.

In sum, social and cultural capital are strongly linked to a person's economic resources, and lack of sufficient money to join an elite club restricts individuals and families from deriving the benefits that such a membership might provide. One journalist succinctly stated it as follows when writing about "San Francisco's Big-Four Clubs" (the Bohemian, Olympic, Pacific-Union, and San Francisco Golf Club): "None of these clubs admits the poor, except in white jackets" (Lara 2004). As this statement suggests, individuals who earn middle-class, working-class, or poverty-level wages are unlikely to ever enter a elite club unless they are employed by the club or have been invited as a guest to a one-time event, such as a wedding reception hosted by a club member for whom they work. On two occasions during my observational research, for example, I saw several long-term household employees of club members, including housekeepers and nannies, at wedding receptions held by these members at elite clubs. These individuals stood out from the others not only because of class differences but also because they were the only nonwhite guests present at the event. According to the wedding planner for one of the receptions, "[The bride's mother] told me to be sure I invited the 'help' and made them feel welcome at the church and the reception because 'they've been with us for so long we think of them as part of our family.'" For this woman and other club members, however, it is highly unlikely that the notion of being a "part of our family" extends to thinking of these working-class guests as ever being members of "our club."

Old Money versus New Money

Despite laws prohibiting some types of discrimination in private clubs, it is not illegal to discriminate on the basis of class: the law does not consider individuals who cannot afford the membership fees and dues of a private club to be the victims of any forbidden form of discrimination. As a result, most sociological analyses of class-based exclusion have focused on battles between Old Money and New Money families regarding club memberships.

Early in the twenty-first century, the ideas of earlier social scientists that the upper (capitalist) class in the United States contains two divisions—the upper-upper class and the lower-upper class—are still relevant. The upper-upper class (Old Money) is made up of people from prominent families that possess great wealth that they have held for several generations. Persons in the upper-upper class tend to have strong feelings of in-group solidarity that frequently are reinforced by membership in the same exclusive clubs and support for high culture (such as the symphony, opera, ballet, or art museums). Children of the upper-upper class attend prestigious private schools and top-tier universities, and they are expected to marry within their own class (Kendall 2002; Warner and Lunt 1941). Some upper-upper class, Old Money club members in Texas, for example, describe themselves as being "Old Austin," "Old Highland Park" (Dallas), or "Old Alamo Heights" (San Antonio), which means that their families have lived in these cities or neighborhoods for many years and that they consider themselves to be part of the Old Guard. These individuals have little or no interest in meeting most newcomers to the city, even if the newcomers are very wealthy. Moreover, the Old Guard in Texas does not want the "new rich" to take over their exclusive neighborhoods by tearing down large, impressive old residences so that they can build much larger McMansions "that block out their neighbor's sunshine" or to invade their private clubs so that the "nouveau riche" can impress their friends or business acquaintances by calling them from "my club" on their cell phone. One upper-upper class city club member in his late forties stated that a "no cell phones in the club" policy (with the exception of an area where public phones were located) had been passed by the club's directors because some "new climbers rudely answered their cell phones during lunch, and, even when they got up and moved closer to the large glass windows [for better reception], they were still talking so loudly that we could hear everything they said." Although it is entirely possible that some members of the upper-upper-class, Old Guard faction of that club also might have answered their cell phones at lunch or dinner, this member and others on the club's executive committee attributed the need for this new rule to a lack of good manners among wealthy newcomers "who don't know any better."

The second category within the upper class, the lower-upper class (New Money) is made up of people who may be extremely wealthy but have not attained the same level of social acceptability and prestige as members of the upper-upper class. Sometimes referred to as the "new rich," these individuals have earned most of their money in their own lifetime as entrepreneurs, entertainers and sports celebrities, and top-tier professionals (see Gilbert 2003; Warner and Lunt 1941). Recently, author and *Wall Street Journal* reporter Robert Frank (2007) referred to the new rich in the United States as "Richistanis" who have a household net worth ranging from $1 million to $1 billion. However, according to Frank, the *truly wealthy* have a household net worth between $100 million and $1 billion, and most made their money by starting their own companies and selling them. As latter-day members of the lower-upper class, the so-called Richistanis did not inherit their wealth but rose up from the ranks of the middle or upper-middle classes by making a fortune of their own and creating their own "new culture of wealth that's vastly different from Old Money" (Frank 2007:4). For many years, some sociologists and novelists have written about the tensions between Old Money and New Money, and Frank (2007:104) suggests that these conflicts remain in the 2000s:

> Richistanis are pouring into the nation's wealthy communities and creating a new social hierarchy built on money and more money, rather than breeding and lineage. They're building giant homes to eclipse the old estates in Palm Springs, Martha's Vineyard, Palm Beach and Greenwich, Connecticut. They're lining up to join the historic golf clubs, yacht clubs, polo clubs and lunch clubs, and when they can't get in [and they usually cannot] they're starting clubs of their own.

As discussed previously, rapid population growth in Texas cities such as Dallas, Houston, Austin, and San Antonio has brought about an "invasion" of new money (particularly from the northeastern and western states) that has not only changed many old, established residential neighborhoods and Old Guard charities and arts organizations but also put new pressures on the membership committees of exclusive city clubs, country clubs, and wall-less men's clubs. These changes have led some members of the old upper-upper class, including one respondent in my study, to make comments such as the following: "Their money's welcome when it comes to supporting the arts, research for the diseases, or raising money for the hospitals, but I'm not sure they [individually] are!"

As Frank (2007) and other journalists and sociologists have found in their research, some of the new rich actively seek membership in Old Guard social institutions such as private clubs, while others are content to create their own club or join a very expensive "nouveau" club that shows their prowess at conspicuous consumption. According to Frank (2007:111), for example, "the New Money [in Palm Beach], prefers Mar-a-Lago, which takes anyone willing to pay the $150,000 membership fee, regardless of religion or last names." Members of the Old Guard typically look down on clubs such as Donald Trump's Mar-a-Lago in Florida and David Murdoch's Sherwood Country Club outside Los Angles because of the people who are members and the "nouveau riche" nature of the clubs. According to one rumor, Trump bought Mar-a-Lago, the old Marjorie Merriweather Post estate in Palm Beach, and turned it into a luxury membership club after he was turned down for membership in Old Guard clubs such as the Palm Beach Bath and Tennis Club and the Everglades Club. It is often a joke among Old Guard club members that "the likes of Donald Trump" would never be admitted to their club. However, the new rich counter that clubs such as Palm Bath and Tennis Club should be referred to as "Bed, Bath and Beyond" because of the "silver-haired preppies in white sweaters, polo shirts and khakis" who make up the club's aging membership (Frank 2007:111). This issue is further discussed in chapter 6.

In Texas, some of the Old Guard have a slightly more welcoming attitude toward some of the new rich who want to join their exclusive clubs, particularly when the new rich, many of whom have become exceedingly wealthy from high-tech enterprises and lucrative investments, are willing to spend generous amounts of money on good causes in their communities. A wealthy Texas political lobbyist in his fifties described why he thought some new rich individuals (and in this case, one specific person) had been invited to join an exclusive club that previously had been a bastion of the Old Guard:

> Well, we've finally had to acknowledge that things are changing around
> here. A lot of the older members have died out or are living at [a retirement

community] and can't make it to the club anymore. In the good old days, we wouldn't have given people like [name of an individual] the time of day, but he came rolling in here with a ——— load of money and started giving it to the symphony, the opera, the ballet, the hospitals, and other groups that put their hands out. He built a huge house and threw lavish charity parties that he practically underwrote himself. Then, he gave enough money to get several [nonprofit organizations'] buildings named after him or his wife. Frankly, I think we were worn down by the time he got "mentors" to put him up for club memberships, and the next thing I knew, he was showing up on the "New Members" lists of my favorite clubs. But, I'll tell you one thing: Some of us try to hide when we see him coming toward us at a party: We still don't like his "know it all" attitude or all his bragging about the benefits of owning his own jet.

Although this lobbyist's comments focused primarily on one person, his observations may hold true for others who consider themselves to be a part of the Old Guard and who do not approve of the brash manners or over-the-top conspicuous consumption displayed by some of the new rich. We should also note that greater inclusion of more people with recently acquired wealth does not significantly change the racial or ethnic composition of most elite clubs, which remain almost predominantly (if not exclusively) "white." We now turn to the issue of exclusion based on religion, race, and ethnicity.

EXCLUSION BASED ON RELIGION, RACE, AND ETHNICITY

As we saw in chapter 2, many of the most prestigious clubs in the United States were originally founded by and for affluent white Anglo-Saxon Protestant (WASP) men. The primary religious divide was between non-Jewish and Jewish individuals, although some clubs also excluded Catholics, whether on the basis of religion or ethnicity. By way of example, Irish Americans and Italian Americans were not welcome as members of the exclusive clubs of Boston, New York, Chicago, and San Francisco (Hornblower 2000; Lara 2004). A few clubs excluded everyone *except* individuals of a specific ethnicity and/or religion: St. Andrews, the oldest golf club in the United Kingdom, by way of example, limited membership until the 1970s to Scottish Presbyterians (Brenner 1997).

White privilege and racial exclusion were part of an unwritten and often unspoken "gentlemen's agreement" among WASP club members. As a result, some white ethnic males founded their own clubs, had their own social functions that centered on Irish or Italian customs and holidays, presented debutantes from their own ethnic group, and generally conducted business in the same manner as members of the WASP clubs, including having their own gentleman's agreement that certain categories of people, particularly Jewish Americans and African Americans, were not welcome in their clubs. In turn, some Jewish Americans founded their own country clubs and excluded individuals who were "not our kind of people." Let's look briefly at the issue of religious exclusion before we examine racial and ethnic exclusion in more depth.

Religious Exclusion: No Jews Need Apply

Historically, religion was a key factor in the exclusion of many Jewish Americans from elite WASP clubs such as New York City's Union Club, the Chicago Club, and the Los Angeles Country Club. A few city clubs were willing to make exceptions for extremely wealthy Jewish men of high social standing, such as August Belmont, a leading New York financier who become one of the few Jewish members of the Union Club in 1847. Some non-Jewish elites viewed the members of merchant Sephardic families favorably for club membership because they represented the oldest Jewish families in the United States, their ancestors having arrived in 1654 on the *St. Charles*, often referred to as the Jewish *Mayflower* (Mayo 1998). By contrast, German Jews and other European Jews were not accepted into the most prestigious city clubs or country clubs, and they began to create their own clubs, including the Harmonie Club in New York, the Standard Club in Chicago, and the Hillcrest Country Club in Los Angeles, which continues to be referred to sometimes as "the Jewish country club" (*New York Times* 1886).

Some clubs were very blatant about their exclusion of Jewish Americans. In the late 1960s and early 1970s, for example, the Baltimore Country Club (BCC) had signs posted that read, "No Dogs, No Coloreds, No Jews." To cope with such patterns of overt discrimination, Jewish Americans in Baltimore formed their own club. In the words of the Jewish owner of a construction company in that city, "We gave up trying to integrate with the BCC crowd. We built our own club instead. It was better than hearing the room go quiet whenever a Jew walked in" (Jeffreys 1999).

Early in the twenty-first century, some influential Jewish Americans still tell "jokes" about anti-Semitism at city and country clubs. For example, the Rabbi Edward Feinstein (2000) frequently told this story about the Los Angeles Country Club:

> Groucho Marx [a well-known Jewish actor and entertainer] was once invited to visit the Los Angeles Country Club. While his children were splashing in the pool, the president of the club quietly informed him that the club was restricted and [his] children would have to leave the pool. "They're only half Jewish," [Marx] replied, "let them go in up to their waist."

Although we do not know if this interaction between Marx and the club president actually occurred, Feinstein's anecdote highlights the blatant discrimination against Jewish Americans by many country clubs and further explains why they chose to start their own clubs.

Some commentators have pointed out the psychological damage that comes to Jewish Americans when they feel the need to engage in one-upmanship because they have been excluded by dominant group members. Consider this "joke" by the comedian Jackie Mason (1997) that was published in the *Jewish World Review*:

> When a Jew walks into a country club, he does not have to look at faces to know he's not welcome. . . . However, [Jews] have convinced themselves they didn't want to be members of those country clubs in the first place. So every Jew decided he would build a club on the highway across the street that would be ten times better and bigger so that when the Gentiles drove by, they would be nauseous from looking at it.
>
> If the Gentile country club had a swimming pool, the Jews would have a lake. If the Gentiles had a 10-foot-high diving board, the Jews would have one 50 feet high. If the Gentiles had a piano bar, the Jews would have a 32-piece orchestra. If the Gentiles had a picnic in the park, the Jews had a cruise to the Caribbean.

Although the one-upmanship described by Mason is told as a joke and constitutes a vast exaggeration, it accurately reflects the fact that successful Jewish Americans have been excluded from many elite WASP clubs since the early days of this nation and have had to cope with that exclusion.

Some clubs have included statements in their bylaws excluding Jews from membership; others have used either blatant methods (such as those of the Baltimore Country Club) or subtle methods to discourage them from applying for membership. According to James D. Nowlan's (2004:107) history of the Union League Club of Chicago, for example, "When a Jew might express interest in membership in the Club, he was told, 'Oh, you don't want to belong here. You'd prefer the Standard Club [the "Jewish" club], which is next door. The food is better there anyway.'"

In Texas, the clubs that I studied had no overt statements in club publications or their bylaws about the exclusion of Jewish Americans from membership; however, most clubs had only a few, if any, Jewish members. Jewish Americans account for less than 1 percent of the total population of Texas, and, according to some analysts, they have experienced less anti-Semitism in this state than in states such as New York. However, my research reveals two specific patterns of discrimination against Jewish Americans in Texas that have affected their ability to join elite, "non-Jewish" clubs: (1) categoric exclusion of Jewish Americans from country clubs through restrictive covenants on residential properties that were linked to prestigious clubs and (2) the accommodations many Jewish Americans made in their efforts to gain acceptability among dominant group elites. An example of the categoric exclusion of Jewish Americans from country clubs is found in the River Oaks section of Houston, where a gentlemen's agreement originally excluded Jews, blacks, and other minorities from purchasing property when the subdivision was new and the River Oaks Country Club was being created. Because memberships in the club initially were linked to ownership of property in the River Oaks subdivision, many affluent Jewish Americans were categorically excluded not only from purchasing a residence in that exclusive enclave but also from joining one of the city's top country clubs. An example of the accommodations many Jewish Americans made in their efforts to gain acceptability among dominant group elites is found in Dallas, where city leaders were more willing to "bestow" whiteness and its privileges on those Jews who were willing to accommodate elite demands, including adopting more Protestant forms of worship and not participating in the black civil rights movement of the 1960s and 1970s. However, despite their efforts at accommodation, Jewish Americans continued to be excluded from the city's most prestigious country clubs and other elite groups (Phillips 2006).

Although several Jewish Americans have become members of elite social clubs in Austin, Texas, some non-Jewish members (usually after consuming a number of alcoholic beverages) make private (and supposedly "joking") comments about Jewish members that they most likely would not have made about a Baptist, a Methodist, an Episcopalian, or a member of another Protestant denomination. At one formal dinner that I attended, for example, a Jewish club member who had been talking rather loudly while telling lengthy jokes about people with "lots of money" was described as "acting like a Jew" by an Old Guard, non-Jewish club member. On another occasion, the same Jewish member was complaining about a problem he had, and a non-Jewish member stated that the person had "an oppression mentality"—a derogatory term sometimes used to describe Jews who have experienced centuries of genocide and discrimination. As a sociologist, I took these comments to mean that at least a few non-Jewish club members have a heightened awareness of the "Jewish" club members and more quickly think of them as "acting" Jewish than they would believe that club members might "act like" members of Protestant denominations.

Although representatives of some prestigious city and country clubs state to the media that they have Jewish American members, it is difficult to determine how many there are. Information derived from the media is often piecemeal and haphazard. Spokespersons for elite clubs often refuse to talk to academic researchers and deal with reporters only when they are trying to defuse criticism of their organization. Consider, for example, the following situation when a past president of the Dallas Country Club was attempting to curb media criticism of that club for having no African American members. The club's past president stated to journalists that his club is "committed to diversity" and that it is "one of the few that has full women memberships, and Jewish members, and Hispanic members, and members working very hard to attract a diverse list of applicants" (Ranshaw 2007). It is very unlikely that members of the Dallas Country Club would ever make a public statement about the composition of that club's membership if it were not for the continual questioning of reporters regarding a specific situation. The following statement by Steve, the chairman of the membership committee of one elite Texas club, is a good example of how officers and club members attempt to deflect criticism of their clubs for not having Jewish members:

> We don't care where you go to church or if you even do. We believe in separation of church and state, and some of our members prefer the golf course to the inside of a church on Sunday morning. I'd guess we have a pretty high percentage of Episcopalians, Methodists, Presbyterians, and Baptists. And probably some Catholics and a few independent, nondenominational types. But no Jews that I can think of and definitely no Muslims. . . . I might draw the line there myself given the current state of the world!

Based on this statement, we might assume that this club does not ask prospective members about their religious affiliation; however, this would be an incorrect assumption because both the organization's application form to be filled out by the candidate and the sponsors' recommendation forms ask about "church preference" and "How active are you and your family in church-related activities?" Obviously, as in other areas of social life, the line is blurred between religion and race/ethnicity in regard to Jewish Americans, and for club members and nonmembers alike, the question remains as to whether being "Jewish" is a religious or an ethnic classification. A similar issue sometimes arises regarding Latinos/as (Hispanics) who trace their origins to Mexico or Central America and are identified as all being Catholic because of their ethnicity by some white (non-Hispanic) people. This brings us to the topic of the racial and ethnic exclusion of African Americans and Latinos/as by elite clubs.

Racial and Ethnic Exclusion: African Americans and Latinos/as

In my research, I examined club archives, newspaper articles, and book-length histories (often written by a club member) for more than sixty clubs in the United States, of which twenty-five were in Texas. From these data, I found that no African Americans and few Latinos were members of such clubs until very recently, and a number of prestigious clubs still have very few, if any, people of color on their membership rosters. From the Gilded Age (1880–1920) to the late 1960s, for example, if an African American was mentioned at all in written materials by or about an elite club, it was because the individual had provided many years of "faithful service" to the club in positions such as a porter, golf caddy, or bartender. Among the numerous examples that I found where African Americans were described in this manner, the stories of two men—Pat Flanagan of Dallas and Ben Brieger of Austin—are representative and worth repeating to reveal the two-tier structure of race in elite clubs: white people are the club members; people of color are the service personnel who wait on the white members.

At the Dallas Country Club, where wealthy, white family memberships traditionally have been passed down from one generation to the next, Lee Patrick ("Pat") Flanagan, an African American, is mentioned throughout a lengthy history of the club, *Dallas Country Club: The First 100 Years*, not because he was a club member but because of his sixty-one years of "faithful service" first as a caddy and then as a locker room attendant at the club. On his retirement in 1969 and again on his death in 1993, club members praised Flanagan extensively for his service to the club, stated that "he was everybody's best friend," and illustrated his devotion to the small tasks in life by pointing out that he had polished several thousand pairs of his best friends' shoes and given more than a million back rubs during his years at the club (see Galloway 1996).

Similarly, Ben Brieger of Austin was widely praised in Headliners Club publications and the local media for his many years of service at the club, which is often referred to as Austin's most exclusive city club. Starting as a bartender long before the club admitted to membership a few African Americans from the corporate, academic, or political sectors of the community, Brieger rose through the ranks to become the club's long-term night manager (Flynn 2000). On Brieger's retirement and again at his death in 2000, a number of club members stated that the loss of Brieger represented "the end of an era" in the club's history (Flynn 2000). These tributes to the lengthy and faithful service of Flanagan and Brieger to elite, predominantly white city and country clubs are not isolated examples: for many years after the eras of slavery, reconstruction, and de jure (by law) racial segregation had ended in Texas and throughout the South, African Americans continued to be thought of as service personnel, not as equals or potential members, by elite clubs. In my study, I found that, in the late 1990s and early 2000s, some elite white club members were still making derogatory comments about "Negroes" or "niggers" while in the presence of African American waiters, bartenders, or other club service personnel. Most club members making the racist comments were white males in their eighties or nineties, and the other individuals present with them typically looked very embarrassed and tried to quiet them down or deflect the situation by changing the subject. When a young African American waiter at one of the city clubs was asked what he thought about such behavior, he stated, "I don't like it, of course. But I just ignore it. They're just a product of their generation, and it will soon be gone."

As we shift our focus from African Americans who have served in elite clubs for many years to those who might seek membership in such organizations, we find that many elite clubs, at one time or another, had specific provisions in the bylaws that excluded African Americans from membership. By contrast, other clubs operated on the basis of unwritten rules that not only precluded people of color from joining the club but also did not allow them to visit the club as the guest of a white member. Both written and unwritten codes about race have been rooted in club members' strongly held beliefs, past and present, that they have a God-given (and legal) right to freedom of association. This issue is reflected in the official documents of clubs that refused service to white members if they came to the club accompanied by an African American guest. Consider, for example, this excerpt from a letter written in the 1940s by F. A. Hathaway, then general secretary of the Young Men's Christian Association of Chicago, to the board of directors of Chicago's prestigious Union League Club: "I was greatly surprised to get your report with respect to the policy of the Union League Club in refusing to accept reservations for service in the private dining rooms [when] Negroes are included" (Nowlan 2004:111). Although African American men eventually were permitted to *visit* the club as the guests of white members, being a member of the club was out of the question for people of color until the early 1970s. For example, Union League Club members in the 1960s wrote letters, such as the following one, stating their deep concerns about admitting the first African American member:

> I feel very strongly, and I know my opinion is shared by others, that electing Mr. [Frederick C.] Ford to membership could result in great harm to our Club. A good many of our finest members, in my opinion, would gradually drift away and eventually move elsewhere. I realize full well the situation confronting our Country today but on the other hand the Union League Club is a private organization and is under the direction of the President and Board of Directors. Their responsibility, as I see it, is to act in a way which strengthens the Club, not weakens it. I urge you to refrain from electing this negro [sic] to membership in the Club. (Nowlan 2004:117)

This letter is representative of the kinds of organized opposition that many people of color faced if they were nominated for membership in elite clubs.

Even in the era of so-called political correctness, some club leaders continued to make public remarks about not wanting American Americans (or "blacks") in their club. Less than twenty years ago, for example, when a Birmingham, Alabama, reporter asked Shoal Creek Golf and Country Club founder Hall Thompson about his views on race, Thompson replied, "We don't discriminate in every other area except the black. . . . The country club is our home and we pick and choose who we want. We have the right to associate or not associate with whomever we choose" (Lieber 2003). Since the Professional Golfers' Association (PGA) Championship was scheduled to be held shortly thereafter at Shoal Creek, Thompson's statement initiated a crisis. PGA officials decided that the tournament should not be played at a racially segregated club, and they became particularly convinced in that regard when they saw that large corporate sponsors were quickly pulling millions of advertising dollars from the tournament. Despite the fact that Thompson went on the record as stating that neither he nor any other members of Shoal Creek would be pressured into accepting "the blacks," a compromise was reached by the PGA of America, Shoal Creek, and the Southern Christian Leadership Conference that called for the club's gradual racial integration. The first African American member was to be invited to join immediately, and the PGA tournament would go on as planned. As a result, Louis J. Willie, an avid golfer and president of the Booker T. Washington Insurance Company, became Shoal Creek's first African American member. Although a few more affluent African Americans have joined Shoal Creek in the ensuing decade, media reports suggest that the racial and ethnic composition of the club has not shifted dramatically in the aftermath of this "unfortunate incident" (Chambers 2000).

Faced with the threat of losing prestigious golf tournaments, a number of other elite golf and country clubs began to admit people of color as members. In the words of Darwin Davis, a well-known African American corporate executive, "When they want to host a tournament, all of a sudden there's room for black members." However, as Davis related, prior to the Shoal Creek debacle, he had a quite different experience with elite white club members:

> Either one or two things used to happen if you asked a guy to sponsor you at his club. Either you never heard from him again, or he'd come back and say, "Darwin, I don't believe this. I'm shocked. The club members don't even want to discuss this. They told me that if I don't like it, then get the hell out. There's nothing I can do." (Clay 1996)

In the first decade of the twenty-first century, more African Americans have become members of elite city and country clubs, including some that were formerly all-white bastions, such as Augusta National in Georgia; The

Country Club in Brookline, Massachusetts; Baltusrol in New Jersey; Winged Foot, Shinnecock, and Westchester country clubs in New York; and the Los Angeles Country Club. The better-late-than-never acceptance of some African American club members was explained in this way by Paul Dillon, a Winged Foot member and president of the Metropolitan Golf Association: "I think Shoal Creek opened the eyes of all of us, whether we were golfers or not. Maybe we blindly went about doing things our way without really thinking. In general I think it made us all aware of the need to examine our policies. And in some cases, clubs didn't even have policies" (Weinman 2003).

However, many elite clubs have not moved beyond having several token members who are people of color. For many African Americans and Latinos/as, being a token club member or having only a few other African American or Hispanic members to associate with does not have much appeal. According to affluent minority members, white club members typically cling to their inner circle, maintain their homogeneous identities, and continue to use the same methods for selecting new members. All these influences, taken together, do not bring much change to the club's racial and ethnic composition.

Despite the presence of outstanding African American golfers such as Tiger Woods, some African American golfers find that, even though more elite clubs claim to be inclusive, people of color sometimes feel out of place when they use club facilities. According to Pat Pierson, a member of a Pomona golf club and a competitor on the Master's tournaments, "Some people still look at you funny. I've gone into locker rooms and people have asked me, 'What are you doing in here?' because they think I'm a caddie" (Weinman 2003).

In Texas, some city and country clubs still have few, if any, African American or Latino/a club members. In 2007, the *Dallas Morning News* reported that both the Dallas Country Club and the Brook Hollow Golf Club, the city's two most prestigious, Old Guard clubs, still had no African American members (Ranshaw 2007). This information became public knowledge when Kneeland Youngblood, a prominent African American businessman, was proposed for membership in the Dallas Country Club. If his membership is approved, Youngblood will become the club's first African American member. However, Youngblood's application, which required two club sponsors and six club references, is now in its sixth year of consideration by the membership committee. Club representatives blame the slowness of the membership process on the fact that club has a waiting list of between 250 and 275 people, and only twenty to twenty-five new members are admitted per year to fill vacancies that become available because of the death or resignation of an existing member (Ranshaw 2007). Youngblood's friends fear that his application is being held up by the membership committee because of his involvement with the Reverend Jesse Jackson's Rainbow/PUSH Coalition, but unofficial comments from club insiders suggest that the problem may be that he did not list his involvement with Jackson on his application form (Ranshaw 2007). On the other side of the argument, Roger Staubach, a white real estate investor and former Dallas Cowboys quarterback, told reporters that clubs (such as the Dallas Country Club) "find all kinds of ways to rationalize it. But at the end of the day, they just don't want to break the [color] barrier" (Ranshaw 2007). Youngblood's membership application at an all-white, highly prestigious country club is but one of many possible examples showing the barriers that many wealthy, high-profile African Americans and other people of color experience, even in the twenty-first century, when they attempt to join elite, Old Guard social organizations.

Rather than blaming their exclusion from elite clubs on racism or discrimination, most upper-middle- and upper-class African Americans attribute their absence from elite (white) club memberships to the fact that white friends simply do not think of them as potential club members or invite them to visit the club. For example, Joseph, a wealthy African American man who is on several prestigious corporate and nonprofit boards in his city, stated,

> No, we aren't members of ——— club. We know [club members], but they've never invited us to their club. We get lots of party invitations from them if they're trying to raise money for the symphony, or the opera, or the ballet, or some hospital or other. Sometimes I wonder, if I'm good enough to give money and sit with them at these fund-raisers, why aren't my wife and I ever invited to their homes or clubs?

As this individual suggests, elite club members often distinguish between "public" events such as charity fund-raisers, where affluent people of color are welcomed as both givers and guests, and "private" events hosted by club members within the confines of their own residences or clubs. In the latter case, African Americans and Latinos/as are often overlooked as potential guests or prospective club members.

However, some elite clubs are now placing more emphasis on racial and ethnic diversity in their membership. This change may be attributed to a number of factors, including declining memberships in some clubs due to resignations or deaths of older members, changes in laws that have made club dues and many club expenses no longer tax deductible, and the number of corporations that have cut back on paying for their executives' club memberships. As a result, city clubs especially have become more proactive in recruiting new members across racial and ethnic lines. Some members believe that diversity is important for the survival of the club; others see a more diverse membership as an important asset in an era of globalization and rapid change in the U.S. economy.

From my research, I found a representative example of how even a slight increase in the diversity of an elite club's membership may produce a few leaders from underrepresented minority groups. Since 2000, for example, Austin's Headliners Club has had two club presidents who identify themselves as Latino or Mexican American. In 2000, Arnold Garcia Jr., then editor of the *Austin American-Statesman*, was the first person with a Hispanic surname to be a Headliners Club president. When asked if he was proud of that fact, he stated, "Sure, but I'm more proud of the fact that I am the first working journalist for many years to be chosen president" (Powers 2000:1). In this statement, Garcia played down his ethnicity by focusing on the fact that this exclusive club originally was formed to include members of the press and electronic media as well as the city's Old Guard and important "movers and shakers" in business, politics, education, and the professions. When Hector De Leon, a Mexican American attorney and adjunct law professor, was elected president of the Headliners Club in 2007, he was more open about the obstacles of race/ethnicity and class he overcame to be president, as this excerpt from his open letter to members shows:

> It is an honor to be asked to serve as President of the Headliners Club. That being said, I have to add that I am truly amazed and humbled that I would ever be considered for this position. You see, growing up in East Austin, I could only imagine what took place at the Headliners Club. My father and mother ran many restaurants in Austin, but nothing like the Headliners Club. While my father would have made today's Club chefs proud to work along side him, he could only talk about what he had heard about the space where well-dressed people could look out over our city and the restaurants he ran. . . . Who would have thought that 32 years later, I would be standing [here] as your president? Who would have thought that this kid from East Austin would actually be a part of the history of the Club that his father and mother could only talk about. Isn't life ironic? (*Headlines* 2007:1)

Although city clubs such as the Headliners now include more African Americans and Latinos/as who are professionals, corporate leaders, academic administrators, and politicians, many country clubs and wall-less city clubs have remained virtually all-white. As previously discussed, the most prestigious country clubs often are located in exclusive urban or suburban enclaves where most residents are white (non-Hispanic) and live in million-dollar-plus homes. In cities such as Harlingen, Texas, located about ten miles north of the Mexican border, where Latinos/as (Hispanics) make up more than 85 percent of the city's population, country clubs frequently have had to make adjustments in their membership procedures if they wish to survive. However, according to one wealthy Latino respondent who was invited to join the Harlingen Country Club, that club sometimes focuses more on getting (white) retirees and "snowbirds" (people who migrate from the North to warmer climates in the winter months) to join the club as regular or seasonal members than really welcoming Latinos as members of the club (see also *Club Management* 2003).

In sum, although the white members of elite clubs may argue that African Americans and/or Latinos have no real interest in joining their clubs, many people of color believe that they lose important opportunities to gain the kinds of social and cultural capital that reap significant rewards in the larger society. One African American executive explained why he thought that the exclusionary practices of elite clubs not only hurt him professionally and financially but also might harm his children:

> My counterpart [a white executive] and his son and daughter practice and take [golf] lessons at their club. His children grow up with the knowledge of how to use the club for social and business reasons. My children don't get this experience and, once again, the cycle is repeated. Second-class citizenship is perpetuated all over again. (Clay 1996)

For many people, the same might be said for exclusion based on gender or sexual orientation.

EXCLUSION BASED ON GENDER OR SEXUAL ORIENTATION

For most of the history of exclusive clubs in the United States, gender restrictions prohibited women from applying for membership in elite men's clubs. The categoric exclusion of women was based on the notion that men needed a place to call their own, away from the daily toil of work and the social pressures of home life. The private club became a bastion for male bonding, and the exclusion of women became the norm.

Gender-Based Exclusion

In the twenty-first century, a number of prestigious clubs, including the Augusta National Country Club in Georgia, the Haverhill Golf and Country Club in Massachusetts, and the Pacific-Union Club in California, exclude women from full membership. Many explanations have been offered as to why women are refused club membership, including the claim by some clubs that they have no more room to expand their facilities so that they could include women.

Historically, male club members made fun of women when they wanted to join a "men's-only" club. For example, when the male members of a prestigious private Upper East Side club in New York City were asked why there were no women in their club, they replied that the "women will be exposed to harsh language, that they'll giggle in the library or drink too much and fall off the bar stool"(Winfrey 1978:B5). Among the few women allowed on the premises of traditionally all-male elite clubs are the wives, daughters, and the occasional mistresses of members. However, at least in the past, these women were welcome only at certain times of day and in limited areas of the club, such as the "Strangers' Room" at the New York City Racquet and Tennis Club (Winfrey 1978). As a result, some privileged women developed separate clubs and established their own clubhouses and membership requirements. The Colony Club at Park Avenue and 62nd Street in New York, for example, is described as the "establishment women's club" (*New York Times* 1987:E7). With early members such as Mrs. John Jacob Astor, the Colony Club became the domain of privileged, upper-class women who stated that they had no need—or desire—to invade their husbands' private clubs. Rather, the women enjoyed luncheons, swimming and reading, and educational activities rather than having to listen to their husband's "boring" discussions (*New York Times* 1987).

Exclusion on the basis of gender is a topic of concern in some elite Texas clubs. In the most prestigious wall-less men's clubs, it is simply assumed that women's primary roles in the group are as a girlfriend, sister, wife, mother, or grandmother. In other words, women are present at club functions, but they typically are the "arm pieces" or cheerleaders for the male members. Debutantes play a key role in annual presentation balls sponsored by the wall-less men's clubs; however, the young women who are presented have no thoughts of joining the club. They instead feel honored to be asked to participate in this annual black-tie affair. However, this does not mean that privileged women in Texas are not active in their own elite clubs. There is an extensive history of the involvement of upper-middle- and upper-class Texas women in charitable and social endeavors where they not only gain social power for themselves but also are able to socially reproduce the next generation of elites through the socialization of their own children and grandchildren to follow in their footsteps (see Kendall 2002).

As compared with elite wall-less men's clubs, it is far more common for women to be members and sometimes officers of exclusive Texas city and country clubs. Professional women, particularly with expertise in business or law, have insisted that they be invited to join city clubs because these are places where cocktails, lunch, or dinner often serves a business purpose. Changing trends such as the greater inclusion of women members have made the city club a venue for daytime business luncheons and other social events at which women, particularly single women, can derive business, political, and social benefits through their participation. Joan, a well-established woman attorney, described changes she has seen at her prestigious city club:

> When we first started going [to the club], the membership was in [her husband's] name. All of the members were men except a few female journalists because the club focuses on the press as well as on leaders in business, politics, and higher ed. Now, I'm a widow, and the membership's in my name. My daughter holds a membership in her own name, and there are a good number of other women members, although I understand that many of them are the widows of former members.

In sum, it appears that elite clubs have become somewhat more open to women members, with the exception of wall-less gentlemen's social clubs. However, as women's inclusion in some elite clubs has become less contentious, the issue of sexual orientation has become more controversial.

Exclusion Based on Sexual Orientation

Throughout the history of elite WASP clubs, the norm for inclusion required that members, at least overtly, should be heterosexual. Since the men in some elite clubs swam and showered in the buff, they felt that it was important for members to demonstrate a macho, heterosexual attitude toward each other so that no one could be accused of being "queer" or gay. In the 2000s, a number of elite men's clubs still have members who swim together naked (Vachon 2005). In New York City, for example, the University Club and the Racquet and Tennis Club have members who relax after a stressful day's work by swimming without their clothes. Most participants are unwilling to talk about such practices; as one investment banker informed a *New York Times* reporter, "It's a matter of the WASP ethic. What goes on at the R.T.C. stays at the R.T.C. We don't want the general public having a peek at the last bastion of old-school pleasure, the last oasis" (Vachon 2005:E1). Clubs where male members swim naked have resisted both female members and male members of "uncertain sexual orientation." The unspoken norm of heterosexuality among male club members was not questioned until more gay men and lesbians began to come out of the closet in the 1960s and 1970s. At that time, some gay men and lesbians began to demand equal treatment by exclusive clubs, and clubs were forced to deal with issues of sexual orientation as well as gender, race, ethnicity, and religion.

Although some barriers have fallen in a few elite private clubs and some overtly gay members have joined, new questions have risen about the membership rights of the partners of gay or lesbian members. Although some gay men and lesbians originally hid their sexual orientation when they were seeking elite club memberships, more now inform directors and club committees of their sexual orientation and request that their partners (and sometimes their children) be given all the benefits and privileges that a family membership grants to the spouses and children of heterosexual members (Chambers 2004). A pivotal point in the discussion at many clubs is whether homosexual partners are considered to be legally married. As the club manager and chief executive officer of the Country Club in Brookline, Massachusetts (one of the oldest and most exclusive in the United States), explained, "If you are married, you are married. If you are not, then you are in the guest category. Now that the state of Massachusetts is allowing gay marriage, fine. It doesn't matter to us if you are homosexual or heterosexual" (Chambers 2004:A32).

As more women have gained membership in private clubs, lesbian members have found that club rules sometimes prevent their same-sex partners from having the same privileges of a family membership that are enjoyed by heterosexual couples. In a 2001, Birgit Koebke and her partner, Kendall French, filed a lawsuit against California's Bernardo Heights Country Club: Ms. Koebke bought a $18,000 family membership, and club officials would not allow her registered domestic partner, Ms. French, to have the same membership privileges as the spouses of heterosexual club members. At this country club, members' spouses can golf for free, but unmarried guests must pay $40 to $75 per round of golf, and they are allowed to play on the club's course only six times a year. In 2005, the California Supreme Court ruled in favor of Koebke and French on the basis that they were domestic partners registered under the California Domestic Partner Rights and Responsibilities Act of 2003. According to the court, the club engaged in impermissible marital status discrimination because the two are registered domestic partners in the state of California. At the conclusion of the case, Koebke called the decision "a great victory for California families" and claimed, "Kendall and I are one step closer to being able to play golf at Bernardo Heights on an equal basis" (Egelko 2005).

The question of what legally constitutes a spouse and what constitutes a private club appear to be the primary issues in a number of cases involving same-sex partners and club memberships. In a case involving the Druid Hills Golf Club in Atlanta, the club president informed a lesbian couple that the organization had its own definition of marriage and that "creating an exception to our longstanding policy regarding what constitutes a spouse is not an exception we are either required or willing to make" (Chambers 2004:A32). However, the plaintiffs in this case prevailed when Atlanta's Human Relations Commission ruled against Druid Hills, stating that the club is a public accommodation and not a private club because it allows major corporations, local businesses, and Emory University to rent its facilities for their functions.

In Texas, the issue of same-sex partnership has not received much publicity or been an issue in court cases. When I sought information about this, I found that some elite clubs have known lesbian or gay members but that they joined on the basis of "don't ask, don't tell" and that these members "act just like any other club member," in the words of one club manager. Gay and lesbian club members in Texas apparently have not raised the question of full privileges for their domestic partners. Either they have taken out club memberships individually so that both persons could participate fully or one partner goes as the guest of the other to club-related social functions. In the club membership directories, these individuals typically have not been listed as partners or as spouses. Because of conservative religious and political ideology in Texas, it is possible that gays and lesbians who hold high corporate positions or who serve as officials in higher education or health care believe that it is in their best interest to conceal or deemphasize their sexual orientation when they join clubs or participate in club events. Larry, a wealthy gay philanthropist who is a member of an elite city club, stated that he believed there were more important things for the gay community to be concerned about than club memberships:

> The gay community in Texas has more important issues to think about, ranging from redneck prejudice and discrimination to the constant need of some politicians to undermine the few gains that gays and lesbians have made over the years. Maybe we will get around to dealing with homophobic country club members some day, but, for now, there are more pressing things on the agenda, like a constitutional ban on gay marriage and denying domestic partners health benefits and prohibiting gays and lesbians from adopting children who have no parents.

As Larry suggests, many issues remain unresolved for gay and lesbian couples, and their treatment by elite clubs is no exception.

As we have seen in this chapter, the practices of elite clubs are far from the strictly private matters that many club members describe them as being. Issues of inclusion and exclusion based on class, religion, race/ethnicity, gender, and sexual orientation are not as much a "thing of the past" as social elites would like to claim. As we enter the second decade of the twenty-first century, elite clubs may serve as one microcosm through which much larger issues of social and economic inequality play out in the United States.

In chapter 4, I examine how new members are introduced to club life. I then look at the privileges that are associated with club membership, including a variety of ways in which members enhance their social and cultural capital through club events. Finally, I examine club gatherings and rituals to show how these unite a number of individuals into one unified body of members who share certain goals, ideals, and traditions that they believe are important not only for themselves but for future generations as well.

· 4 ·

Membership Has Its Privileges

Some things in life I might give up; others I wouldn't want to be
without. My [club] membership is one of the things I want to
keep. When I come here, I'm treated very well. The manager and
the help call me by name. They know what I like to drink, where
I want to sit, and, even more important, they know when to
strike up a conversation with me and when to leave me alone.
Prior to becoming a member, I went to a number of [club] functions, but my feelings about the club really grew when I was invited to join—I now belong to the club, and the club belongs to
me: It's "my club."

—"Chuck Jones," a white attorney in his fifties,
describes how he feels about his club

To the outsider, the club to which the upper class man or woman
belongs is a badge of certification of his status; to the insider, the
club provides a more intimate or clan-like set of exclusive groupings which places and characterizes a man. Their core of membership is usually families which successfully claim status by descent. From intimate association with such men, newer members
borrow status, and in turn, the accomplishments of the newer
entrants help shore up the status of the club as a going concern.

—C. Wright Mills (1956:61), a highly respected
twentieth-century sociologist, describes the benefits
of club membership based on his research findings

These descriptions of elite club membership—by a current club member and
a prominent sociologist who extensively studied upper-class organizations—
highlight the privileges associated with being a member of an exclusive club.

Although the slogan "membership has its privileges" was popularized by the American Express Company in its credit card advertisements, this motto is useful in a sociological analysis of the immediate and longer-term benefits of club membership. Being a member provides individuals with a variety of scarce resources, such as access to an extensive social network of wealthy and influential people ("These are *my* kind of people!"); a feeling of personal ownership in the city's most prestigious dining, entertaining, and health and fitness facilities ("Let's meet for drinks at *my* club."); and an increase in prestige and social standing in the community because of the member's known association with the city's blue bloods, political leaders, or most successful investors and businesspeople as a result of club membership ("I recently I saw 'Mr. Big Bucks' at *my* club, and he said . . .").

According to C. Wright Mills, club membership is as a "badge of certification" of a person's status to *outsiders* and a "more intimate or clan-like set of exclusive groupings which places and characterizes" a person to *insiders*. From this perspective, both newer members and established members derive benefits from their association with one another: new members gain prestige and enhanced status by associating with established members who are part of the Old Guard; in turn, new members reenergize the club through their accomplishments and their social and financial contributions. As Hal, an established club member of long standing, stated, "Those young pups keep us old dogs looking good. They get elected, win philanthropy awards, and are named outstanding doctor, lawyer, and this and that. We can sit around the bar and say, 'Oh yeah, he's a club member . . . a really great guy,' and we don't have to do a lick of work to take credit for what he's done."

In this chapter, I examine the privileges and benefits that new members gain when they join an exclusive club and the process by which these novices learn about their club privileges and responsibilities. Next, I describe the methods by which newer and established members enhance their social and cultural capital through their participation in the club's programs, social events, and organizational activities. Finally, I address an underlying sociological question regarding privilege in elite clubs: if members ("insiders") have much to gain from their clubs, what—if anything—do nonmembers ("outsiders") lose by not being members?

LEARNING THE ROPES: PRIVILEGES AND RESPONSIBILITIES

Although social elites are members of a variety of clubs throughout their lives, each organization tends to socialize new members, regardless of their pedigree and social status, to the club's way of doing things. Becoming a member of an elite city, country, or wall-less social club is no exception: whether the group conducts a new-member orientation session or simply delivers printed information about the club and its rules to the newcomer, new members are expected to know certain things about the club and to follow its norms and expectations. How new members learn about their privileges and responsibilities varies based on the type of club they join and the social customs of other clubs in their region; however, three immediate privileges for new club members may be identified: access to insider information, approval and acceptance by established club members, and gaining higher prestige in the eyes of non-members.

Privilege: Access to Insider Information
Responsibility: Not for Public Consumption

Exclusive clubs typically are secretive about their members' names and personal information, about club policies and procedures, and about social relations that are developed within the club setting; however, when a person joins the club, he or she receives a virtual Pandora's box full of information that is not available to outsiders. This information includes a membership directory, club newsletters, a calendar of upcoming club events, and (when applicable) a list of reciprocal clubs that are affiliated with their own club so that they will have a "club home" even when they are in another city or country.[1]

The membership directory is perhaps the single most important source of information regarding *who* the club members are, *what* they do for their economic resources and in their leisure time, *where* they may be contacted, and *how* long they have been club members. Sociologists who study the upper class, such as G. William Domhoff (2005, 2006), have long lamented the fact that the membership directories of elite clubs such as California's Bohemian Club are virtually impossible to obtain unless they are very old (and often quite irrelevant) copies that have been donated to a library or university collection on the death of a club member.

A club's membership directory typically contains the member's full name; his or her spouse's name (listed in parentheses after the member's name); first, second, and third home addresses; business names and addresses; numbers for landlines and mobile phones; and fax and e-mail addresses. Some directories list the names of minor children and the children's phone numbers, especially in golf or country clubs where young people actively participate in age-specific activities and intermural sports. University club directories often indicate the degrees held by their members and list current academic commitments, such as serving on their alma mater's board of regents. Some directories have elaborate lists of members' residences year-round, such as contact information at the "yacht," "lake house," or "summer residence." In Texas and other states where upper-class publications like the *Social Register* have not been as widely available or as influential as in other areas of the country, the membership directories of elite clubs have often been used by privileged people as a *Social Register* of sorts. According to one prominent Highland Park resident who holds membership in a number of city and country clubs, "Being listed in the DCC [the Dallas Country Club] directory is like being in the *Social Register*, except we don't really have one."[2]

In addition to information about other club members, most membership directories contain lists of the club's board of trustees, past presidents, bylaws, house rules, and sometimes the club's history. Although this is not of great relevance to outsiders, club members and officers do not want this information to be widely published because of their belief that, in popular lingo, "what happens at the club, stays at the club."

The second-best source of insider information at the exclusive club is the monthly newsletter because this publication usually has photographs and descriptions of the latest social events at the club. From the newsletter, it is possible for newer members to see who is participating in various events at the club and to attend similar events in the future if the person is interested in similar activities or would like to become acquainted with other members who seem to enjoy such events. The newsletter provides a calendar of upcoming events so that it is possible to plan ahead either for leisure purposes or for opportunities to enhance one's social and/or cultural capital. As you will recall from chapter 1, social capital refers primarily to the nature and kind of social connections and networks an individual possesses, whereas cultural capital refers to widely shared, high-status cultural signals (attitudes, preferences, formal knowledge, behaviors, goods, and credentials) that are used in social and cultural inclusion or exclusion. Thus, a new member who decides to benefit from attending a social function at the club is likely to gain in both *social capital*—by becoming better acquainted with other members who share a similar interest in wine, for example—and *cultural capital*—by becoming more knowledgeable about some marker of upper-class taste, such as the best of this year's French or Italian wines or highlights from the latest book by a prize-winning author.

The membership directory and the club newsletter are only two of many sources of insider information that are available to new and established members. When members are around the club and participating in social and sports activities, they see and hear things that may tell them something about other club members that is not widely known to outsiders. Even clubs that are not considered to be a secret society, like the Ivy League drinking clubs or a chapter of the Masonic Lodge, are based on the assumption that members will share mutual respect and be able to trust each other. By joining an exclusive club, a new member implicitly agrees to respect the privacy of others and not to reveal information he or she learns within the club. For this reason, many clubs do not permit reporters or photographers to be present at the club's events. However, clubs such as Austin's Headliners Club invite prominent journalists to become members, and in that case, journalists are present at some functions but are not thought of as working journalists (meaning that they should leave their notepad or computer at home) when they are enjoying a meal or social event at the club.

All club members are responsible for protecting insider information about their club and its members. As is evidenced by the popularity of tabloid journalism and the numerous "tell-all" exposés that are available on television, so-called insider information (regardless of its accuracy) is a valuable commodity. Outsiders who are able to acquire a club's membership directory and copies of newsletters and other publications may garner an array of personal information that a member may not wish to share with nonmembers. As a result, new members not only gain the privilege of easy access to this information but also are informed about the importance of confidentiality and the prohibition against revealing information or handing out copies of the membership directory to other people. According to Fred, a new-member coordinator at an exclusive Texas country club, the officers decided that it was going to be necessary to deal explicitly with the problem of leaked information in their club after several unfortunate incidents occurred:

> At the welcoming orientation, we specifically ask new members not to give out the information we provide them. I point out that other members will be displeased if you inappropriately use this information or give it to someone else who tries to make social connections or money off of it. We had problems a couple of years ago when we had more new members than usual and some of 'em were new to our city. I guess they were used to making money from their club and church connections, but we don't do things that way. Pretty soon, VIPs were getting phone calls on unlisted lines and piles of e-mails about investment opportunities and fund-raising for charities from people who were acting like their best friends but they'd never heard of 'em before. When they figured out that the information was from our club directory, they got really hot under the collar and called the [club] manager and chewed him out. Then the trustees had a big discussion about whether we should have a directory or not and if members should be able to be "unlisted" in the club directory also. To make a long story short, we kept the directory, asked people to list only those numbers where they would be willing to be contacted, and focused on teaching new and old members alike about their responsibilities to other members.

According to this respondent, violations of privacy were particularly subject to scrutiny when it involved the members' children. One new member used the club directory, which listed children's names and phone numbers, to create a "get-acquainted list" for her own son and daughter because she thought these contacts might be useful for her children. In interviews with members of other clubs, I heard a limited number of similar stories; however, club members for the most part value their privacy and expect other members to do likewise.

The disdain that established club members feel for people who do not respect the privacy of others was expressed by an influential club woman from an Old Guard family: "Only social climbers *use* information from the club in an inappropriate manner! Club directories and websites are *not* to be used for one's personal gain. Shame on those who try." This member pointed out that although most people who join exclusive clubs still come from her city's "better" families and understand that club rules are to be followed, a few "bad apples"—by which she meant wealthy "arrivistes with more money than class"—had to be frequently reminded of the club's behavioral norms. This problem exists at many private clubs, a large number of which have printed statements similar to the following example (in all capital letters) in one club's house rules:

WRITTEN RULES ARE EMPTY RHETORIC WITHOUT THE FULL UNDERSTANDING THAT EACH MEMBER AND GUEST SHALL AT ALL TIMES ABIDE BY THE UNWRITTEN RULES OF COURTESY, DIGNITY AND GOOD CONDUCT EXPECTED OF ALL PEOPLE. (Headliners Club 2006)

Words such as "courtesy," "mutual respect," and "dignity" are used in club statements regarding the responsibilities that come with a member's privileges in the club. A statement in The California Club's house rules reminds not only club members but also their guests (and visitors from reciprocal clubs) that they are expected to behave themselves while on the club's premises: "In order to preserve the customs and traditions at The California Club, all the Members, Privilege Holders and their Guests are requested to conduct themselves with decorum and in keeping with the Club's traditional concepts of dignity and mutual respect."

In sum, members of elite clubs expect other members to abide by written and unwritten rules regarding courtesy, dignity, and conduct. In return for their good behavior and proper decorum, newer members gain the approval and acceptance of established members.

Privilege: Acceptance by Other Members
Responsibility: Dress Right and Act Right

One way in which new members benefit from club membership is through the acquisition of a sense of belonging (in-group solidarity) that comes from being fully accepted as a member who deserves to be a part of the club. Although individuals are invited to join an exclusive club, they may not know many of the established members. As exclusive clubs have grown larger and have sought to provide a wider diversity of activities and services, it is not unusual for many members not to be acquainted with one another.

One way new members can become better acquainted with existing members is through attending club functions and giving established members "a chance to look them over and see if they fit in." A new member's club sponsor and the organization's orientation sessions are used to encourage novices to look and act like other club members to ensure their greater acceptance and to make other club members comfortable in their presence.

Nowhere is this statement more accurate than at the orientation sessions held by wall-less elite men's clubs during which new members are introduced to the dress code and behavioral norms of the club. This typically is no surprise to new members because they often have attended numerous social functions hosted by the club before they were invited to membership. However, at the new-member orientation, the expectations of the club are formalized for new club members. At these orientation sessions, new members are informed about club regalia that they will wear at formal social events to signify their membership in the organization. Let's look first at a club where members enjoy wearing a distinctive club uniform on formal and semiformal social occasions.

The Admirals Club originally was formed as a sponsoring organization for Austin's annual Aqua Fest celebration, which included a summer concert series, motorboat races, beauty pageants, and an elaborate, by-invitation-only debutante ball at which the daughters of Admirals Club members and other social elites were presented as the Queen and Court of Aqua Fest. Although the Aqua Fest celebration has not been held in almost a decade, the Admirals Club continues to flourish, and members and their wives present an annual debutante ball at which the members wear their specially made naval uniforms to commemorate the club's traditional association with the Aqua Fest celebration.

Knowing the dress code of the Admirals Club helps new members show up appropriately attired for social events, and established members appreciate how novices respect the club's tradition by showing up in full-dress regalia for formal occasions and in semidress for cocktail parties. On full-dress occasions, members wear a powder blue nautical jacket with gold trim, a lightly starched tuxedo shirt, a black silk bow tie, black tuxedo pants, and black patent dress shoes (no laces, tassels, or buckles). For semidress (cocktail) occasions, members wear their nautical jacket with a white dress shirt, regular black necktie, black suit pants, and well-polished black leather shoes. On formal occasions, club officers such as the Fleet Admiral wear dress whites that set them apart from rank-and-file club members. Since formal social events like the annual debutante ball are open to nonmembers by invitation from the members, it is easy to identify club insiders from men who are outside the club because the dress code for nonmembers is "black tie"—a standard black tuxedo. According to one journalist's description of the history and demise of the Aqua Fest celebration, the uniforms of Admiral's Club members are a defining feature of this organization and also a source of ridicule for some nonelites in Austin:

> The all-male, by-invitation-only Club itself, with its formal dress whites for every member [*sic*], comprises Austin men who cut ice—doctors and lawyers, car dealers and real-estate barons, UT leaders and once and future mayors. That men with means spent their energies dressing up in fake uniforms, throwing theme parties, and parading their marriageable daughters surely seems silly—which is why the same rituals have been adopted as camp staples by drag artistes—but basically harmless. It sure did, though, make Aqua Fest an easy target for populists, progressives, greens and radicals ... even though the same moneybags in the sailor suits worked [hard] to put on the Festival. (Clark-Madison 1998)

As this reporter suggested, many Admirals Club members worked hard to make Aqua Fest successful even if they enjoyed themselves as they did so. Now the club is purely social in its goals and objectives.

Of course, most wall-less elite men's clubs in Texas and elsewhere do not have club uniforms: the most popular attire for men at a formal occasion is a standard suit-length tuxedo jacket, pleated tuxedo shirt, black silk bow tie (hand tied, not a clip-on), wide fabric cummerbund at the waist, black tuxedo pants with a silk stripe down each leg, and black patent evening shoes. A number of wall-less men's clubs have other means to designate club members and club officers by their attire at formal social occasions sponsored by the club. One of the most popular membership designations is a shoulder sash—a brightly colored loop of fabric that is draped from the member's left shoulder down across his chest to the edge of the right hip so that the material will lie flat across the front of the tuxedo shirt and otherwise be hidden from view by the person's tuxedo jacket. Some organizations emboss the club's emblem on the shoulder sash in gold or silver.

New members who wear their club's shoulder sash for the first time typically describe a sense of pride in belonging to the organization because the sash sets them apart from nonmembers. Following the custom of British aristocracy and some gentlemen's clubs in London, the members of U.S. clubs who wear these wide, brightly colored (usually red, purple, or gold) sashes think of this as a unique form of identity ("we-ness") among club members.

New members learn about the shoulder sashes through informal discussions with other members. When they arrive at their first formal function after joining the club, new members are presented with a sash and shown how to attach and drape it. In some clubs, officers, active members, and associate members have different colors of sashes, and sometimes officers have more ornate sashes that are made from a fine brocade and trimmed with elaborate braiding to honor them for their service to the club.

Wearing a specially designed club sash or a uniform is a privilege of elite club membership because it is not only a physical item of clothing or an accessory but also a symbol of belonging, of membership in a club that does not accept everyone who might wish to join. Wearing a shoulder sash also signifies to other club members that a person they may not know is "one of us" and should be treated as an equal. Sashes and other visible indicators of club membership may serve as powerful symbols. According to Arthur, a thirty-year member of a prestigious wall-less men's club, the shoulder sash provides outsiders (and sometimes insiders as well) with a visible "who's who" of the club:

> In [name of club], the officers wear a gold sash printed with the club's insignia and gold braiding around the edges. If a person has on a white sash with the club's insignia, he's an active [a younger, single member]. A red sash means the wearer is an associate [an older, married] member. We wear our sashes at the ball to show we're proud of our club's tradition. The debs' parents and friends and the guests we invite can tell from our sashes that we're the ones in charge, and the sashes read like our club's "who's who."

Exceptions to the uniform or shoulder sash do exist. One of the most prestigious Texas men's clubs has chosen to use a very subtle indicator of club membership for black-tie events. Members of the Idlewild Club of Dallas wear a discreet red ribbon pinned on their lapel to identify themselves as past or present club members at their annual debutante ball (Heap 2006). Although the ribbon is similar to those used in fund-raising for cancer and other diseases, the thin red ribbon signifies to the Old Guard and to more recent affluent newcomers to the city that the individuals wearing these ribbons are members of a club that, for about 120 years, has held the most prestigious ball in that city and has its own Idlewild Waltz (Heap 2006).

Although casual events held by wall-less men's clubs typically do not have a specific dress code that sets members apart from outsiders, some clubs create T-shirts or caps that members and guests can purchase to wear at a specific function. Similar to the T-shirts worn at theme parties given by college fraternities and sororities commemorating some event and the individual's involvement in it, elite men's social clubs have specially made shirts for members at some special events. The Dervish Club of Dallas, for example, sells members a white T-shirt to wear at the club's annual All Club Crawfish Festival, which has the following written on the front:

ALL CLUB CRAWFISH BOIL
Barley House
"PINCHIN' TAILS
ALL DAY LONG!"

In addition to the crawfish shirt, this club—like many other elite men's social clubs—has a signature golf shirt and cap with the club's insignia printed on it. Although such things as club T-shirts and caps may seem like a very small thing to nonmembers, the typical member of an exclusive club, whether it be a wall-less men's social club or the city's premier country club, believes that clothing and other accessories with the club's logo or the commemoration of a special social event are visual representations of that person's membership in the organization and association with other influential individuals who add to his or her own resources and social capital.

Wall-less men's clubs are not alone in having a dress code that sets members apart from outsiders. Although, as clothing norms in the larger society have become more relaxed, the leaders of some elite clubs have felt the need to modify the dress code of their club, and most have agreed that there is a minimum standard of appearance norms that should be adhered to by all members and their guests at club facilities and functions. For this reason, clubs print a club dress code in their newsletters and as part of their house rules. The following is a typical example of such a dress code:

A. At lunch, coats and ties are not required. Casual attire accepted in any part of the Club. (No shorts anytime.)
B. On private party occasions, the dress code is set by the host or hostess, depending on the occasion or theme of the event.
C. After 6 p.m., coat required (ties optional) in the main Dining Rooms.
D. After 6 p.m., coat required (ties optional) in the Main Lounge.
E. Coats and tie are not required in the Press Box[3] in the evening.
F. It is understood that ladies who come to the Headliners Club will dress with dignity and decorum by their own choice. (Headliners Club 2006)

As the policies of this club show, club dress codes often vary by time of day, specific rooms or areas of the club, and the nature of a social event. In the past, most exclusive city clubs required men to wear a coat and tie for dinner, but this rule has been relaxed because of changing social norms and the climate in some areas of the country. Clubs such as Pittsburgh's Duquesne Club, which is considered to be one of the nation's top city clubs by many club analysts, specifically establish a distinction between "club traditional attire," which refers to a coat and tie for men and comparable attire for women; and "club casual attire," which is as follows: "collared shirts, turtleneck sweaters, or knit or golf type shirts with collars, tucked into tailored trousers or khakis. Ladies may wear blouses or sweaters with tailored skirts or slacks." Children's attire is described in this way: "Children should be conservatively dressed at all times. The Club's adult dress code applies to children ages 12 and older." Unacceptable attire at the club is defined as "jeans, denim, tee shirts, sweatshirts, shorts, mini-skirts, athletic clothing and athletic shoes (except in the Health and Fitness Center), leggings, spandex, informal leather attire, halter tops, casual hats, casual sandals, hiking boots and recreational footwear." According to this club's rules, "No one will be admitted to the Club in unacceptable attire" (Duquesne Club 2006).

Although I could provide many examples of dress codes in elite clubs, my central point in this discussion is to show that club rules about dress constitute a benefit for club members—even though, to outsiders, such policies may appear to be a liability associated with membership—because if new and established members follow the dress code and behavioral norms, they feel that they truly belong and that they fit in with other members. They also show their support for upper-class social norms and values that they may believe have been largely lost on people in the middle and lower classes of contemporary society. In other words, new members have an opportunity to impress on established members and outsiders alike that they are part of the Old Guard or a "blue blood," based on how they look and how they behave, even if their social credentials are not as impeccable as they might like. Perhaps this is the American modification of the earlier British notion of "clubability" and the "true gentleman," as discussed in chapter 2. Clearly, visible indicators of membership, such as items of clothing or accessories, produce a "consciousness of kind" among members and a sense of community where, in the description of one exclusive Minnesota country club, "everyone in your family makes friends for a lifetime" and all members have "sense of neighborhood" (Edina Country Club 2007).

Of course, as members bond with each other and develop their own social networks and sources of cultural capital, nonmembers are left outside the social equation. Outsiders who aspire to join an elite club often develop an increased and perhaps grudging respect for people who are invited to join one of their city's most exclusive clubs whether or not these individuals have actually done anything to deserve this heightened level of prestige.

Privilege: Prestige from Outsiders
Responsibility: Deference to Established Members

Members of elite clubs pride themselves on their social position in the larger society and within their own private club. New members particularly believe that their status—their relative position within one or more hierarchies—is enhanced by their affiliation with a prestigious organization and that they may be admired or at least looked favorably on by outsiders because they possess this club membership.

Elite clubs operate on the principles of admiration and deference: members are admired by other members and outsiders, and members are given at least some deference by individuals on the club's staff who refer to members using their formal names ("Welcome, Mr. Adams. How may we serve you tonight?") but are spoken to by their first name, usually followed by a command ("John, please bring me another class of wine").

In a classical sociological study of social status and prestige, the sociologist Emile Benoit-Smullyan (1944) suggested that wealth alone is not sufficient to make a person feel important. Although possession of wealth may make it possible for individuals to enjoy certain "creature comforts," they do not receive "any delight of domination" from their wealth other than in how they choose to spend their money (Benoit-Smullyan 1944:157). Possessing high prestige based on status makes it possible for a person to see himself or herself as possessing power over others and having the ability to dominate them, even if no overt efforts are made to control others. According to Benoit-Smullyan (1944), a person who possesses high prestige becomes an *object of admiration* because that individual holds a place of honor in significant organizations and participates in important ceremonies. Similarly, a person of high prestige may be the *object of deference* because people of lower prestige address that individual in a distinctive way and typically give the person favored treatment in a specific social situation, such as the former president of the United States who is always given the VIP table at his private club even if he has not informed club personnel in advance that he will be dining at the club that evening.

People with high prestige may become an *object of imitation* because their behavior becomes the model by which others think that they may achieve the same level of social success. Outsiders who aspire to join an exclusive club, for example, may model their behavior on that of individuals who are members of the club, knowing that their appearance and behavior apparently were successful in winning their approval from established club members and hoping that it will do the same for them. Similar types of modeling behavior are also evident in relationships such as between attending physician and medical residents or between top partners in a law firm and first-year associates. Similarly, aspirants to exclusive club membership may imitate the appearance and behavior of established members in order to gain favor with those who will make future decisions about membership in the club.

Although there are a number of benefits, such as increased prestige, from joining an exclusive club, the downside of this new affiliation is that acquaintances and friends become aware that they are now "outsiders" in an important aspect of the new member's life. One feature of new-member orientations at elite clubs is the emphasis that is placed on camaraderie among members and in participation in the social events of the club. However, what is not mentioned is how a person's nonmember friends may respond to the new member's increased involvement in club activities and his or her commitment to an organization where he or she is now an "insider." To allay this concern, some clubs emphasize that friends may be brought to the club as guests on certain occasions, which typically are spelled out. Some club invitations, however, state specifically that an event, such as the club's annual Christmas party, are "for members only" and emphasize that the capacity of the club makes it impossible for a member to bring more than one guest for this special event.

Members have the privilege of entering the club by providing their member card or unique number to the personnel at the front door or the reception desk if they are not immediately recognized by the staff. For nonmembers to enter the club, the outsider must be formally invited by a member to be his or her guest, and information about the guest must be left at the reception area so that this individual can be escorted to the location where the member is waiting for the guest. As a result, membership in by-invitation-only clubs make the distinction between insiders and outsiders more evident to all parties involved: clubs formally define "in-groups" and "out-groups" or "we-groups" and "they-groups," and it is impossible to shift from one category to another without successfully going through the membership process.

For millions of people who have no interest in being a member of an elite club, distinctions between insiders and outsiders are meaningless; for people who desire to become a member and participate in the same activities that their member/friends do, being defined as a nonmember labels them as an "outsider," while the member/friend is identified as an "insider." One nonmember in my study explained how he felt when his best friend became a legacy member of an exclusive country club where he was on a lengthy waiting list with about 150 people in front of him:

> Bud had every right to get in. I don't resent that. His family has been in the club for three generations. But I never realized how I would feel when he started playing golf with his new friends at "his" club and only occa-

sionally invited me to play a round. Bud and I've done so many things together from our college days on, but now he spends time at a club I'm not
a part of. I respect him for getting in, but I resent how this is affecting our
friendship and making our wives act stiff around each other. Going as a
guest (and repaying them for tickets) isn't the same as if we were members.

As this individual's statement points out, membership does have specific privileges that do not accrue to guests, particularly in regarding to feeling a sense
of belonging, being able to run a tab at the club that will be billed to the
member's account at the end of the month, and having others acknowledge
that you are one of them.

Although a central theme of city, country, and wall-less men's clubs is
having a good time together as club members and building useful social networks, how outsiders feel about a person's membership is ignored as a topic of
interest. One central factor is the heightened esteem some outsiders give to a
person chosen for membership in an elite club because of the old adage, "It's
not what you know, but who you know." Knowing the right people is considered important among elites from all areas of social life, including the financial, political, academic, and social sectors.

Through the eyes of an outsider, elite club membership may be its own
badge of honor, and for insiders, membership may become a way of life. Being a member of an exclusive club may mean that a person has reached a
higher social status than he or she formerly occupied: the person has been determined to be acceptable by the "inner circle" of social elites in the community. According to Frank, a male attorney in his thirties, when one of his
friends learned that Frank had joined one of their city's most exclusive private
clubs, he said, "Well, now you're a big fish in an even bigger pond. Being in
[name of the club] says you're a big fish, but I have one word of warning: be
sure an even bigger fish doesn't come along and gobble you up!" For this new
member, being invited to join an Old Guard club was a social compliment to
him; however, he soon realized that his friend both admired and disdained
him for being accepted by this group. In a club, members are at least loosely
bound to each other by name and reputation, but they do not accept similar
responsibility for outsiders. In the words of a manager of one of San Antonio's elite city clubs, "You don't just blow into San Antonio from out of town
with a hunk of cash and get into Club Giraud. If you are sponsored, that
means other members put their names on the line to vouch for you. *People are
tied to other people.* That's a good recommendation" (Bragg 2004:6H). Similarly, a president of San Francisco's Bohemian Club once told new members,
"You have joined not only a club, but a way of life" (Domhoff 2005). It is this
way of life that brings both honor to members and potential frustration to

outsiders because club membership may create a sharp divide between insiders and outsiders: an exclusive club is not just a club; it is a way of life that reflects who you are and reveals your financial, political, and prestige statuses.

Like other privileges that accrue to new members of an exclusive club, the benefit of enhanced social prestige must be balanced with a sense of responsibility to established members who expect that newcomers will remain deferential for a period of time as they learn the history, traditions, and operations of the club from longer-term members. Although a newer member may join a club with high recommendations and fulfill all the expectations of existing members in terms of appropriate attitudes, appearance, and behavior, it is also expected that newcomers will "pay their dues" before seeking to be a "voice of authority" or to take over leadership roles within the club.

Some expectations of deference pertain to becoming officers in the club, but others relate to less formal matters, such as which members are chosen to escort the debutantes who are being honored at the club's next presentation ball. In one wall-less men's social club, several established members commented about the "audacity" of a new club member who thought that he should be allowed to escort one of the debutantes during his first year of membership. According to club tradition, which he apparently had not learned as yet, the honor of escorting a debutante is reserved for current club officers, longer-term members who have "paid their dues" by chairing the ball or distinguishing themselves in other activities of the club, and any member (regardless of his length of membership) who is the brother of a young woman being presented as one of the club's debutantes that year.

In this section, we have examined how new members learn about the privileges and expectations of elite club membership. In the following sections, we look at how elite club memberships provide individuals with unique advantages in regard to the accumulation of social and cultural capital.

WHO YOU KNOW: ACCUMULATING SOCIAL CAPITAL AT THE CLUB

Although private clubs offer a wide variety of benefits for members, one of the primary advantages of membership is the member's access to other club members and sometimes to their personal acquaintances and business associates who may assist the member in a variety of ways, such as acquiring a new business investor, finding the member's college-aged child a summer internship, or raising money and heightening political support for an election campaign. These are examples of gaining and utilizing the social capital that is an important part of elite club membership.

Although some scholars believe that social capital is a *collective attribute* that is possessed by an entire group or community used in various ways, I found in my study that it is easier to demonstrate how social capital is a *resource* that is *possessed by individuals*. This utilization of the term coincides with the work of other social theorists, such as sociologist James S. Coleman (1988), who identified social capital as a resource that accrues to individuals by virtue of their access to contacts, connections, and linkages. Similarly, French social theorist Pierre Bourdieu (1986) focused on the relationship between the volume of social capital an individual possesses and the size of the social network that the person could effectively mobilize if he or she desired to do so.

Exclusive clubs bring together people who have the "right credentials" in a variety of areas, ranging from individuals with "old" family money and backgrounds to those who have more recently earned their wealth through entrepreneurship or gained prestigious positions in politics, top corporations, or influential universities. The integration of diverse elites in a private club setting helps produce social homogeneity, value consensus, and personal interaction (Putnam 2000) even among individuals who do not share a long history together. As Anthony Giddens (1975) has pointed out, an integrated elite is one in which members of different elite groups frequently interact as acquaintances, friends, or kin. Elite private clubs facilitate this integration because they make it possible for members to enjoy each other's company and work cooperatively where they otherwise might have remained largely encapsulated and fragmented (see Moore 1979). This is especially true regarding the inner circle in such clubs. The social cohesion within the inner circle has been described as follows: "Social cohesion implies that the inner circle is truly a circle: acquaintanceship networks are dense, mutual trust and obligation are widespread, and a common sense of identity and culture prevail" (Useem 1984:63).

Although an elite private club does have a collective identity in regard to the group's prestige or influence within the local community and sometimes the state or nation ("the prestigious XYZ Club"), the social capital that comes from club membership accrues to the individual members.

Some members may never "spend" the social capital they accumulate, whereas others may use it in a time range from immediately to a number of years later. One club member—Charles—explained how social capital he had accumulated at his city, country, and wall-less men's clubs was useful when his son decided to pledge a different fraternity from the father's own Greek organization:

> When I went to UT, I was a Delt, so I thought Charles Junior would have no problem getting in if he wanted to . . . after all, he was a legacy. But his high school friends wanted to pledge Fiji, so I felt some degree of apprehension because I didn't know how well my son was known among the Fiji

actives and alumni. I checked around at my clubs and found a number of men whom I've known for years and some I've helped out in the past and quickly came up with enough supporters to make sure that he got in. It's nice to have good friends who won't let you down when you need 'em.

The kinds of social networks that this individual described could be made in a number of social, religious, and work-related settings; however, when people are bound together with formal social ties, such as membership in a highly prestigious club, they often feel more duty bound and purposeful in meeting the needs of other members. In order for the club to be prestigious, it must be composed of members who can—and will—help one another in ways that nonmembers are unable to do.

Although it may seem odd that some of the most privileged people in our nation would desire to accumulate additional social capital, many top-tier political and moneyed elites believe that a person can never possess too much social capital because they never know when they might want to draw on that "bank" reserve. For social elites, superior connections (and wealth) have paid off in the past, and they have every reason to believe that these networks will remain important not only for themselves but also for their children and grandchildren.

However, when I suggested to a number of elite club members that accruing social capital (although I did not use that terminology) is a distinct advantage of being a member, many of them denied that this was one of the reasons why they are involved in a private club. When I asked one member about how a person might improve his social networks by joining his club, he tersely replied, "Networking is a buzzword for digital-age 'high-techies' and new-rich social climbers. The members of [his club] don't need—and definitely don't want—any of this."

Although some Old Guard club members may assert that networking is not appropriate in exclusive clubs, this belief is not shared by other club members, who think that it is important to develop social networks and put social capital to work for the benefit of oneself and one's family members. Some clubs, for that matter, formally recognize that networking is one of the benefits of membership. The Petroleum Club of Houston (2007) has the following statement posted on its website: "Networking—Every day hundreds of potential clients are entertained, transactions discussed, problems analyzed and business agreements confirmed all in the confines of the club." The congenial environment of elite clubs, including their hushed service, efficient and courteous food and cocktail servers, and a panoramic view (discussed in a previous chapter), suggests that the club members have arrived, allowing them to enjoy existing social networks and forge new ones. This is enhanced by the various types of activities available at the club or at social events that the club holds.

Eat, Drink, and Be Merry: Camaraderie and the Social Capital Account

Although drinking a glass of wine or having a cold beer is an enjoyable activity in itself, one of the most profound pleasures of many elite club members is visiting with other club members while having a favorite drink. City and country clubs universally are equipped with a bar, cocktail lounge, or other comfortable room specifically set aside for serving cocktails and appetizers to members and their guests in a setting that encourages conversation and social bonding. Like the gentlemen's clubs of London and the "old-line" northeastern and western United States, it is a "given" that alcoholic beverages will be served in the most exclusive clubs of Texas.

"Let's Have a Drink, Y'all"

Today, drinking and socializing among members and guests are closely linked in the city, country, and wall-less men's clubs of Texas, and this camaraderie helps individuals build and enhance social networks that are valuable to them in their social, academic, business, and political pursuits. According to one member of an exclusive Dallas golf club, "Drinking is to friendship as gas is to my SUV: alcohol serves as a lubricant to keep a good conversation moving along."

Wall-less men's clubs are particularly known for providing their members with social events where they can enjoy a good conversation and share information while imbibing beer, wine, and/or cocktails. The officers of these clubs often schedule social events where the consumption of alcoholic beverages is a key ingredient so that members can relax, "let down their hair," and get to know each other better. For some members, these events remind them of their days in a college fraternity before they had high-powered jobs and major family responsibilities.

It is socially acceptable—and even expected—that most club members will drink a few beers or have several glasses of wine at social events such as a "Beer 'n' Barbeque" night, a St. Patrick's Day "Green Beer Celebration," an "Open Bar" sporting event such as a skeet shoot (a target sport where the shooter uses a shotgun to hit a moving clay target that has been propelled into the air to simulate the flight pattern of a live bird), or a "Texas Hold 'Em Poker Tournament" in which competitive poker playing and gamesmanship are facilitated by the club's "Bar Service Available" sign throughout the evening. Although alcohol consumption contributes to social bonding and serves as a means of building social capital among younger club members, it may also be helpful to established club members as they seek to renew old friendships, make new ones, or "shake hands" on a business deal.

It is difficult to establish a direct relationship between how members enhance their social capital through involvement in an elite club and the routine practice of consuming alcoholic beverages when socializing with other members. However, my content analysis of more than 100 elite club websites, monthly newsletters, and other club-related publications revealed a recurrent pattern of emphasizing the availability of alcoholic beverages at various club functions. Many club members believe that alcohol consumption helps with social bonding and that drinking is part of having a good time with each other and forging new social networks. For example, the symbolic importance of offering a toast in celebration of a special occasion was often mentioned as a club ritual by various members. A toast is made by raising one's filled glass in the air and making a statement that praises a person (or group), a new friendship or partnership, or a special family occasion. In some situations, each person then lightly touches ("clinks") his or her glass to the side of other individuals' glasses, as some say, "Hear, hear!" or "Cheers!" Offering a toast with an alcoholic beverage symbolizes the members' regard for one another and their bonding as a group. Although toasts are made in many social settings, toasts that are offered by members of private clubs appear to have great significance to members because they build an extended family relationship among those who share membership in the same exclusive organization. In the words of one club member, "Sure, we pay dues to belong, but it's more than that. Getting together lets us know that we aren't alone even though our kids are grown and have moved to another state. We toast each other and our way of life."

Even though drinking is a favorite pastime of many elite club members, excessive alcohol consumption is frowned on, particularly when a person is "falling down drunk" or "making lewd and lascivious comments about the ladies," as one respondent stated. In the wall-less men's clubs, for example, although it is considered appropriate for club members to have a glass of wine to toast the young women who are being presented at the club's annual debutante ball, it is unacceptable for members to become drunk or to be physically aggressive toward a young woman or another guest.

Members who come to a city or country club alone typically are incorporated into the evening's activities by the club's bar personnel or other members so that they will not feel alone. Some of the nation's top city clubs have comfortable bar chairs at a designated area where solo members can chat with the bartender while having a drink, or these clubs set aside a specific "bachelor's table" where individual members can visit with one another or have dinner rather than sitting alone in the formal dining room. From my observations, I found that gender differences persist in such seating arrangements in elite city clubs: male club members easily sit alone at the bar or in the cocktail lounge, but female members or the wives of male members are more likely to be seated by club personnel in a parlor or dining area for their predinner drinks and conversation than in one of the designated bar areas. Today, many Texas clubs appear to have an unwritten norm that women without men present should bond with each other in a more "feminine" setting, whereas solo male members can feel more free to engage in social interaction at a location where the alcohol flows freely.

From my research, I also learned that "having a drink at the club" has special significance for members who like to invite nonmember guests to join them: inviting an outsider to one's club is a way in which many members assess whether they want to develop a social or business relationship with that person. Carl, a real estate developer in his fifties, explained why he invited people to his club for a drink before he entered into a joint real estate venture with them:

> Sure, you can invite a potential investor out for a drink anywhere, but there's something special about taking him to your own club. You begin to see him through the eyes of the bartender you've known for thirty years, and you introduce him to several of your lawyer pals who are celebrating a recent court victory, and you start to see this person more clearly: Does he fit in with people I know and like? Would they trust him? Should I trust him? The club visit with a few stiff drinks is my litmus test for whether I want to get more involved with a person or forget about it.

Although many members enjoy having a drink at their club and engaging in social or business conversations with members or invited guests, club members also see dining at the club as a means of social bonding and thereby enhancing their social capital.

Dining as "One Big, Happy Family"

The nation's top city and country clubs pride themselves on creating a dining experience for their members that provides them with outstanding gourmet cuisine in a prestigious setting where they can visit with other club members and friends. Most clubs have a full-service Main Dining Room and at least one less formal dining room, such as a Grill Room, that has a more casual atmosphere and serves "down-home cooking" such as hamburgers or meatloaf. Although elite clubs have not always been known for serving gourmet cuisine, many clubs now recruit the finest gourmet chefs from five-star restaurants and luxury hotels to design their menus and oversee meals for club members. For example, one chef at Houston's River Oaks Country Club received more than sixty national and international culinary awards and won three gold medals with the U.S. Regional Culinary Olympic Team. Newer country clubs such as Cimarron Hills Country Club (outside of Austin, Texas) advertise that their "credentialed staff" includes as "a Four Seasons–trained chef" and a food and beverage director from Donald Trump's famed Mar-A-Lago Club (*Texas Monthly* advertisement, August 2007).

Most city club members frequently eat at their club on Monday through Friday when there is a weekday luncheon buffet featuring an elaborate array of courses that are set out appealingly on long, wide tables with elaborate tablecloths and massive floral arrangements. Having duplicate sets of food on each side of the table and two serving lines makes it possible for members to quickly choose what they would like to eat. Franklin described his club's buffet as follows:

> One of the things I like about the daily buffet is how great the food looks all spread out. First, there's the nice variety of cheese and crackers and the fresh fruit on silver platters, and then there's a variety of salads like chicken, tuna, and lobster. Then you get to the "heavy stuff" like King Ranch Chicken, roast beef, ham, and other meats. At the end of this huge table, there's a beautiful display of the best desserts you've ever seen—key lime pie, brownie pecan pie, chocolate cake, and about anything else you might want.

But Franklin also indicated why he really liked having lunch at his club: it was because members could engage in conversation with other members with whom he or she was not having lunch at the time because they could "talk across the food":

> I enjoy eating the buffet lunch instead of ordering off of the menu because I like to *talk across the food* to other members as they are getting a plate or loading it with food. With members I know, I exchange greetings like, "How are [the person's wife or husband] and [the kids]?" or "Let's get together soon." Sometimes I meet new people I may want to know better. When I see another member eating with somebody I don't know, he may ask me, "Franklin, have you met Ralph? He's the new managing partner at Smith and Brown." That brief intro gives me a chance to meet Ralph in a setting where we are both connected to Chuck and in a nice club. Seeing others informally over food helps me keep in touch with old friends and meet new ones where I otherwise wouldn't have these connections.

And connections are what it's all about in elite clubs. As much fun as a member may have when he or she participates in club events, most members want to share in the camaraderie that goes with club life: it reassures them of their privileged status in society and helps them maintain social ties to other elites.

Drinking, dining, and building social capital go together at elite clubs. In addition to their regular luncheon buffets and seated evening dinners, most elite city and country clubs offer fifteen or more annual holiday celebrations featuring elaborate food service. Among these festive celebrations are the Valentine's Day Dinner, Easter Champagne Brunch, Mother's Day Brunch, Father's Day Brunch, Grandparents' Day Brunch, July 4th Dinner and Fireworks Display or Independence Day Pool Party and Picnic, "Scary" Halloween Buffet, Thanksgiving Day Brunch, Santa Brunch, Christmas Holiday Luncheon, and New Year's Eve Adult Cocktail Party and Dinner Dance. Between these special dining occasions, many clubs offer an array of dining events featuring local food favorites or some of the club's most popular recipes, such as Prime Rib Night, Lobster Night, and Family Casual Dinner Night with such "kid-friendly" food as fried chicken, barbecued brisket, homemade cookies, and do-it-yourself ice cream sundaes.

Although food is important at these social occasions, enjoying the company of other club members and making new friends is a priority for most members. This statement by one woman who is a legacy member of an exclusive country club is representative of statements by many respondents about their shared memories of private club life:

> As I was growing up, I think we ate more meals at the club than we did at home. I don't recall my mother cooking, and the woman who worked for us did cleaning, washing, and ironing, but she didn't cook anything except grilled cheese sandwiches when we were sick. I loved going to the club. There we had it all: Santas dressed up and giving away little presents, clowns blowing up balloons and doing face painting, fireworks on the Fourth, and, most of all, having fun with friends who went to other schools but whose parents were members of my family's club. Some of them are my best friends now, and many of my adult friends are women I first met in the club's tennis association.

As this woman suggests, elite clubs help individuals build friendships and social networks that last for many years because members are together in a comfortable and relaxed environment: children and young people are with others who are being brought up in a similar manner, and they share a privileged lifestyle associated with the upper-middle and upper classes. Adults are among like-minded individuals who typically have similar family and educational backgrounds and who have economic security from their wealth and/or earned income. With a nice wine, good food, and a pleasant social environment, the principle of homophily—"similarity breeds connection"—survives and thrives (see chapter 1 and McPherson, Smith-Lovin, and Cook 2001).

Recent generations of privileged elites often have moved many of their social gatherings and family celebrations from their residences to an exclusive city or country club. One benefit of using the club to celebrate is the ease and efficiency with which professionals can plan and prepare the event with little effort (but much expense) on the part of the hosts. However, the downside to having most social gatherings at the club is that "outsiders" are less likely to be invited for some events because there are plenty of *members* available to include in the activities. Consider, for example, one male club member's description of his club's annual Fourth of July celebration where members and guests can eat "fancy and plain" holiday fare, ranging from prime beef to hot dogs, and watch the city's fireworks display in air-conditioned comfort:

> My wife and I used to throw a big Fourth of July party at our house . . . have our friends and neighbors over. But it's so easy to come up here. The work's done for us. Decorations, food, fireworks, good folks to talk to, everything. . . . All we have to do is show up and celebrate, and the bill is added to my monthly club statement. I do miss some of our old friends we had over for the backyard party, but they wouldn't know the other members.

Although it is easier for many people to attend their club's Fourth of July celebration, it may leave out "old friends" unless the member specifically invites them as his or her guest and pays an additional fee for them to attend. Like the individual quoted previously, many elite club members want their clubs to be a place for camaraderie but one that requires little work on their part to bring a special event together.

As members eat the elaborate gourmet meals and enjoy alcoholic beverages, they frequently talk about how they need to spend more time at the club's fitness center or on the golf course or tennis court to "burn off" the excess calories they are consuming, and the most exclusive clubs are set up so that members can do just that. Some who seldom share meals at the club regularly use its state-of-the-art sports and fitness facilities to enhance their physical fitness, improve their golf and/or tennis games, and build stronger ties with other members and guests.

Networking while Sweating

Although golf and country clubs have the most elaborate sporting and fitness facilities, many city clubs in high-rise office buildings are equipped with spa and gym facilities that offer early morning workouts, cutting-edge gym equipment, weight machines, cardio equipment such as treadmills and stair steppers, and group fitness classes including indoor cycling and Pilates training. These clubs employ personal trainers and massage therapists, and they provide members with plush locker rooms. Typically, there is less time for social interaction among members at a city club while exercising because many come to the club before or after work or during their lunchtime. A few respondents indicated that they invited guests or other members to play hand-ball or racquetball at the city club because they could decide if they wanted to do business with them:

> I can tell more about a man by playing racquetball with him than I can by talking to him for hours. Watching him play tells me whether or not he is impetuous. I can see how his mind works when the ball's coming toward him. What strategies he will use . . . I've made some really good friends and some very bad enemies on the racquetball court at the club.

According to this individual, people use similar skills in sports and business, and he is able to assess their abilities on his club's racquetball court. Using the club as his home turf, he is able to build a business relationship or a personal friendship with those whom he so chooses and "gently" let down others with whom he believes he has little in common. Other male club members indicated that they used their golf or country club in a similar manner because of the availability of excellent facilities that would impress the other individual and give him a chance to show his best side.

Unlike city clubs that typically do not have golf facilities, golf and country clubs provide their members with top-tier golf courses designed by professional golfers. Golf and country clubs typically have one eighteen-hole golf course, but two or more courses are now common at some exclusive clubs, offering at least thirty-six holes of golf, and a few have as many as ninety-nine holes. Clubs such as the Augusta National Golf Course are so proud of their facilities that each of the holes on the course is named after a famous person or, in the case of Augusta National, a particular tree or bush that grows there, such as the Pink Dogwood, Flowering Peach, or Holly. Terms such as "lightning fast and perfectly conditioned A-4 bent greens" are widely used by members of these exclusive clubs to describe why the course at their club is the best. At the bottom line, many club members are most impressed by other members and by the professional golfers who play their course. Since private golf clubs largely remain out of the public eye except when televised tournaments are held there, and some clubs allow no reciprocity with other golf clubs, it is difficult for an outsider to gain entree to these settings. It remains clear from interviews with members, however, that eating, drinking, and playing golf at one's private club is all about networking, particularly for men. Tim provided this description of "fun and fellowship" at his prestigious Dallas golf club:

> There's nothing like a good game of golf for fun and fellowship, followed by eating Donnie Ray's seafood gumbo in the nineteenth hole. We sit in that air-conditioned room in those deep, leather chairs and watch the Golf Channel

on that big flat-screen TV and talk about who's the best golfer among us and how we compare to the pros on TV. It's a load of laughs . . . now, we don't take ourselves seriously, but we do take golfing and our club seriously. I'd be making an understatement if I said "It's the best in Texas."

Similarly, golf club members in other cities and states describe with similar affection how much their club means to them. Consider, for example, this statement by Keith Bambel regarding the Colonial Country Club near Memphis, Tennessee:

> In comparison to the litany of places I've played, our golf course is something special and I am very proud to consider it my home course. The tradition and layout of our South course especially is right there at the top of the list, like a little Heaven on Earth to a golfer.
> I am happy to play with a large group of guys affectionately known as "The Goats." Although not known for their golfing prowess, the competition, laughs and utter enjoyment playing together is a highlight of my life and our friendships continue to grow. However, I must admit that my alcohol consumption has increased significantly after being welcomed into this group of golf nuts. (Colonial Country Club 2007)

This person's statement, as recorded on his club's website, is representative of the sentiments of numerous members of golf clubs and country clubs about the fun and friendships that they have as a result of playing golf and sharing in social activities at their club.

Golf and country clubs offer private and group golf lessons with top pros (for an additional fee) and organize amateur leagues and competitive tournaments for children starting at the age of five years and continuing through seniors in their eighties. In addition to outstanding golf courses and other golf-related facilities, country clubs also feature tennis as a sporting and social activity. Most clubs have ten or more lighted courts that are surfaced for all-weather play, and some clubs have indoor facilities as well. To offer members the widest array of experiences, the best clubs have both clay and hard surface tennis courts that meet the standards for professional tournaments. Tennis leagues and women's and men's tennis associations are a popular means through which members and their families become acquainted with others and develop relationships that may last for many years.

Pro shops at golf and country clubs help people establish a group identity as members of the club by selling clothing and other sporting equipment emblazoned with the club's name and logo. Wearing the club's logo symbolizes an "in-group" identity with other members; however, when such clothing is worn away from the club's premises, the merchandise shows individuals in the outside world that this person is affiliated with a prestigious, members-only club. Ironically, a 1980s brand of clothing, Members Only, played off of country-club elitism in clothing by selling jackets with a "Members Only" tag and having an advertising tagline stating, "When you put it on, something happens." This popular consumer item may reflect what members believe happens when they wear their club's T-shirts, warm-up suits, and shorts: "something happens" that binds them together and sets them apart from outsiders.

In addition to golfing and tennis, swimming is a favorite activity at country clubs because the entire family can enjoy the fun and make new friends through informal contacts around the pool and through lessons, leagues, and swimming competitions across elite clubs. Most country clubs have at least one Olympic-size pool as well as sunning decks and outdoor dining areas for members' before- or after-swimming pleasure. Women respondents in this study particularly recall fond memories of leisurely summer afternoons spent around the pool at "the club":

> Anywhere from four to seven or eight of us would get together in the late morning for "fun in the sun." We'd put bottle after bottle of gooey baby oil on our faces and backs and order icy lemonade from the snack bar so a cute guy working there would bring it to us at poolside. We swam and sunned for several hours, and then we went inside to the Grill Room and ordered fries, burgers, and hot dogs. We didn't need money: we just signed a ticket that charged it to our parents. Years later, I can tell you, some of my oldest and dearest friends are the same girls I shared those hot summer days with at the club.

As this person's statement suggests, swimming pools and other sports facilities at elite clubs provide members and their families with a social environment in which they can have fun and build endearing and enduring social relationships. Membership in an elite club excludes individuals who have been identified as "not our kind of people" while it helps young people identify "our kind of people" and accumulate social capital in the process. Being a member of an exclusive club suggests that an individual is relatively evenly matched with other members in regard to one's lifestyle and social status, and this may become a social marker for children and adolescents without their parents having to make any verbal distinction between their preferred "in-group" as opposed to "out-groups."

Finally, networking while sweating does not end after a golf game, tennis match, or aerobics class at the club: more exclusive clubs now offer full-service beauty and spa facilities where members can refresh themselves before leaving the club. Some clubs offer a wide array of beauty treatments, including hair-styling, makeup, massage, manicures and pedicures, and waxing. These services are particularly appealing to women members because they can go to business, social, or family activities without having to return home or go to a public salon. Social interactions among female members at a club's beauty and spa facilities are a key means of bonding and building social and business networks, as Patricia, a longtime very successful real estate broker, described:

> I'm a Realtor, and you wouldn't believe what I can learn while I'm having a pedicure at the club. I find out who's thinking of buying or selling a house, who's getting—or might get—a divorce, and "where the skeletons are hidden," so to speak. I wouldn't think of having my beauty treatments anywhere else because the members are in the know about everybody and everything that's going on. I wouldn't trade our family membership for anything because the cost is nothing compared to the people I've met and the business connections I've made.

Although clubs officially frown on members conducting business on the club's premises, many social interactions contain information that might be construed by some as business related. As Patricia pointed out to me, the fine line between business and pleasure that existed in the past is now a totally artificial distinction:

> So, I ask you, is this business or pleasure: I'm playing on a tennis league with a friend, and between sets she tells me about someone she knows who just got engaged and will be looking for a Realtor. My friend wants me to have the first shot at working with the bride-to-be. Playing tennis at the club is a leisure activity, but when we briefly talk about business, what's wrong with that? I think business and pleasure blend together. Isn't this what men have always done? Now women are finally getting a chance to play the same game.

As Patricia's statement suggests, a fine distinction between business and pleasure exists in the minds of many elite club members who believe that social and economic networking are one and the same thing: under certain circumstances, accrued social and cultural capital may be readily convertible into economic capital when they participate in club-sponsored events and programs.

WHAT YOU KNOW: ACCUMULATING CULTURAL CAPITAL AT THE CLUB

Members accrue cultural capital through their investment of time in club activities and programs that give them priority access to well-known connoisseurs and experts who possess specialized knowledge in fields ranging from the "finer things in life"—such as high culture, fine arts, classical music, gourmet food, and wine—to recognized authorities in business and leisure pursuits who provide information on topics such as investing, creating tax shelters, and the best locations for vacations or ownership of second or third homes. Club-sponsored encounters between established authorities and club members help members accumulate additional *cultural capital*, which refers to the ideas, knowledge, and cultural style that individuals draw on when they participate in social life. Based on my data, I classified club events and programs that help members accumulate cultural capital into two categories— those that foster *appreciation* and those that enhance one's *knowledge* by providing insider information on selected topics of interest.

Appreciation of the Finer Things in Life

Although privileged people usually have been socialized to appreciate high culture and the "finer things in life," such as the best works of art and the finest wine, elite club members often learn how to make subtle distinctions in taste that they believe set apart the inner circle of social elites from others in the upper class and from those in the lower classes. Being able to make fine distinctions also helps elites identify and classify themselves and other people in regard to location in the class structure. French sociologist Pierre Bourdieu (1984:56) thought of these distinctions in terms of "taste" when he wrote, "Taste is the basis of all that one has—people and things—and all that one is for others, whereby one classifies oneself and is classified by others." According to Bourdieu, physical things (such as food preferences) and social behaviors (such as table manners) are indicators of people's class-based lifestyles and tastes, and people use the indicators to identify themselves and to evaluate others who do not share their tastes. For Bourdieu, taste is a class-based phenomenon: what people accept as *legitimate taste* is not genuine good taste but rather the *taste of the ruling class*. Other social analysts disagree with this notion and suggest instead that there is no unified whole when it comes to taste. There are numerous "communities of taste" continually being born and dying out, thereby leaving standards of taste in a perpetual state of change (Gronow 1997). Regardless of that distinction, privileged people have enhanced their appreciation for the "finer things in life" over the past several centuries by participating in social events and programs at their exclusive clubs that foster camaraderie among the members by bringing together groups of art lovers, opera enthusiasts, wine connoisseurs, or world travelers to broaden their horizons regarding objects and activities of interest to them.

Club activities and programs seek to foster *appreciation*—an understanding of the meaning or quality or magnitude of an object, such as a work of art: Members gain new insights on the *aesthetic* value of an object ("Beauty is in the eye of the beholder") and also on the *economic* value of the object ("This sculpture is worth a specific amount of money now, but it may be of greater worth in the future"). An article on art appreciation in *Private Clubs Magazine*, a publication for members of certain elite clubs, makes the following distinction in regard to art appreciation:

> The term "art appreciation" is increasingly understood to have more than one meaning. Art is universally regarded as an asset. But how much is that asset worth now, and how much will it be worth in the future? . . . Knowing how—and why—to buy is the key to having art that is appreciated now, but also is an asset that appreciates in value over time. Whether purchasing a single substantial work, building a collection, or investing in a managed fund, buyers should begin their personal art adventure by gathering some good advice. (de la Rosa 2007)

Through interesting and informative programs that feature experts on art-related topics for private club members, people enhance their appreciation of the arts. Members of elite clubs also form art societies within the larger club so that they may host guest lectures, artists' receptions, tours of private collections, and local, national, and international tours to visit top museums. Some arts-related events provide members with "fun facts" about top local or regional artists; others have a distinguished artists series in which acclaimed artists and sculptors describe their works and invite questions from the audience. Some clubs plan members-only tours of art exhibits, museums, and galleries. In these settings, a celebrated art historian or other expert in the field may spend extensive amounts of time discussing the topic with club members:

> For me, art is strictly for pleasure. I enjoy art, and I like to learn more about it, but I'm not interested in purchasing highly acclaimed works of art or building an impressive collection. The club has tours where we start with a Sunday brunch and drinks, then we take a private bus and head to a new exhibition at the art museum or the latest gallery opening. A local art historian or an expert from the university gives us insights on the art and serves as a tour guide. Some members have taken international tours to Italy, France, and elsewhere to see the finest art in the world together.

Although contemporary art lovers and buyers have numerous sources, such as gallery owners and museum websites, to learn about art, many club members enjoy learning from experts about why certain works of art are more highly valued than others. Art world insiders provide members with tips on how to determine the worth of a painting or sculpture, how to have it authenticated, and why it is important to have the piece appraised. According to *Private Clubs Magazine*, "Art is an asset class with its own unique measurements of satisfaction and value. It is an investment with the potential to add a special dimension of pleasure and beauty to a buyer's life" (de la Rosa 2007). However, art appreciation not only enhances members' cultural capital and brings them into the realm of pleasant and beautiful objects but makes them more aware of how fine art may be turned into economic capital as well.

Art appreciation is beneficial for elite club members because they assume that a person who is able to fully appreciate a valuable object also is able to make delicate discriminations among a variety of similarly fine objects: in other words, this individual has the perceptiveness to identify the *best* even when it is surrounded by a number of other really fine things. For some members, possessing this kind of discernment sets them apart as being better or more sophisticated than other people and may serve as a foundation for snobbish attitudes or behavior. For other members, discernment is linked to greater understanding of the object and a true appreciation of its real meaning and significance as a cultural object. As Bourdieu suggested, cultural capital may exist in an *objectified state*—meaning that a work of art, a vintage wine, or a first-edition book may be owned by an individual because the object has been physically transmitted, or sold, to him or her as an exercise of economic capital; however, the individual cannot fully understand the true importance and cultural meaning of the object if he or she does not possess the proper cultivated and class-bound knowledge that individuals acquire through class-related socialization that specifies how one should think about a specific object.

Many elites pride themselves on being connoisseurs—persons who possess extensive knowledge about high-cultural objects such as the fine arts, outstanding wines, and other collections where it is important to be an expert judge in matters of taste. In the private club, members learn how to evaluate objects of art on their aesthetic merits and sometimes on their economic worth. Likewise, some members learn how to evaluate wines and identify outstanding varieties, labels, and even the best wine glasses for consuming various types of wines. For this reason, elite clubs such the Petroleum Club of Houston host a series of wine tastings and dinners in which various wines are paired with gourmet cuisine. These events have names such as A Taste of France Wine Dinner, A Taste of Australia Wine Dinner, The Classic Wine Experience, and New World Wine Dinner. At these dinners, members enjoy wines from various countries and form their own opinion about which ones they prefer. As discussed in chapter 3, sociologists have suggested that the wine connoisseur is a good example of how cultural capital serves as a high-status cultural signal: to be a connoisseur, a person must possess the following: (1) the correct *attitude* (knowing what a good wine is supposed to be), (2) *formal knowledge* (knowing how to evaluate wines), (3) *preferences* (knowing how to identify the *best*-tasting wines), (4) *behaviors* (knowing how to consume wine appropriately and tastefully), and (5) *possession of the right goods and credentials* (having a wine cellar full of exceptional wines and/or achieving recognition as a top wine connoisseur).

Exclusive clubs offer their members wine dinners, tasting courses, and organized wine societies where connoisseurs and regular club members alike can find out about the latest varieties of wine, keep up on wine terminology, visit the best vineyards around the world, and even study options in wine glasses. According to one respondent who is a member of several elite clubs, including the prestigious wall-less club known as the Knights of the Vine,

> I grew up in a family where wine was always served at meals, and we visited vineyards in northern California and southern France when I was young, so I thought I knew quite a lot about wine until I became involved with some of the wine aficionados in the Knights. There were many grape varieties and wines I knew nothing about before experts told us about them, and I didn't realize that some wines, like Pinot Grigio, are trendy for a while but then lose their popularity. Words to evaluate the smell and taste of wines—like bouquet, fruity, grassy, oaky, smoky, and buttery—are tossed around by those in the know about wine, and if you want to be one of them, you need to know what the terms mean and be able to apply them correctly to the wines you taste. Otherwise, you reveal that you are a wannabe, not a connoisseur, when it comes to fine wines.

The extent to which this club member's statement is accurate is revealed in the exacting terminology and expected knowledge of individuals who are wine aficionados. Consider, for example, this review of a wine by James Molesworth (2006): "CHÂTEAU DES FINES ROCHES, 2003 is dark and lush, with blackberry and currant fruit followed by hints of prune, cocoa, tar and tobacco. Licorice and smoke on the finish. Drink now through 2018. 750 cases made." To understand what he means by this description, a person needs to be knowledgeable regarding wine terminology and appreciate how this combination of taste sensations might be pleasurable to a person consuming this wine.

The idea that knowledge of fine art or of the best wines is convertible into a social or economic advantage for the possessor of that knowledge is not a new idea in the social sciences and humanities. One historian who examined the passion of nineteenth-century Americans in South Carolina and Georgia for collecting madeira wine concluded that madeira was an important form of cultural capital that also could be easily turned into economic capital:

> Madeira is a good example of cultural capital in the objectified state. It demonstrates highly cultivated and class-bound knowledge that is aesthetic

and esoteric. . . . Madeira consumption as social ritual is a prime example of the objectified state of cultural capital as it is an object (wine) that through consumption allowed a planter . . . to show his specialized knowledge to others. Cultural capital is important in signifying class identity and even position within the class. Moreover, it requires economic capital to generate and is readily convertible back to economic capital. (Tuten 2005:175)

Just as contemporary club members benefit from their knowledge and possession of fine wines, privileged planters in the South prior to the American Civil War benefited from their knowledge of madeira wine and their possession of the finest blends of this wine. Prior to the war, the wine was a form of cultural capital for the planters, who showed their good taste and elevated position in the class hierarchy through their specialized knowledge of this wine. After the war depleted their financial status, the planters converted the wine into economic capital by selling it to wealthy northerners. As this example demonstrates, elites across time and place often have the opportunity to use their knowledge about the finer things in life not only to signify their upper-class status but also as an economic resource when they desire to do so. Elite club members have many opportunities to learn more about the finer things in life if they actively participate in club events and programs. They can also gain new insights on public issues, politics, business, education, and other hot topics by attending speakers' events and special presentations planned by their club.

Knowledge Based on Insider Information

The most prestigious clubs present many educational events for their members throughout the year. Members hear and meet the most coveted business and political personalities in the world through speakers' series, forums, and informal "meet-and-greet" gatherings at the club. Former and current national and international leaders; well-known politicians and political strategists; business leaders; nationally recognized physicians, surgeons, and other medical specialists; and high-profile journalists and authors all present the latest information in their respective fields and give their personal insights on issues in an informal club atmosphere that makes it possible for members to interact with them.

Recent topics of several speakers' series at elite Texas clubs show the range of insider information that is available to participating members: Business Strategies for the Twenty-First Century, The Challenge of International Terrorism, and The Future of Politics are only a few of the many issues discussed by authorities in various fields. Members are impressed with how much "inside information" they get from these presentations. After a discussion on terrorism by the chairman of the Congressional Homeland Security Subcommittee on

Investigations and a former director of the National Security Agency, for example, one club member stated, "It was a fascinating, if somewhat sobering,
evening." This statement captures the essence of numerous comments by
members who participate in such programs because they are fascinated by
what the insiders tell them about past and current events or about politics of
the past, present, and future. As this person suggested, however, some information may be "sobering" because the speaker has had the opportunity to view
firsthand the situations that they describe for their audience.

The fine line between accumulating additional cultural capital and enhancing one's economic capital by participating in elite club events is evident
in the clubs' many educational programs that focus on wealth. These wealth
management programs provide members with the latest information on investments and tips for building an investment portfolio, engaging in financial
planning, and understanding tax law, estate planning, and philanthropy. Having experts talk on these subjects in an environment where they are not
overtly trying to sell something to anyone gives club members an opportunity
to gain information about wealth management without having to give their
business to a specific person or company to learn this information.

In recent years, entrepreneurial philanthropists and other major givers
have been interested in learning about how to get the greatest value for how
they invest their money and whether their philanthropic endeavors will have
tax benefits. Speakers series at exclusive clubs often address issues such as this
because they are of interest to club members, and, in some cases, members
and their acquaintances are the ones who have the knowledge and expertise
in this field to make the presentations themselves.

A board member of one elite Texas club explained that when he served
on the committee for determining which programs and speakers his club
would present each year, they broke the topics down into types of capital assets that they thought members might be interested in hearing more about:

> I had a double major in college—business and economics—so I think in
> terms of capital assets. We bring in speakers to talk about human capital,
> such as how the labor market is changing, what kinds of knowledge our
> kids and grandkids need to be competitive in the global economy, and so
> forth. Then we have experts in natural capital, such as land, water, wildlife,
> and biodiversity. Some members are professors or corporate types who
> know a lot about this, so we get suggestions from them about national and
> international authorities we can bring in. Then we have some speakers who
> talk about financial capital, such as savings, investments, and pensions, and
> others who talk about physical capital, including what water, energy, and
> communications are going to be like by 2020 or some other futuristic
> topic. You'd be surprised how many people show up for an evening of din-

ner, drinks, and conversation on these hot topics. But, as you can guess, some members never show up for lectures and other "stuffy affairs." They see their membership as giving them access to the best golf course or dining facilities in town and nothing else.

Although most clubs do not have as many speakers' and seminar series as are offered by this individual's club, the majority of city and country clubs have talks by engaging and important public figures on current issues such as the climate change debate because hearing presentations by distinguished speakers, followed by time for questions and discussion, has great appeal to elite club members who desire to enhance their cultural capital and perhaps to benefit financially or politically from the information they gain in this manner.

In chapter 5, I describe how political capital is amassed in elite clubs through events such as a distinguished speakers' series, receptions for political candidates and incumbents, and elaborate luncheons or black-tie dinners at which prominent political figures are "toasted" or "roasted" by their colleagues and club members, and I discuss the reverential manner in which the physical images and nonvisual legacies of both living and deceased political leaders are displayed or recalled in elite clubs for the benefit of newer members and for the next generation of social, economic, and political elites.

NOTES

1. Reciprocal club privileges refers to agreements that are established among specific clubs in various cities under which a member of one club who is in "good standing" (meaning that he or she has paid all club bills and has not been negatively sanctioned for any reason by the home club) will be allowed full club privileges at a reciprocating club by having the home club submit a formal letter of introduction.

2. This respondent was referring to the traditional *Social Register*, a 120-year-old directory that has been published in a number of cities to keep members of "polite society" or Old Money families in cities such as Boston, New York, Philadelphia, and San Francisco informed about other members' names, addresses (both winter and summer residences), club and society affiliations, alma maters, and yachts, as well as current information about births, debuts, engagements, marriages, and deaths. Although a few cities still publish modified versions of this directory, today a single national publication known as *The Social Register* is published by *Forbes* magazine. Although a number of Texas families are included in this single-volume directory, many contemporary elites in this state believe that this publication is a "relic of the past" that has been supplanted by listings such as private clubs' membership directories.

3. The "Press Box" is a room at the Headliners Club containing a full bar and tables at which members and their guests may enjoy drinks.

· 5 ·

Making Connections:
Clubs and Political Networks

I earned capital in the campaign—political capital—and now I
intend to spend it. It is my style.

—President George W. Bush, in the first press conference
following his 2004 reelection, suggests that "political capital"
is something that can be earned and spent like money.
(Nagourney 2004:A1)

Political capital shouldn't be taken lightly! It's something you either have or you don't have. And, it isn't just about the money either. It's an intangible thing that includes trust, mutual back-
scratching—what other people have done for you and what
you've done *lately* for them—and this can all change shape real
quickly. That's why I keep in touch with my people. You know,
invite them to join me for lunch at the club or play several
rounds of golf while [the legislature] is in session . . . that kind
of thing.

—A former Texas legislator and current lobbyist
describes how he uses his multiple club memberships
to maintain and enhance his political capital

*A*lthough widespread debate exists about whether *political capital* is a distinct form of capital or if it is merely a type of social capital, political leaders
and other players in the political realm are convinced that political capital is
something that can be accumulated, stored, and used. Recent usage of the
term political capital by high-profile individuals such as President George W.
Bush has differed from previous academic definitions of the term that have
focused on factors such as the representative and reputational capital of legis-

lators. Representative capital includes the powers that stem from holding political office such as the legislator's committee assignments, seniority within those committees, lobbying contacts, and lawmaking acumen: legislators who possess limited representative capital are at a comparative disadvantage when it comes to having influence on the outcome of a specific issue. By contrast, reputational capital refers to a politician's standing with voters and other unorganized interests and might be measured by factors such as the person's political party affiliation, voting record, and name recognition, which voters may assume are a way in which they can predict the person's future performance in office (Lopez 2002). Although there is great utility to applying the concepts of representative and reputational capital when a researcher is investigating topics such as the legislator as political entrepreneur (see Lopez 2002), in order to examine how elite clubs help members and their associates accumulate political capital, I have focused primarily on a popular usage of political capital that is more easily understood by elite club members, including President Bush—who possesses a lengthy history of involvement in such exclusive clubs, dating back to his years at Yale University.

In this chapter, I examine the ways in which elite clubs serve as a political networking point for members and invited guests. By creating the appropriate sociopolitical environment, private clubs help politicians accumulate political capital and encourage members who are not players in the political arena to view themselves as "insiders" because they participate in club activities where they get to rub shoulders with the club's movers and shakers or meet famous guests brought in for special events.

THE LONG HISTORY OF PRIVATE CLUBS AND POLITICAL CAPITAL

From the prime of London's gentlemen's clubs and the distinguished men's clubs of New York, Boston, Chicago, and San Francisco, politics has been deeply intertwined with club life. Throughout their history, some of the gentlemen's clubs in London have been political in nature. The United Service (established in 1815), for example, was formed as a military club and has included many generals and other British military and political leaders in its ranks. Similarly, the Carlton (established in 1832) has had many members who were Conservative members of Parliament and the House of Lords. Political insiders could be distinguished from outsiders by their membership in the Carlton, as was the case when one older member of the Carlton stated that he "always lunched at the Carlton," meaning the club, and a younger companion stated, "I prefer the Ritz" (a public hotel restaurant). As one social historian noted in regard to this exchange,

> It was quite clear that the [younger individual] had not the slightest knowledge of politics, since in political circles, the Carlton has always connoted a sort of forum of the Conservative conscience. As a social institute, the Carlton would have won repute. Its politics have ensured its fame. (Graves 1963:61)

Even more political in nature as an elite club is London's Junior Carlton Club (established in 1864). Members of this club published political pamphlets on topics such as the common market, sent out teams of members to support candidates and raise money during political elections, and held huge election-night parties where the results were broadcast and a buffet supper was served until dawn (Graves 1963).

In New York City, alliance with a specific political party was not uncommon among elite men's clubs. The Manhattan Club was long known as a Democratic Party bastion, while the Union League served the same purpose for the Republican Party. Regarding the Manhattan Club, for example, social historians have stated, "The club made no attempt to conceal its purpose, and specifies that its objectives shall be to advance Democratic principles, promote social intercourse among its members, and provide them with conveniences of a clubhouse." Apparently, the club did all of this within an opulent Fifth Avenue palacelike setting in which wealthy individuals such as Cornelius Vanderbilt and August Belmont were "regulars" who gossiped, hobnobbed, and talked about the latest business and political events of their day (Fairfield 1975). Likewise, at the Union League Club, receptions were held for military leaders and the top politicians from the Republican Party. In its elegant club house on Madison Avenue, the Union League Club served as the venue for many lectures and discussions about state and national politics, even though the stated purpose of the club was social in nature (Fairfield 1975).

For several centuries, elite northeastern men's clubs have been filled with political elites who originally were affiliated with the most exclusive Ivy League clubs at Harvard, Yale, Princeton, and other prestigious universities. In *The Proper Bostonians*, Cleveland Amory (1947) described the close ties between the upper classes of Boston and the Harvard University clubs that were modeled after London's gentleman's clubs. According to Amory, social life and politics were inseparable in these clubs and their postgraduation counterparts, such as New York City's Harvard Club. Fifty years later, author and journalist Alexandra Robbins (2002) documented how private university clubs such as Yale's Skull and Bones have served as the breeding grounds for future politicians such as Presidents George Herbert Walker Bush and George W. Bush as well as other "Bonesmen" who have gone on to positions of power and influence. Although politics may not be a constant topic of discussion among members of Ivy League clubs or other elite organizations, the social connections that are built and the political alliances that are forged in these clubs contribute to a political aspirant's ability to achieve his or her goal of political leadership and power. These linkages also help individuals who become the so-called power behind the throne to make the connections they need to achieve this level of influence over the political process and public policy decisions.

Across the nation, California's Bohemian Club and its summer camp, the Bohemian Grove, have received more scrutiny than any other elite private club as a result of the webs of political power that are found therein. The Bohemian Grove has brought together many of the nation's top political leaders, particularly members of the Republican Party, for many years. As its presence and influential members became more widely discussed in the national and international media and on the Internet, top government officials such as the president of the United States and the holders of top-level cabinet positions have become more hesitant to participate in the events of the club. However, this has not kept many other politicians, lobbyists, and top corporate executives whose companies directly benefit from close alliances with elected politicians and other government officials from attending annual events at the Grove encampment. From his study of political networks at the Bohemian Club, the sociologist Peter Martin Phillips (1994:100) reached this conclusion: "Collectively, Bohemians offer political candidates a concentrated network of potential contributors and influential contacts in the U.S. corporate world." According to Phillips (1994:104–5), although many Bohemian Club members are not in positions of power that give them immediate access to action on social issues or the shaping of political policies, they do have a shared sense of elitism that contributes to the formation of reactionary attitudes toward various progressive movements and certain kinds of social change: "The homogeneity of the Club and the close interrelationships of the men, allows for the articulation of shared values and beliefs on numerous sociopolitical topics." Many nonpolitician members are influential enough in other arenas—because of their wealth and established positions in business, education, or other venues—to bring their ideologies and preferences to bear on those individuals who do make key political decisions. In other words, they have accumulated political capital even though they are not named players in the political realm.

ACCUMULATING POLITICAL CAPITAL AT THE CLUB

Those who believe that political capital is a type of social capital suggest that political capital refers to informal institutional arrangements that may either benefit a wide cross section of people through effective representation, accountability, and participation or that may harm specific categories of people through exploitation, clientelism—an oppressive relationship between wealthy patrons and poor clients—and exclusion. By contrast, recent popular usage of the term *political capital* has suggested that it is distinct from social capital per se. From this perspective, political capital may be social in nature, but it goes beyond that: it involves the resources that a person or group controls and can use to influence public policy in what the person or group believes to be his, her, or its own best interests.

Regardless of which perspective we accept as to the nature of political capital, elite club members who are involved in politics—including elected officials, unelected advisers who serve as the powers behind the throne, major campaign contributors, top lobbyists, and others with political clout—believe this form of capital does exist in the political arena. They also show through their actions that membership in exclusive clubs is a useful tool in helping them accumulate this type of capital because such clubs provide the right setting for political bonding to occur. Just as there are the "right families" who go to the "right schools" and live at the "right addresses," there are also the "right" city and country clubs where the social environment is such that some members come to believe that they deserve to rule, and they gain a crucial sense of entitlement that is the most valuable form of political capital (Birmingham 1968; Dee 2007).

Although the general notion of political capital has been used for a long time, the idea of this type of capital returned following the 2004 reelection of President George W. Bush, who stated that he had accrued a great deal more political capital as a result of winning the election. Political pundits and other social observers quickly adopted this term and began to suggest to the president that there were many ways in which he should spend his newly enhanced "political capital," including immigration reform, national security reform, appointment of conservative Supreme Court nominees, and obtaining peace in the Middle East (Suellentrop 2004).

Since much of my study was centered in Austin, the capital city of Texas—one of the fastest-growing states in the nation—I specifically investigated how privileged people gain greater access to powerful positions in the local, state, and federal branches of the government. I found that they do this partly through extensive social networks among elite club members, networks that they have laboriously built, strengthened, and locked into place. Although there are many ways for political candidates and potential political appointees to gain monetary and nonmonetary support (such as people who volunteer time, goods, and services) without any involvement in an exclusive club, I found that the use of private clubs expedited the process of "getting the right people together at the right time for the mutual benefit of all" (in the words of a prominent political consultant who is a member of a number of prestigious clubs in several Texas cities).

To analyze the relationship between the privileges of elite club members and the development of social capital in its political form, I conducted a case study of one prestigious Austin, Texas, city club where several generations of state and federal officials and lobbyists have held memberships or been invited as frequent guests. According to the *Austin Business Journal*, this club tops the list of prestigious clubs because it has the most "movers and shakers" on its membership roster: "For more than 50 years, the Headliners Club has been at the top of the Austin social scene in both stature and station with its high-rise location on the 21st floor of the Chase Tower downtown" (Orman 2007:1). This club is a mainstay not only for politicians but also for prominent members of the local and state business community, national and international corporate executives, top higher-education administrators, leading community leaders, and respected journalists who meet and dine there. Through this research, I am able to show how social capital is transformed into political capital through one's membership affiliations and regular participation in special events and informal activities at prestigious clubs such as Austin's Headliners Club.

Although this chapter focuses on examples of political capital at one club in one city, similar illustrations might be found in many other elite clubs. However, Austin remains the political hotbed of Texas because it is the capital city of a rapidly growing and diversifying state that produced three contemporary U.S. presidents. Occasionally, I will also include examples from the Austin Club, which is also a favorite "watering hole" and lunch and dinner location for state politicians and lobbyists. Like the Headliners Club, the Austin Club serves as the site for many political fund-raisers when the state legislature is not in session. The *Houston Chronicle* explained how the process works:

> Legal shakedowns may be an accurate term for the stacks of invitations on the desks of most Austin lobbyists and a long list of lunches and receptions filling up some prime venues as the private Austin Club, a few blocks from the state Capitol.
>
> Years ago, legislators decided it would be too unseemly—and awkward— to accept political donations while they were deciding which contributors would win or lose favors. So they enacted a law prohibiting most state officials, from the governor on down, from accepting political contributions during and immediately preceding or following a regular legislative session. (Robinson 2006)

Because political figures must raise as much money as they can before the moratorium takes effect, which occurs when the Texas legislature convenes, the schedule of fund-raising events typically is packed, and politicians are frantic to bring in as many supporters as possible. One evening alone, for example, simultaneous fund-raisers were held at the Austin Club for three state representatives, while several others were held at the Headliners Club. Not all fundraisers are held at city clubs: some are paired with golf outings at top golf or country clubs or with hunting trips, but city clubs provide some of the most popular and convenient venues for attracting influential supporters and raising significant sums of money because of their proximity to the state capitol building and to the downtown offices of high-priced lobbyists, top political consultants, and major political contributors (Robinson 2006). From my research, I have identified four specific types of events that are related to political capital in elite clubs: (1) political insider talks given for club members and invited guests, (2) soft-sell political events that introduce new players in the political arena or entertain local and statewide candidates and officeholders, (3) hardsell political events for major contributors, and (4) fun events with political overtones that may raise money for scholarships, for a nonprofit foundation, or for charitable endeavors in the community. Let's look more closely at how these types of club functions help members and well-chosen nonmembers accrue political and economic capital that makes it possible for them to gain or maintain their privileged positions atop influential political, economic, and social hierarchies within their city, state, and nation.

POLITICAL INSIDERS TALK TO MEMBERS

The importance of political insider talks at elite clubs was first called to public attention by sociologists such as G. William Domhoff (2005) and Peter Martin Phillips (1994), who studied California's Bohemian Club and its Lakeside Talks at the club's summer encampment. Since 1932, Bohemian Club members have invited top government officials and politicians to participate in talks to provide intellectual stimulation and political enlightenment. Some of the speakers are club members; others are invited guests of the club. The speakers typically provide new insights on how a particular problem will be handled or what current issues are most important among political or military insiders. In the 1980s, for example, General John Chain, commander of the Strategic Air Command, spoke at the Lakeside Talks about how the United States needed the Stealth B-2 bomber: "I am a warrior and that is how I come to you today. I need the B-2" (quoted in Weiss 1989). Throughout the Grove's history, noted military and political leaders have provided club members with their views on everything from the atomic bomb to international monetary policy to universal health care and federal tax laws, and, in turn, members have made their views on these topics known to the speakers. As one journalist stated, "The important men come out for the Lakeside Talks, and each speaker seems to assume that his audience can actually do something about the issues raised, which, of course, it can" (Weiss 1989). Even if no inside or secret information is divulged at these Lakeside Talks, club members still gain from the events, as noted by Domhoff (2005): "Whatever the value of the talks, most members think there is something very nice about hearing official government policy, orthodox big-business ideology, and new scientific information from a fellow Bohemian or one of his guests in an informal atmosphere where no reporters are allowed to be present."

As we shift our focus to elite Texas clubs that have similar types of political chats for members, it might appear to outsiders that spending an evening listening to talks by elected politicians, government officials, or other people who are influential in the political process would not be particularly entertaining or beneficial for members. However, this is not true for many members: older members come to visit with former political allies or to relive an era in which they had strong ties with those in power; younger members often find these insider talks relevant because they find out how the political game is played and who the movers and shakers are in the political, military, and business arenas. Gaining access to these individuals and their ideas provides members with a chance to learn from political elites and to turn their own weak social/political ties into stronger ties that may be useful for them in the future.

Obviously, accumulating political capital through involvement in club-sponsored events is related to building economic capital for political incumbents, candidates, and parties because of the need for contributions; however, in the sense that I am using this concept, political capital refers to advantages that are more encompassing than collecting money and pledges of support alone. Among inner circles of social and political elites, political capital relates to trust, obligations, mutual exchanges, political intelligence, and policy advice. As governor of Texas and later as president of the United States, George W. Bush frequently made the statement that he "trusted" someone, whether the individual was one of his advisers, a political ally, a foreign head of state, or other person with whom he came into contact. In regard to the possession of political capital, however, trusting another person is closely related to other factors such as meeting one's obligations or engaging in mutual exchanges of ideas, information, and resources. When a person possesses significant political capital, he or she is able to access the political intelligence of other individuals who have served inside government and know what goes on there, who are particularly knowledgeable about the attitudes and actions of other political leaders, or who can provide unique insights on a pressing social issue or a current "hot spot" somewhere in the world. Political capital also involves access to useful policy advice from insiders about policies that might be instrumental in minimizing or resolving a current crisis. Although elite club activities with a political aspect have only limited utility in bring about dramatic shifts in the political arena, they provide a setting in which past, present, and future political leaders and those closest to them reveal the inner workings of their world to both insiders and outsiders.

Elite private clubs plan events that bring together highly influential individuals who can provide insider information on how the political process works, what can be expected from current and future politicians, and why certain policies are (or are not) working. In elite Texas clubs, this kind of information typically is disseminated to club members at an event that starts with cocktails, followed by dinner, and then a keynote address, forum, or panel discussion featuring high-profile people who are or have been deeply involved in the political process. A specific example will show how the insights of such noted individuals not only are for the entertainment of members but also may serve as a source of information for those who have political aspirations or want to have a voice in public policy decisions.

One of the most popular politically oriented social events at exclusive private clubs is to invite as a speaker a former political leader, adviser and "insider" to a political leader, or name-brand individual who can provide a bird's-eye view of some aspect of the political process that is not known to outsiders or that reflects the opinions of the speaker on the strengths and shortcomings of a leader in handling a political crisis or other major event.

Consider, for example, a lecture delivered by political consultant Mark McKinnon at the Headliners Club in 2006. This keynote speaker clearly had the authority to be discussing the selling of a candidate because he had helped George W. Bush capture the White House in the contested 2000 campaign and managed more than 1,000 political campaigns worldwide. McKinnon not only served as a political adviser to Bush and oversaw advertising for his campaigns, but he also is considered to be a personal friend of the president and has joined him on mountain-biking trips. McKinnon is known by political insiders to be extremely effective in getting out the message of his candidate while undermining the message of opponents. It was natural that the Headliners Club would invite McKinnon to give a talk to its members because he possesses strong ties to the Austin community from his days as a former editor of *The Daily Texan*, the student newspaper of the University of Texas at Austin, as well as his current positions as a lecturer at the Lyndon B. Johnson School of Public Affairs and as vice chairman of Public Strategies, Inc., a public relations and public opinion consulting firm.

The topic of McKinnon's speech to the Headliners Club was "What is in a political message?" As armchair politicians and aspiring politicians in the club's audience listened, McKinnon carefully explained how to effectively get a specific political message across to the public. According to McKinnon, it is important to tell a great story, such as a television advertisement in President Reagan's reelection campaign that featured a bear (which stood for communism) wandering in the wild, and the ad's message was "Prepare for Peace." McKinnon believes that political candidates should be brief and try to not say too much. He pointed out that during the 2004 presidential election, sound bites from candidates averaged eight seconds, whereas in prior campaigns they averaged sixty-eight seconds. To be effective, McKinnon explained, political ads must be emotional because showing emotion will trump an intellectual message every time. He illustrated this point with a Bush campaign ad where a young woman says, "He's the most powerful man in the world, and all he wants to do is keep me safe." However, as McKinnon noted, it is also important for the political message to be relevant. In Lyndon B. Johnson's 1964 presidential campaign, for example, a television ad featured a young girl pulling leaves off a daisy and counting, "One, two, three . . ." followed by a mushroom cloud. The voice-over stated, "These are the stakes—we must either love each other or we will die." In the Cold War era, such a message was truly relevant, according to McKinnon.

Regardless of their own political background or aspirations, club members gain unique insights from hearing well-connected speakers such as Mark McKinnon because of their profound influence on and close proximity to top candidates and elected officials. As one person summarized the importance of McKinnon's speech, "Members were given a unique opportunity to hear and see just what goes into the making of a candidate and his or her message when Mark McKinnon treated us to a personal journey through 'message articulation'. . . . McKinnon informed and entertained the audience with anecdotes and fascinating visual examples of what, literally, makes up an effective message" (Allensworth 2007:8–10). Some club members were seen taking notes during McKinnon's talk because they realized that they had a rare opportunity to gain information from a person *Broadcasting and Cable* magazine referred to as "one of a handful of players behind every big decision, consensus or roadblock in Washington . . . putting a unique, sometimes hidden stamp on the outcome of today's debates" (McConnell 2005). Moreover, president George W. Bush's statement regarding McKinnon shows the high esteem with which political elites such as Bush view him: "I was very impressed with Mark's creativity, and particularly impressed by his honesty. He's a trusted ally" (Public Strategies 2007). McKinnon has returned the favor and shown his insider status in the Bush administration by pointing out that when people vote for candidates in a presidential election, what they really want is to elect "the head of the family." According to McKinnon (2003), "[Voters are] looking to elect someone they can trust to run the country or the state or the city, but they want characteristics and attributes beyond a set of positions on issues. What they're thinking about is, I may not agree with this person all the time, but I trust him to exercise good judgment, to be honest, to have integrity. That was why swing voters found President Bush appealing."

In supposedly nonpolitical clubs across the nation, special events are planned that bring club members in close contact with top politicians and those who advise them. Audience members build their political capital not only by what they learn from the speakers but also from interacting with them and benefiting from the speakers' close connections with individuals in power. As one analyst suggested in regard to the Bohemian Grove's Lakeside Talks, "Whatever the topic, those present emerge with a sense of insider awareness of high-level policy issues and political situations which are often yet-to-be, or perhaps never-to-be, publicly articulated" (Phillips 2001). In some cases, club members are able to put information gained from these talks to use for their own advantage in the political area.

Like speeches given by individual keynote speakers, panel discussions are another way in which political insiders and their messages are brought to members of elite clubs. Although panel discussions involve more participants than talks by individual speakers, these events are also held in the club's intimate physical setting, where the proximity of like-minded people contributes to a feeling of group solidarity. Panel discussions provide newer and less entrenched club members with a chance to meet influential power players and to develop greater cohesiveness with other club members. As Domhoff (2005:35) suggested in regard to the linkages between the members of the Bohemian Club and politically oriented speakers who are in a position to influence public policy, "Social cohesion aids in the development of policy cohesion. . . . But that doesn't make policy cohesion automatic—that's why the upper class and corporate community have also developed an extensive policy-planning network." Panel discussions at some elite clubs include time for club members to express their own opinions and to ask questions of the experts before, during, or after the formal event. In this way, members can make their opinions on important policy issues known to the panelists.

At the Headliners Club, one panel provided members with insights on politics in the past and future. According to the club newsletter, "In a main dining room as packed as the proverbial 'smoke filled back room' of political legend, only without the smoke, the Headliners Club was treated to an analysis of the past and a crystal ball look into the future of Texas and National politics by four superbly qualified and knowledgeable pundits" (Granger and Talley 2006:4). At this forum, former Texas Comptroller John Sharp, current University of Texas Board of Regents Chairman James Huffines, former Lieutenant Governor Ben Barnes, and former chief justice of the Texas Supreme Court Tom Phillips "dissected the body politic to reveal how the process has changed and will continue to change" (Granger and Talley 2006:4).

From the panel discussion titled "Politics: Past and Future," club members heard about the decline of the political party boss as well as a decline in the moderate voter's involvement in both the Republican and the Democratic parties. Panelists described changes in how political leaders and parties communicated with the voter, and they noted the ways in which the changing demographics of Texas and the nation were affecting state and national politics. Some panelists also described the decline in voter turnout at a time when a greater portion of the population was able to participate in the process, and others spoke of the growth in single-issue organizations. Concern was expressed by panelists over the ways in which some state and national congressional districts had been gerrymandered to the extent that no viable contests were possible between political parties in those districts. Along the themes of McKinnon's talk on a previous occasion, panel members described the future of politics in terms of major changes in the methods of communication that are used to reach voters as technology continues to advance. They also described the effects of continuing demographic changes, ongoing reforms in campaign finance at all levels of government, and changes in the method of filling state judicial positions (from the campaign process to a selection process with voter review).

Headliners Club members were interested to learn the panelists' observations about politics and why many recent changes had not been positive. According to one summary of the panel discussion, "There was agreement by all panel members that politics had changed, not for the better, over their collective memories and hope that the changes in the future will be better for all those participating in the political process—both candidates and voters" (Granger and Talley 2006:6). Prior to panel discussions such as this, club members enjoy cocktails, dinner, and visiting with other members. Some former political insiders are able to relive a part of history in which they participated; however, other members can think about their political aspirations and what political connections they might make through the club as well.

Most elite clubs that have politically oriented events attempt to have speakers that reflect local, state, national, and international levels of power. After having recent events that focused primarily on state politics, the Headliners Club sponsored a panel in which international issues were examined from the perspectives of former U.S. ambassadors. Panelists for an evening featuring "The Life of an American Ambassador" included Lewis Lucke, ambassador to the Kingdom of Swaziland from 2004 to 2006; Stan McLelland, ambassador to Jamaica from 1998 to 2001; Lyndon L. Olson Jr., ambassador to Sweden from 1988 to 2001; and Pamela Willeford, ambassador to Switzerland and Liechtenstein from 2003 to 2006.

These panelists have strong roots in the Austin community, but they also possess important linkages to various presidential administrations and to movers and shakers in international politics and business. Club members who desire to forge stronger linkages with business and political elites in the United States and other countries may gain access to these ties through individuals such as these panelists, who have spent part of their careers as ambassadors building strong networks across continents. At these social and informational gatherings, club members and panelists share cocktails, dinner, and formal and informal discussions about current national and international issues. They also share the sense of "we-ness" that was described as follows by one sociologist in regard to Bohemian Club members and their Lakeside Talks:

> Contact with the pinnacles of power, presidents, foreign dignitaries, cabinet officials, and intellectual giants in an informal off-the-record discussion format, gives Bohemians a heady sense of sharing ideas at the topmost levels. Intellectually, Bohemians can agree or disagree with the specific issues of the chats but . . . [the] Lakeside Chats are a shared experiential process that enhances a sense of elite we-ness in union with shared challenges and in opposition to common threats. (Phillips 1994:111)

Although elite Texas clubs do not routinely draw presidents and foreign dignitaries for their speeches and panels, the frequent presence of former presidents, ambassadors, top presidential aides and advisers, and other well-connected political elites is not taken lightly by club members who make their opinions known on issues of importance to them. Consider how Phillips (1994:120) described a similar situation at the Bohemian Grove and Club:

> A Bohemian's belief that he is hearing first hand interpretations of current events could well lead to decisions or considerations on various other interests outside of the Club context. . . . These ideas could well provide advantages for decision-makers' timely use of material resources, political power, or financial capital.
>
> This does not mean that when a banker hears the President of Mexico discuss the North American Free Trade Agreement (NAFTA), that special secrets unavailable to the public will be disclosed. However, it does mean that this banker, politician, or corporate director will have a heightened awareness of NAFTA's implications, that can be immediately shared and discussed with other elites, and that this process will give relative ad-

vantages to Bohemian family members over others in the pursuit of their business and career interests in the everyday world.

As Phillips suggests, the heightened awareness that comes from associating closely with political elites helps other privileged people know where to look for key issues and what to do about national and international concerns as they relate to their own business and professional interests.

Up to this point, we have focused on the influential role of political insiders who give talks or present panel discussions at clubs; however, one of the most significant political activities in elite clubs is the "soft-sell" political event, which is used to introduce new or "up-and-coming" players to political pros and major contributors who wield serious clout in the political arena.

SOFT-SELL EVENTS: "THE CAMPAIGN TRAIL RUNS THROUGH THE CLUB"

Soft-sell political events are organized by club members to introduce political novices to individuals who can be helpful to them in achieving a goal such as winning an election or being appointed to an important political position. The most commonly held functions are a cocktail reception shortly after the end of the workday, a cocktail buffet that includes both an open bar and a large table of elaborate appetizers and small gourmet sandwiches, or a full dinner (usually reserved for introductions to "major players") so that those who are invited will have an opportunity not only to shake hands with the person being introduced but also to become better acquainted with that person by learning about his or her background, finding common interests or overlapping personal histories, and coming to an understanding of why this individual should be supported in his or her effort to win public office or be appointed to a key political position.

Although we hear very little about politically related events when they are held in private clubs, many well-known politicians have accumulated political capital and gained a stronger footing for their careers through participating in these gatherings at elite clubs. In turn, club members also gain specific political and social advantages by getting to know these up-and-coming players before they reach political prominence. In the words of one respondent, "If you knew them 'back when' and were instrumental in helping them get to where they are today, they owe you something for helping them get there. You could say the campaign trail runs right through the Headliners and Austin Clubs." And, this individual might well have added, the political careers of many high-level governmental appointees also have gained momentum from their introduction to elites at top private clubs. A case in point is that of former U.S. Attorney General Alberto R. Gonzales.

Bolstering Alberto Gonzales's Reputation and Credentials at the Headliners Club

In my study of elite clubs and their role in helping people accumulate political capital, I was often reminded by respondents of the rapid ascent of Alberto R. Gonzales, former U.S. attorney general, whose political climb followed that of George W. Bush from the Austin statehouse to the White House in Washington. Receptions and other social gatherings for Gonzales at Austin's Headliners Club played at least a small part in his political ascension because he did not have the typical background for becoming a Bush insider, or a "Bushie," as members of the national press corps labeled individuals who wielded serious clout in the George W. Bush presidential administration.

For individuals not familiar with Alberto R. Gonzales, a brief biography is useful in explaining why he needed to be introduced to and accepted by well-connected political, economic, and social elites in order for his career to move from one level to the next. Although many of Governor and then President Bush's closest political allies had been his close childhood friends, former schoolmates at Phillips Academy Andover, or Skull and Bones fraternity brothers at Yale University, upper-class friends of the senior Bush or the younger Bush's affluent neighbors in Dallas and a few well-chosen outsiders to the Bush inner circle, including Alberto Gonzales, were allowed to play a strong role in his gubernatorial and presidential administrations if they demonstrated their loyalty to Bush. However, Gonzales did not fit the traditional image of a Bush ally, coming as he did from a working-class family (the second of eight children born to a construction worker and his wife). Gonzales was widely described as a bootstrap type who attended the U.S. Air Force Academy, graduated from Rice University, and earned a degree from Harvard Law School. After he made partner at an influential Houston law firm, Gonzales was named general counsel to Governor Bush, then appointed Texas secretary of state, and later named to a position on the Texas Supreme Court (whitehouse.gov 2007a). For this rise in political position to transpire, however, Gonzales needed to become better known among political elites and to bolster his reputation across the state. This is where soft-sell receptions at elite clubs served an important purpose in furthering his career.

At about the time that Gonzales was named general counsel for Governor Bush, influential Republican members of the Headliners Club hosted a large cocktail reception and buffet to introduce Gonzales to key social and political elites. This reception was typical of hundreds of similar receptions held throughout the state and nation for rising political stars, and thus it serves as a case study of how this type of function is planned and what effect such events have on political capital for aspirants and elite club members.

Planning a Soft-Sell Event to Gain Maximum Political Capital

How are soft-sell political events organized in elite clubs? Although elite clubs do not directly sponsor political events, individual club members organize the functions and serve on the host committee. Club members do not overtly state that they are trying to "sell" a future political appointee or that they are raising money for a candidate or incumbent: they typically play down the political aspect of the function and focus on the fun side of the evening by informing invited guests that the event will include an open bar, a lavish buffet, and the opportunity to interact with important leaders. Host committees may name one or more distinguished honorary chairpersons for the event. These individuals may not actually be present at the event, but they lend their name to the function so that it will be appealing to individuals who desire to associate with key players in the political arena. Former President George Herbert Walker Bush and First Lady Barbara Bush, for example, have been used as drawing cards for a number of politically related elite club events, although they often have "last-minute obligations" that keep them from being present on the day of the event. Other well-known individuals who have been used to draw attendees to functions at the Headliners and the Austin Club include former President Bill Clinton, the late Lady Bird Johnson (widow of former President Lyndon B. Johnson), numerous past and present state officials, and former national media celebrities, such as Walter Cronkite, Dan Rather, and Tom Brokaw.

Who is invited to a soft-sell political reception? To compile a guest list for these functions, club members invite their club-member friends, club-member business associates, and other well-connected individuals who are active in politics or in the community. Obviously, the first individuals on the invitation list are club members who are closely linked with the current administration, which in the case of Alberto Gonzales were key players in Governor Bush's statehouse and others with strong ties to the Republican Party, such as members of the Associated Republicans of Texas. However, many influential community leaders in the arts, higher education, and business are also invited to such events because the implicit support of Old Guard club members adds to the credibility of a rising political star.

It is important that the invitation list be large enough to invite (and thus not snub) important elites; however, the list must appear to be highly selective and exclusive in nature. If Old Guard elites believe that "just anyone" will be at the function, they are less likely to attend and lend their credibility to the event. The term "cattle call" is often used by elites to describe social or political events where they believe little discernment is used in regard to the invitation list, and events that fall into this category may be boycotted. As a result, club members hosting politically related events carefully supervise the invitation lists and pass them by elites who are "in the know" about the hierarchical ranking of privileged individuals in a community and who keep abreast of current feuds among elites that might prove difficult or embarrassing if the individuals involved were invited to the same event.

After invitations are sent out, club members sponsoring the event divide up the invitation list so that they can either call or e-mail those who have been invited and encourage them to attend, and these sponsors also arrange for name tags to be made. Since everyone invited to the reception is asked to reply (RSVP) to the invitation by a specific date, follow-up calls may be made to those who have not been heard from, and name tags will be made for those who indicate they will attend. On the day of the event, the name tags are carefully spread in alphabetical order on large tables that also hold one or more elaborate floral arrangements so that reception guests can find them easily but also so that early arrivals can see the many "big names" who are supposed to attend the event. According to Rhonda, a political events planner, name tags may be put out for top elites who have been invited but whose attendance is questionable:

> Well, if they show up, there's a name tag for them. If they don't show up, other guests think that this is a big-deal reception because these guys are going to come but haven't gotten there yet. As the evening wears on, we put the name tags away if they haven't shown up, so they don't look like "no-shows" when people are leaving, and most guests assume that these folks came in and they just missed them. It's a win-win situation: if they come, it looks like we were expecting them; if they don't, it looks like they are supporting the candidate. According to one club member who organized a number of these events, "There's nothing worse than low attendance. It makes it look like your guy look like a 'loser' when you're trying to promote him as being 'one of us.' So, we keep a close eye on numbers [who are planning to attend] and will sometimes invite additional people to pad the attendance at the last minute if we need to."

Like the procedure that is followed for invitations and name tags, there is also a standard format for how the rising star political reception is organized.

As they enter the private club, guests are first greeted by club personnel who direct them to the great room where the reception is being held. When the guests arrive at that room, they pick up their name tags and are asked by the club's black-tie-attired waitstaff what they would like to drink. As guests receive their drink, they are greeted by the evening's hosts who introduce them to the rising star, which in this case was Alberto Gonzales. As the evening gets busier and more guests arrive, reception organizers continue to introduce Gonzales to as many key politicians, major party contributors, wealthy business people, lobbyists, and community leaders as they can. In their introductions of Gonzales, they tell the guests something important or flattering about him and try to reveal any conversation starters they think might exist between Gonzales and the guest. For example, if both individuals attended Rice University, the host may make this fact known. Ultimately, the goal is to inform guests that Gonzales is a "person to watch because of all the great things he is going to do in the future," as one guest stated. The fact that Gonzales was building strong ties to Governor Bush at the time of the reception is not lost on those present at the cocktail reception. As some of those who attended this event pointed out, it was clear that Gonzales was becoming a close friend and confidant of Bush, and those who wanted to get along with Bush also needed to accept Gonzales as a political player who was rapidly accumulating political capital that would be useful in his future and could also be useful for those who got to know him well at this time.

And, indeed, after the Headliners Club reception, Gonzales did become much more widely known not only in Texas politics but also at the national level, where he was named U.S. attorney general and was widely discussed as a possible Supreme Court nominee before he became embroiled in controversies that resulted in his resignation as U.S. attorney general in 2007. As Gonzales's ascent and descent in politics was described by one journalist, "It was a meteoric rise and a spectacular fall" (Gillman 2007). Part of his "meteoric rise" was facilitated by soft-sell receptions such as the one held by members of the Headliners Club, which helped Gonzales move beyond his working-class origins. Clearly, influential club members and other Texas political elites helped facilitate his rapid rise in politics by investing some of their own accrued political capital in an account to be used on behalf of Gonzales.

How are soft-sell political functions, such as the one held for Gonzales, viewed by elite club members? A reflection of how private clubs describe such functions is found in club newsletters where an item may describe the politicians as having been "entertained" or having "visited" the club. Consider, for example, these statements from *Headlines* (2006:21–22, emphasis added), the Headliners Club monthly publication: "With the elections in November, the Club has been very busy *entertaining* local and statewide candidates. In addition, you might have noticed national security in the halls charged with protecting the many national Senators and Governors who have also *visited* the

Club." When candidates or incumbents are entertained at the club or when they come as visitors to the premises, they usually are being introduced to or feted by influential club members and major contributors. Through their presence at elite clubs, politicians and political hopefuls indicate not only that they are accustomed to the lifestyle of elites but also that they are aware of the fact that members expect them to play by the unwritten rule of the upper class ("You watch my back, and I'll watch yours") when they are in public office. As politicians garner political capital at such functions, club members expect to gain political capital for themselves that may be invested when they need a favor from an elected official or political appointee. Although political capital may be accumulated in a wide variety of settings, elite clubs provide a unique venue for this accumulation because aspirants and incumbents come into contact with individuals who possess economic and/or political power and who often find it to their advantage to help a few well-chosen up-and-comers move up the political ladder. For this reason, numerous club members are willing to become involved in soft-sell and hard-sell political events at this club.

THE HARD SELL: SERIOUS FUND-RAISING AND SCHMOOZING

The primary goal of hard-sell political events held at elite clubs (and elsewhere) is to gain major endorsements for candidates and garner significant campaign contributions within an exclusive setting that has the air of affluence and success. The central purpose of these events is not to produce a social gathering for club members but rather to hold the event in a setting that is popular with top campaign contributors and others who might be persuaded to become "big-ticket" donors. As the cost of mounting a successful political campaign has risen drastically in recent years and laws have been passed that restrict the amount of money that a person can contribute to an individual political candidate, more emphasis has been placed on contributions to political parties or to holding events that are not within the guidelines limiting contributions. One popular event in this category is the $2,500-a-plate dinner at an elite club or luxury hotel ballroom.

For events held at elite clubs, facilities are available in one of two ways—borrowing or renting the club. Club members *borrow* or *reserve* the club in their name for the evening's event, make all arrangements for food and drink, and pay the bill. When the club's facilities are *rented* by non–club members such as elected politicians, members of campaign committees, political action committees, or a group of key campaign supporters, the renters pay a fee for use of the club's facilities in addition to paying all expenses incurred, such as drinks, food, and service personnel. Renters pay the club's bill from campaign funds or the resources of a nonprofit political organization such as the Associated Republicans of Texas. When a candidate or his or her representatives rents the club, a public effort is made to distance the candidate from the club, particularly when the club has been accused of elitism, sexism, or racism. Privately, however, it is a different matter: the candidate wants the prestige associated with the "top-tier" club and wants its "movers and shakers" to be associated his or her political campaign. Likewise, club members want the additional political capital that accrues from "rubbing shoulders" with successful political candidates. Some elite clubs do not rent out their facilities to nonmembers because they do not wish to lose their private, nonprofit status and become the object of discrimination lawsuits regarding their membership and employment practices, as discussed in chapter 6.

Similarly, the issue of politicians renting exclusive clubs for their fundraisers and then being held accountable for the club's membership practices has been raised on a number of occasions. For example, former Maryland Governor Robert Ehrlich was accused of being an elitist and a racist when he held a campaign fund-raiser at the exclusive Elkridge Club, which allegedly has no African American members (Foxnews.com 2005). In response to this criticism, Ehrlich stated, "We have no access to the membership information. Obviously, we're *renters*. We come in and we pay our bill and we leave" (Foxnews.com 2005). By making this statement, the governor sought to distance himself from the club's membership practices and day-to-day operations while still giving his contributors access to one of the most prestigious clubs in his state. In the aftermath of this dispute, the *Baltimore City Paper* (2005) jokingly named Elkridge Club as the "Best Place to Hold a Political Fundraiser":

> When looking for just the right place to hold a political fundraiser, you have to consider what kind of message the setting sends to your constituents. So it was especially shrewd of Gov. Robert Ehrlich to hold a $1,000-per-plate fundraiser at North Baltimore's exclusive Elkridge Club on June 20, 2005. Not only did he rake in $100,000 for his war chest, the governor benefited from a perfect locale: good food, wealthy supporters with fat checkbooks, a day of photo-ops, and a top-notch golf course. And while many would have balked that the Elkridge Club has not had an African-American member in its 127 year history, that didn't stop Ehrlich. . . . The club, which in January 2005 finally eliminated gender-based membership [restrictions], was the perfect place to convey a "pro-whitey" message to your more racist supporters without having to actually come out and say "whites only."

As this statement suggests, some of the governor's critics believed that there was a racial message in the selection of this exclusive golf club as the site for the fund-raiser because the location's social geography signified a "whites-only" territory, although the names of Elkridge's members and the racial composition of the group is not public information. After a 1977 Maryland law was passed that prohibited country clubs from getting a property tax break if they discriminated in their membership policies, the Elkridge Club gave up its tax break rather than having to divulge its membership list to the state if requested to do so (Foxnews.com 2005). Over its 130-year history, Elkridge Club has had almost 3,000 members who pride themselves on the club's tradition and do not want to see dramatic changes (McLean 2005).

Like the members of Elkridge Club, members of other elite clubs do not believe that the government has the right to tell them who their members should be or whether they should be able to hold high-ticket political fundraisers within the walls of their club.

Hard-sell fund-raising events are becoming increasingly popular because, as one respondent stated, "Fund-raising season is a lot like hunting season in Texas," and the calendars of elite clubs reveal the intensity of this season by the shear number of political gatherings that are held each day, ranging from breakfasts and luncheons to elaborate cocktail buffets, seated dinners, and other activities that are geared to raise money from big-ticket contributors. For hard-sell fund-raisers, political insiders compile invitation lists on the basis of their access to information about potential guests' political affiliations, prior contributions to candidates, and how much access they are going to want to officials in various political offices. These hard-sell events often last for about two hours, but during that time, large sums of money often are pledged to candidates and political action committees. Organizers look for ostensible reasons around which they can build a fund-raiser. Birthdays of politicians, for example, provide justification for events such as these Texas functions in September 2006: "Martha Wong Celebrates [Texas House Speaker] Tom Craddick's Birthday" at the Austin Club and the "[State Senator] Kip Averitt Annual Austin Birthday Bash" at the Headliners Club (Capitolinside.com 2006). Birthday bashes such as these are only one of the many ways in which political candidates and incumbents are honored or celebrated by their followers or by lobbyists who hope to benefit from their financial support of the candidates. It is not even uncommon for many donors to give money to more than one candidate vying for the same office: regardless of who wins, the donor has chits in with the person who will hold the office. Those who do not give sufficient amounts of money fear that there will be unpleasant political consequences, such as greatly diminished political capital at the time they need to spend it.

Many politicians do not like the fund-raising process but are acutely aware that it is necessary for their political survival. In regard to his fund-raising activities, for example, U.S. Representative Phil Gingrey (R-Ga.) stated, "This is the hardest part of being a member, and we all get weary of it. So much money is spent and sometimes you think, 'Gosh, you know, we need to bring some sanity to this.' But when you've got both sides doing it, it ups the ante" (Allen 2005). Although it is difficult for outsiders to gain entry to these hard-sell, big-ticket fund-raisers when they are held in private clubs, journalists sometimes gain access to these events anyway. Here is one journalist's description of a hard-sell fund-raising event at an Austin club in 2006:

> The setting was a rear room in a private club. Two already-acquainted men in suits met briefly. Pleasantries were exchanged. A check passed between them. This wasn't a business deal or a scene from a gangster movie, but a run-of-the-mill political fundraiser, where lobbyists ply elected officials with contributions, hoping, hinting—though never explicitly asking—for political favors down the road.
>
> Lobbyist Raul Liendo wasn't keen to explain why he forked over $250 to a San Antonio lawmaker in the weeks leading up to the 2007 legislative session. He was just following orders from his client, TXU Energy's political action committee. "I'm just the delivery guy," Liendo said at a Tuesday night fundraiser for Rep. Joaquin Castro, D-San Antonio. . . . "I just work with the system that's in place."
>
> As a hired gun for an energy giant, Liendo was a bit player in the elaborate though rarely displaced ritual of political fundraising. It's a busy time for him: Austin's high season of check writing and catered receptions in the parlors of exclusive clubs. (Sandberg 2006)

The sight this journalist describes is not uncommon during fund-raising season; however, an equally common sight is one where no money visibly changes hands during the event itself but where money is the coin of the realm for participating in the event. Checks for $2,000 and $2,500-per-plate dinners are sent well in advance to reserve a space for top lobbyists and other major contributors.

The extent to which big-ticket fund-raising has been conducted in elite clubs came to light during the Texans for a Republican Majority (TRMPAC) scandal in 2004–2005 when charges were filed and an indictment was handed down against TRMPAC, a political action committee organized by Tom DeLay, then the congressional majority leader. This committee was accused of accepting $120,000 in allegedly illegal corporate campaign contributions shortly before and after the 2002 election, which resulted in Republicans gaining control the Texas House of Representatives for the first time in 130 years and enabled them to redraw the state's congressional districts to the benefit of Republican candidates. Despite a Texas election law prohibiting corporations and unions from making donations to help an individual political candidate, TRMPAC raised and spent $523,000 in corporate funds on such campaigns (Smith 2005:A3). According to media reports, a substantial portion of this money was raised at events held in elite private clubs around the state (Hoppe and Kuempel 2004).

As we near the end of the first decade of the twenty-first century, there is no reason to believe that we have reached the end of major political fundraising efforts in elite clubs and other posh settings in Texas and throughout the United States. Over the past decade, special interests in Texas alone have spent between $1 billion and $2.3 billion on almost 65,000 lobbying contracts, according to reports filed with the Texas Ethics Commission (Texans for Public Justice 2007).

To offset the notion of elitism in hard-sell fund-raising and the idea that influence can be bought and sold, many politicians (including President Bush during his first term of office) have held down-home fund-raisers or thank-you parties for major contributors at public halls or other nonelite settings rather than conveying the image of wealthy city slickers who are very much at home in snobbish private clubs. One example of the counterelite political event was a private barbecue held by President Bush at Hickey Broken Spoke Ranch—located a short distance from the president's Crawford, Texas, ranch—where about 350 top contributors and major fund-raisers who had collected at least $200,000 each from donors were brought in for the evening to eat barbecue and receive personal attention from President Bush and Karl Rove, who was his top political adviser at the time (Lester 2003). For the evening, wealthy and influential individuals acted like they were ordinary, down-to-earth folks even though some of them flew in on their private jets and are members of the very exclusive clubs that were not chosen as the site of that evening's festivities.

Thus far, we have looked at three types of events that are related to political capital in elite clubs: political insider talks, soft-sell political events, and hard-sell political events for major contributors. Now I turn to the fourth and final type of event, which involves the accumulation of political capital in elite clubs, namely, entertainment with political overtones that raises money for scholarships, a nonprofit foundation, or other charitable endeavors in the community.

FUN CLUB EVENTS WITH POLITICAL OVERTONES

Not all politically related events held at elite clubs are related to raising money for political campaigns: some events honor or roast well-known political figures while raising money for a cause such as the club's nonprofit foundation. The tradition of roasting politicians and their top advisers appears to have started in some of the social and professional organizations of Washington, D.C., such as the Alfalfa Club and the Washington Press Club; however, the idea for this special event has spread over the years to numerous city clubs, particularly those located in state capitals or large metropolitan areas.

Regardless of the city or the specific occasion, toasts or roasts are held to honor established political elites or journalists who cover politics, and the proceeds from some of these events are used for purposes such as funding college scholarships, while others are purely for fun. The Alfalfa Club in Washington came to public attention when President Bush and his wife, Laura, attended a $200-a-plate dinner of filet mignon and lobster given by the club. The evening included humorous speeches about politicians, business leaders, and world affairs. Although the club was organized for the purpose of holding an annual banquet honoring the birthday of Civil War General Robert E. Lee, its 200 members are top politicians and business leaders, and the evening has strong political overtones because of jokes told about the president, cabinet officers, White House staffers, and other influential individuals. According to media reports, the club was humorously named for the alfalfa plant because its roots will range far afield to reach liquid refreshment; however, members of the press are barred from the event, and little is reported in the media about what goes on inside the party. It is known that prior to 1994, when Hillary Rodham Clinton attended the event with President Clinton, the club was off limits to women (FoxNews.com 2007).

A more widely known political event that has inspired similar activities at elite city clubs is the Washington Press Club Foundation's annual Congressional Dinner, which is the major fund-raiser supporting the work of the foundation. Invitations go out to members of Congress, elected officials, members of the Washington press corps, and other well-known people or celebrities who happen to be in the District of Columbia at the time of the event. Proceeds from the dinner are used to fund internship and scholarship programs that are awarded to aspiring journalists. According to media reports, this congressional dinner is a "gathering where pols and media types spruce up and poke fun at themselves and each other" (Davis 2006:C2). Many of the speakers tell supposedly humorous stories about other politicians; some tell racy jokes that would not be considered politically correct but are carefully couched in a "Did I hear that correctly?" format.

Political roasts have become popular among members of elite clubs because they can be used for special occasions such as the celebration of the fiftieth anniversary of Austin's Headliners Club to raise money for the foundation's scholarship program and to bring together past and present luminaries in the fields of politics, journalism, business, and education and those who are simply known as "Old Austin" or "high society." To celebrate the club's anniversary, Karl Rove, then top adviser to President George W. Bush, was the honoree at a gala held in a local hotel ballroom because the club's facilities could not handle the anticipated crowd for this $2,000 minimum per table event.

Karl Rove has been closely linked with George W. Bush, first as his chief political strategist in getting Bush elected governor of Texas and then as president of the United States, and has been referred to by many political pundits as "the power behind the throne," so Rove was a good choice for such a roast. Rove has strong ties to political and business leaders in both Austin and Washington, and he is a friend or acquaintance of numerous Headliners Club members. He is also widely known for showing his humorous side at black-tie dinners and once impersonated a rapper at the Radio and Television Correspondents' Association dinner when comics from the television show *Whose Line Is It Anyway?* persuaded him to dance around and refer to himself as "MC Rove" (CBS Broadcasting 2007; Rich 2007).

At the Headliners roast of Rove, former club president Lowell Lebermann greeted the roastee by saying, "Karl we are so glad to have you in Austin . . . hell, we're glad to have you anywhere other than Washington, DC." Mark McKinnon (previously mentioned in this chapter as having managed President Bush's media campaigns in 2000 and 2004 and giving a talk at the Headliners Club about his endeavors) then presented a slide show of the "Best of Karl Rove," including still photos of Rove throwing snowballs at the national press corps' bus while on the campaign trail. Although President Bush was not present for the roast, he sent along a video message with a three-year "To-Do List" for Rove, which included such activities as taking "Barney [the president's dog] to drug sniffing training at Homeland Security" and "I hope you finally finish reading the Cliff Notes of the Constitution" (Copp 2006:B3). Other highlights of the evening included recorded messages from former President George Herbert Walker Bush and his wife, Barbara, who were also honorees for the evening but unable to attend. For his part of the evening, Rove responded with his own brand of humor to comments made by various speakers, including Mary Matalin, who formerly served as assistant to President George W. Bush and counselor to Vice President Dick Cheney simultaneously. Matalin is quite popular as a speaker at roasts held by elite clubs: she frequently appears as a presenter at events held to honor Washington insiders, including the Headliners Club evening honoring Rove. When his turn came at the microphone, Rove told club members and their guests that he missed living in Austin, and he thanked Bush for the opportunity "to work for a man with vision, a man with guts" (Copp 2006:B3). Rove also stated that, just for the record, he wanted everyone to know that "not a single snowball got within five feet of the press" when he attempted to throw snowballs at their bus (Copp 2006:B3). The evening's roast was summed up as follows in the club's newsletter:

> In the tradition of the old Headliners Stag Luncheon roasts, everyone on the dais took a shot at everyone else on the dais in a free-for-all that had the audience rolling in the aisles. Hard to discern which laughed last or best. Karl Rove did end, however, by addressing his roasters, *"Is that the best you could do?"* (Granger and Greig 2006:9)

Evenings such as this one share certain common features. There is a local but well-known master of ceremonies who usually is a club member and has media or public relations experience. He and other speakers tell funny stories and jokes about some of the club's top members and about individuals seated at the head table or on the dais. There are videos featuring important people who cannot attend, such as the two Bush presidents and their wives. Still photos or home movies of the honorees when they were younger are shown, and comments are made about the baby and kiddie photos that suggest that their future careers were already apparent in these childhood endeavors. What was not known at the time of the Headliners' 2006 roast was that Rove would resign slightly over a year later in the wake of a congressional investigation and that he would not get to complete Bush's three-year "to-do list" that he had jokingly been given at the roast.

Despite the jokes and humorous repartee, political roasts at elite clubs typically end with a big love-in and much glad-handing by honored guests, club members, and others who desire to maintain their political, business, and social ties with one another. If there are any hurt feelings, they are carefully hidden because, after all, "the evening is for a good cause, and people with a sense of humor live longer," in the words of one club member.

Exclusive private clubs, limited-purpose social clubs such as Washington's Alfalfa Club, and professional associations such as the Radio and Television Correspondents Association sponsor lighthearted social events with strong political overtones to raise money for a good cause or to pay tribute to outstanding individuals in politics, journalism, or other fields. However, these events often involve pointed remarks and a contest to see which person can outdo the others. The presenters frequently use insults as terms of endearment and to show appreciation for what the individual has done for them and others who have benefited from close ties with the person. This is what the relationship between money and politics is all about, and this relationship can be furthered in many elite clubs in the United States and other nations where diverse members of the top tiers of economic, political, and social elites are brought together for their mutual benefit.

WHY MAKING POLITICAL CONNECTIONS MATTERS

As previously described, many elite city and country clubs are comprised of diverse categories of elites who come from a wide variety of backgrounds, ranging from "trust fund babies" who have inherited large sums of money to "New Rich entrepreneurs" who have recently made millions or even billions of dollars and to those individuals who are known as top players in the fields of philanthropy, politics, higher education, law, and medicine. From the common experiences they share in elite clubs and the events sponsored by these organizations, these diverse players become part of an *integrated elite*—an overarching elite in which members of diverse elite groups regularly come together and develop intertwining social networks. Social interactions between Old Guard club members and younger, rising elites, for example, make it possible for several generations of members to become acquainted and to work cooperatively on joint tasks such as endowing a nonprofit foundation for the club or a community organization.

Private clubs provide a means by which elites from various sectors of the upper classes are united among themselves rather being fragmented and working at odds on some business, political, or social issue without consciously realizing that they are doing so. Accumulating social, cultural, and political capital through club life keeps elites from becoming encapsulated within their own limited circles, and club life makes it possible for them to have a wider sphere of influence and greater social cohesion. According to sociologist Michael Useem (1984:63), "Social cohesion implies that the inner circle is *truly* a circle: Acquaintanceship networks are dense, mutual trust and obligations are widespread, and a common sense of identity and culture prevail." For elite club members, social cohesion provides a sense of belonging, loyalty to other members, and a desire to participate in events that enhance the members' social, cultural, and political capital. Participating in the same events, sharing laughs with one another, and knowing that you too are a political insider, at least when you need to be, builds strong group ties and social cohesion. For outsiders, all this is nothing more than something caught on an occasional YouTube.com clip or a newspaper article describing a "fundraising bash" held by members of the privileged classes.

In chapter 6, we examine attempts to reign in some of the elitism, racism, sexism, and homophobic behavior that allegedly has occurred in private clubs over the past fifty years and assess how much, if any, change has occurred in the "insider" and perhaps above-the-law mentality of some members of our nation's most prestigious clubs.

· 6 ·

Change and Resistance to Change in Membership Policies

London, England:

"I think it's wonderful," said Rachael Heyhoe Flint, the former England women's cricket captain, outside Lord's [Cricket Ground in London] last night as Marylebone Cricket Club members walked past in various states of humour [following a vote to admit the first women members to the club in its 211 years of history]. "It's very important for cricket around the world that the MCC can now be considered with the utmost respect. It's important for sponsorship and the development of the game." But as she spoke, a middle-aged member of the club walked past, turned to look at her and said, "Life as we know it is over."

Ms. Heyhoe Flint responded: "It's not surprising there are people who still don't like it. It is 211 years since this club has been formed. I can now apply as a member, though with a 17- or 18-year waiting list, I'll probably be dead and buried before I can join my husband who is a member in the Long Room" [a famous clubroom where paintings of MCC's best-known players are displayed]. (Fenton 1998)

Blue Bell, Pennsylvania:

Meadowlands Country Club of Blue Bell, Pennsylvania, a private/members only club, was recently sued by a former female member, who alleged that the club treated her in a discriminatory manner by giving preferential treatment to men over women. Among her complaints were that the club illegally barred women from a men-only dining facility, refused to grant women club voting rights and forbid women from access to the golf course at certain times. The case settled at the end of September [2004] for an undisclosed sum and certain concessions by the club. (Ewing 2004)

$\mathcal{T}$he granting of full membership status to women at the United Kingdom's 211-year-old Marylebone Cricket Club and the Meadowlands case in the United States challenging the second-class status of women at an elite club have been widely proclaimed as victories for women and as prime examples of how elite clubs are changing their membership practices. However, there is much more to the story of change—and a corresponding resistance to change—in the most exclusive clubs of England and America.

In this chapter, I first examine laws in the United Kingdom and in the United States pertaining to discrimination by private clubs and discuss how those laws are changing in both countries. As laws have been enacted prohibiting discrimination on the basis of such things as race, ethnicity, religion, and disability status, one of the factors in determining whether those laws apply to private clubs has been whether a particular club is a place of public accommodation (and thus subject to those laws) or a private association that usually is not subject to those laws. Next, the reaction of many private clubs to ongoing changes in antidiscrimination laws is discussed. Finally, the chapter describes what some people do when they are excluded from membership in an existing club: start their own club. Let's turn first to antidiscrimination laws in England and the United States as they relate to private clubs.

DRAWING A FINE LINE: ANTIDISCRIMINATION LAWS IN THE UNITED KINGDOM

As we have seen in earlier chapters, many of the elite private clubs in the United States—from this nation's earliest times through the current date—were patterned on the exclusive gentlemen's clubs of London. Part of what was adopted in this country's adaptation of the English club environment was the belief that a private club is a *voluntary association* that is entitled to discriminate in any way it chooses with regard to both its membership practices and the use of the club's facilities. However, antidiscrimination laws have been passed over the past few decades in the United Kingdom dealing with the "six equality strands" (sex, "including gender reassignment"; disability; religion or belief, including the freedom not to have a religion or belief; sexual orientation; age; and race, including nationality, ethnicity, and national origins), and these laws have increasingly been made applicable to private clubs.

Applying Antidiscrimination Laws to Private Clubs

Originally, the United Kingdom's antidiscrimination laws as they related to private clubs applied only to those clubs that offered their goods, services, or facilities to the general public, such as by renting out their premises for banquets or conferences or for sporting events (Department for Work and Pensions 2004), a distinction still made with regard to private clubs in the United States. The rationale was that, if a club's facilities could be used only by the members themselves (and by the members' bona fide guests when accompanied by a member), the facilities were private, whereas if the club from time to time rented out its facilities to nonmembers, the facilities lost their private nature and became places of (at least sometimes) public accommodation that should not be allowed to discriminate on a forbidden basis.

More recently, however, the antidiscrimination laws in the United Kingdom have been extended to *any* private club with twenty-five or more members if admission to the club is regulated by a written or unwritten constitution (BBC Action Network 2005; United Kingdom Parliament 2004). Likewise, the antidiscrimination laws at first applied only to discrimination on the basis of race and ethnicity but over time were extended to discrimination on the basis of disability status. However, these laws provided little if any protection to women with regard to private clubs until 2006, when a proposed European Union directive—applicable to all nations that participate in the European Union—would have made it unlawful for private clubs, regardless of whether or not they provided goods and services to the general public, to discriminate on the grounds of sex. When early drafts of the proposed directive became public, strenuous opposition was voiced by many individuals, including members of some of the most exclusive men-only clubs in the United Kingdom. Members of these clubs feared that the sanctity of their group would be violated by the directive's provisions, and they used their social and political power to resist this change. As a result, before the final directive was adopted, a paragraph was added allowing differences in the treatment of men and women if they were "justified by a legitimate aim." Among the various legitimate aims specified was "freedom of association, in cases of membership of single-sex private clubs" (Rennie 2006). In other words, elite men's clubs—such as White's and Boodle's in London—and women's clubs can still discriminate on the basis of sex as long as they have no members of the opposite sex, whereas a *mixed-sex* club (one with both male and female members) is forbidden to engage in such practices as denying women seating or service in the "men's" grill room or bar, limiting women's tee times on the golf course to "off-prime" hours, or engaging in any other act that treats women members as second-class citizens.

Have these laws resulted in elite private clubs in the United Kingdom no longer discriminating on the basis of age, race, ethnicity, religion, sexual orientation, and (except for single-sex clubs) sex? The answer is no, they probably have not. Many of these clubs have long lists of people waiting for a membership position to become available, and it is hard to tell what factors go into each club's membership selection process. Likewise—as is true in the United States—these clubs do not make their membership lists (or the race, ethnicity, or religion of their members) public, with the result that it is virtually impossible to tell whether they are complying with the antidiscrimination laws.

The Future of Elite British Clubs

Since English law and the latest European Union directives regarding discrimination by private clubs on the basis of sex apply to mixed-sex clubs only, many British clubs continue to categorically deny women membership, and the members of other clubs that have considered becoming mixed-sex clubs have decided against such a change because of the directive. Ironically, in the short term, the European Union directive will probably have little influence on the exclusionary practices of the most prestigious gentlemen's clubs in London, but it may affect the extent to which historically men-only private clubs offer women "associate" or "restrictive" memberships in the future.

However, some social analysts suggest that changing times in the global economic community will eventually catch up with these "dinosaur" clubs and force them to change or die. For example, members of some prestigious British golf clubs apparently have realized that change is inevitable and that women must be granted full rights. Michael Endall, chairman of the Gay Hill Golf Club, which was the center of a 1990s controversy when a female golfer was denied the right to sit at the club's bar, recently told reporters that his club allows all members to socialize over drinks and that women can now serve on the club's board: "We're in the year 2007. It's time that everyone understood it," said Endall (CBSSports.com 2007). Similarly, according to Lord Lester of Herne Hill, who tried but failed to open the doors of the prestigious Garrick Club to women, it is possible that male members of mixed clubs will find that they actually enjoy having women participate in their clubs: "There might be some reactionary Neanderthal men who may form more such [single-sex] clubs [as a result of the European Union directive], but if they do, I think they'll have a rather miserable existence, because mixed golf is more fun" (quoted in Rennie 2006).

Although a number of differences exist in antidiscrimination laws and in the treatment of women by elite clubs in the United Kingdom and the United States, we can identify two significant commonalities. First, laws and courts in both nations have focused primarily on very specific exclusionary acts (such as women's limited use of club facilities or their restricted tee times) within a single type of club (typically a highly prestigious country or golf club) while larger patterns of overt discrimination regarding membership policies and practices have been ignored. Second, the focus of individual lawsuits and media coverage has almost exclusively been on practices that harm affluent women while little attention has been paid to problems of exclusion based on class, race/ethnicity, or religion.

ANTIDISCRIMINATION LAWS AND THE EXCLUSIONARY PRACTICES OF U.S. PRIVATE CLUBS

In a nation that prides itself on an ideology of equality and justice for all people, why are members of elite clubs allowed to engage in patterns of overt discrimination that appear to defy federal and state antidiscrimination laws? The answer may vary depending on the geographic location of the private club and on the nature of the discrimination. By way of example, although there is no federal law banning sex discrimination by private clubs, some cities have adopted laws prohibiting such discrimination, especially by business-oriented private clubs, in recent years. And although private clubs in this category generally may discriminate with regard to *membership issues*, they generally are prohibited from unlawful discrimination with regard to *employment issues* and must comply with other nonmembership laws, such as the Americans with Disabilities Act.

A central issue with regard to antidiscrimination laws and private clubs, however, is whether any particular club is truly *private*. Historically, private clubs were exactly what that term implies: groups of individuals who voluntarily chose to associate with one another for a wide variety of political, social, economic, educational, religious, and cultural purposes or some combination of those purposes. Being able to voluntarily choose to associate with one another also meant that the group had the ability to exclude those individuals with whom the club's members—or at least a majority of the members—did not wish to associate as members of the same club. Thus, private clubs were allowed to determine the criteria for those who could—or could not—become a member, and the law and the courts did not interfere with such matters, which were considered privileged under the freedom-of-association provisions of the U.S. Constitution.

The U.S. Constitution, Personal Association, and Private Accommodation

The U.S. Constitution does not contain the words "freedom of association." Rather, the courts have held that freedom of association—the right to associate with persons with whom one chooses to associate and the right to *not* associate with those persons with whom one does not desire to associate—is implicit in the First Amendment's guarantee of the freedoms of religion, speech, and assembly. This guarantee applies to groups—and their membership practices—as well as to individuals. According to the U.S. Supreme Court, there is "no clearer example of an intrusion into the internal structure or affairs of an association than a regulation that forces the group to accept members it does not desire" (*Roberts v. United States Jaycees* 1984:623). The principle of not forcing a group to "accept members it does not desire" clearly applies to private clubs because of their "members-only" nature and the highly selective manner in which new members are chosen in some of those clubs. As a result, discrimination that may be unlawful in some types of organizations may be lawful in the membership practices of private clubs. Congress has exempted these clubs from the public accommodations provisions of the federal civil rights laws, provided that certain requirements are met by the clubs. One of those requirements is that the club be one of "intimate association."

Expressive versus Intimate Association.   What is meant by associational rights or freedoms in regard to private clubs? Members of private clubs may have the protected freedom of *expressive association*, or they may have the protected freedom of *intimate association*. Expressive association refers to people getting together for the purpose of engaging in activities, such as speech, assembly, and the exercise of religion, that are protected by the First Amendment. Freedom of expressive association typically is not an issue in private clubs because members typically join these organizations for recreational, sporting, or social opportunities rather than for the purpose of engaging in free speech or expressing their religious beliefs (Jolly-Ryan 2006).

The key issue for private clubs in regard to protected associational rights is the freedom of intimate association. Citizens of the United States have the constitutional right to enter into and maintain certain intimate human relationships without undue intrusion by the government. However, the Constitution does not protect all interpersonal relationships: they must qualify as "intimate associations." This term usually refers to relationships involving family life, such as marriage and child-rearing arrangements; however, the Supreme Court has ruled that some relationships outside the family may also qualify as intimate associations:

> [C]ertain kinds of personal bonds have played a critical role in the culture and traditions of the nation by cultivating and transmitting shared ideas and beliefs; they thereby foster diversity and act as critical buffers between the individual and the power of the State . . . [T]he constitutional shelter afforded such relationships reflects the realization that individuals draw much of their emotional enrichment from close ties with others (*Roberts v. United States Jaycees* 1984:618–19).

What club members do inside their own clubhouse may be protected by the Constitution, much like what the members of a family do within their own home is protected. The Court assumed that interactions among club members provide them with emotional enrichment that is possible only by maintaining close ties with other people, based on a set of shared ideas and beliefs, and without the external interference by the state.

To determine if a private club qualifies as an intimate association, courts consider a number of characteristics, including the organization's size, purpose, policies, selectivity, congeniality, and other relevant characteristics (see *Roberts v. United States Jaycees* 1984). In regard to size, for example, organizations with vast numbers of members are less likely to qualify as protected private clubs because their members have fewer opportunities to establish the intimate relationships that come from close interaction with a relatively smaller number of homogeneous individuals. Consequently, nationwide or worldwide clubs such as the Jaycees or the Lions may not be entitled to constitutional protection from antidiscrimination laws because of their size, diffusion of membership, and relative impersonality.

In addition to size, a club's purpose, policies, and selectivity in membership are also factors in determining whether a club has protected associational rights. To be considered a private club with protected associational rights, a club must have written bylaws, stated admissions and expulsion procedures, and a formal membership roster. The club must hold formal meetings because it cannot be claimed that a private association exists if the members do not meet together on a regular basis.

If a club meets all these criteria, it may be exempt from the public accommodations provisions of Title II of the Civil Rights Act of 1964, which provisions prohibit discrimination or segregation in "places of public accommodation." According Title II, "All persons shall be entitled to the full and equal enjoyment of the goods, services, facilities, privileges, advantages, and accommodations of any place of public accommodation . . . without discrimination or segregation on the grounds of race, color, religion, or national origin" (42 U.S. Code § 2000a[a]). It is important to note that Title II expressly exempts a "private club or other establishment not in fact open to the public" from its antidiscrimination requirements (42 U.S. Code § 2000a[e]).

Public versus Private Accommodations.   Although Title II and other civil rights laws appear to be clear on the matter of public versus private accommodations, distinguishing between places of public accommodation and private accommodation may be difficult under some circumstances. If a city sells its public golf course to a racially segregated private club, does the golf course cease to be a "public" place and instead become a facility owned by a private club to which the public accommodation laws do not apply? If a public restaurant, faced with a challenge to its asserted right "to refuse service to anyone," chooses to do so, may it become a whites-only "private club" of which any white person may become a member? Questions such as these demonstrate the difficulties that legislatures and courts have continued to face in determining what constitutes a place of public accommodation and what should be considered a place of private accommodation that is allowed to operate under a different set of rules and guidelines regarding membership practices.

To gain more insight on this issue, let's briefly examine the evolution of the notion of public versus private accommodations during the past sixty years in the United States. Prior to the 1950s, private clubs were treated in largely the same manner as business establishments. It was considered permissible for a proprietor of a business that was generally open to the public at large to post a sign that stated, "We reserve the right to refuse service to anyone" and to refuse such service on any basis that the proprietor might choose to enforce, such as that the would-be customer was too loud and boorish or smelled bad or even that he or she appeared to be of a race, religion, or national origin that the proprietor did not wish to serve. By the 1950s, however, some states began to impose limitations on the right of a proprietor to deny access to "public accommodations," particularly if the denial was based on factors such as an individual's race or ethnicity. In the mid-1950s, the federal government also began to protect the rights of historically disadvantaged groups (such as African Americans) in the area of public accommodations.

Although these "civil rights laws" were strenuously challenged in court, they generally were upheld: the right of an individual to choose with whom to associate—or not associate—did not include the right to deny any person access to *public accommodations* on the basis of race, religion, or national origin (or, subsequently, other characteristics, such as gender, sexual orientation, or disability). However, these laws did not apply to private clubs, which were private associations rather than public accommodations. On the national level, that distinction largely remains in effect today with regard to the membership practices of private clubs.

In recent years, the issue of discrimination in private clubs most often has been raised as a result of a challenge to one club's exclusionary membership practices under state civil rights acts or city ordinances prohibiting discrimination in public accommodations. Those local clubs most likely to be the target of a successful antidiscrimination action on the basis that their facilities are "public accommodations" are those clubs that own and operate a facility such as a country club or golf club, a boating or yacht club, a sports or athletic club, or a dining club where the club's facilities are rented out or used by nonmembers who are not the guest of a member who is present at the time the nonmember is physically on the club's premises.

Attempts to Keep Private Clubs Private

Because of the changing nature of antidiscrimination laws, many private clubs and the associations that represent such organizations have carefully sought to meet all the legal guidelines that keep a private club beyond the reach of state and federal antidiscrimination laws. Professional associations of elite club administrators provide regular updates on legislation and lawsuits that might affect elite clubs, and they offer advice regarding what clubs must do to comply with the latest regulations. For example, private clubs that do not want interference from the courts regarding their membership policies are advised by professional club managers to follow guidelines such as these (based on Ewing 2004):

- Place a cap on the total number of active and associate members allowed in the club's membership and abide by those limits.
- Demonstrate genuine selectivity in the admission of any new member rather than giving the appearance of denying membership to any person on the basis of race, ethnicity, religion, gender, sexual orientation, disability status, or other personal attributes.
- Strictly control operations by following all the club's established rules, including membership requirements and procedures.
- Have a written mission statement, goal, or purpose that appears to be worthy and nondiscriminatory.
- Operate strictly on a nonprofit basis: do not allow club facilities to be rented out to nonmembers for any purpose.
- Require that club facilities be used only by current members in good standing; nonmembers should be allowed access to the club only when they are bona fide guests of a member.

Although numerous examples could be provided to demonstrate how this kind of advice is used by elite clubs, one further illustration will suffice to make the larger point about the protective nature of elite clubs and their professional associations. Consider the following advice that was provided to clubs regarding a suggestion that some clubs might reduce to *one* the total number of sponsors required to put up a new member so that the clubs could streamline and speed up their membership process. In regard to this suggestion, the publication *Private Club Advisor* quickly suggested that such a change was not advisable for several reasons:

> We believe reducing the number of sponsors to one to be potentially antithetical to the selectivity requirement for distinctly private clubs. That is, if one of the major considerations regarding a membership candidate is the

candidate's perceived likely compatibility with the existing membership and perceived congeniality, are the club's interests well and best served by taking the recommendation of but one member?

. . . We have always believed that requiring two or more sponsors shows the club is genuinely interested in being selective. Having only one sponsor ostensibly "cheapens" the process and may tend to create the appearance that the club isn't particularly fussy about who joins. Having somewhat a gauntlet to run . . . creates an impression that gaining membership is something of an achievement and recognition of personal worth, not merely an economic acid test. We advise clubs wishing to protect their private status to have a well-defined admissions procedure in place, to follow the procedure assiduously, and to include in the procedure certain evaluation criteria relevant to the club's mission and purpose. If the process is too streamlined, to accommodate impatient candidates, it risks not being deemed a genuinely selective process. (Somers 2003)

As a result of professional advice such as this from private club experts, club managers, directors, and ordinary members make every effort to avoid any legal challenge to their membership policies.

Are individuals ever successful in challenging the discriminatory membership practices of elite U.S. clubs? We have previously touched on this issue in chapter 3; however, two cases that were decided in favor of women plaintiffs are instructive at this point. Although a number of discrimination suits in federal and state courts have been decided in favor of private clubs, two cases— *Warfield v. The Peninsula Golf and Country Club* and *Borne, et al. v. Haverhill Golf and Country Club, Inc.*—were decided in favor of female plaintiffs who contended that they had been discriminated against by private clubs.

In *Warfield*, the California Supreme Court ruled that a private golf club cannot discriminate against its women members. Mary Ann Warfield, the former spouse of a club member, challenged the legality of a San Mateo private club's policy that only men could own a family membership in the club. Warfield—a women's golf champion at the club and a real estate agent who used the club's facilities to generate clients for her business—was awarded the club membership as part of her divorce settlement. However, the Peninsula Golf and Country Club refused to recognize her membership after the divorce, claiming that only men could hold voting, proprietary memberships. Based on Warfield's claim that the club denied her the proprietary membership based on what was, at that time, the club's official policy, the California Supreme Court found that, at the time that the alleged discrimination occurred, the club was a business establishment under California's public accommodation law because of these aspects of the club's operations:

- The club permitted unrestricted access by more than 700 people, including members, guests, and others to golf and tennis tournaments, weddings, bar mitzvahs, fashion shows, and special luncheons and dinners.
- Host members were permitted to receive reimbursement from employers for charges incurred for the entertainment of invited guests.
- Golf and tennis professionals offered instruction to the public with the use of the club's facilities and pro shops.
- Local high school golf teams used the golf course without charge, during limited off-peak hours. (Hart 2007)

Warfield established the principle that clubs, whether private or not, that operate as businesses cannot discriminate against a class of people based solely on their gender, race, religion, national origin, or disability status.

Legal issues pertaining to gender-based discrimination in private clubs were also raised in *Borne v. Haverhill Golf and Country Club.* In this case, nine women who held limited club memberships alleged that they were routinely denied—because of their sex—prime tee times on the golf course, even at various times when male members were not playing on the course. The plaintiffs also noted that only one woman had been accepted by the club as a primary (as opposed to a limited) member in the previous five years. At Haverhill, primary members had the broadest range of access to the golf course and facilities, while persons designated as limited members were restricted to certain off-hour times when they could reserve the facilities. According to the lawsuit, when the women sought to change their membership status from limited to primary so that they could gain full access to the club's facilities, the club's rules for making such a change fluctuated widely, and no explanation was given to the women about why they could not become primary members. At trial, the jury found that the club was a place of public accommodation because its facilities were available for hire by the general public for social functions. As a result, the jury awarded the nine plaintiffs $1.9 million in damages plus an additional sum for attorneys' fees. The award for damages included amounts for the breach of an implied covenant of good faith and fair dealing, compensatory damages based on emotional distress, and punitive damages to deter the club from pursuing a course of action in the future similar to that which had damaged the female plaintiffs in this case. According to one legal analyst, there was evidence in the Haverhill case that warranted a finding that "the Club had been cavalier and callously indifferent about failing to treat women golfers as equal. The conduct persisted in the face of warning shots in the form of letters to the board of governors about what it was that the plaintiffs were aggrieved" (*Commonwealth of Massachusetts and Borne v. Haverhill Golf and Country Club*).

Court cases such as those involving the Haverhill and Peninsula clubs provide a small window through which we can see the kinds of activities that go on within some of our nation's most exclusive clubs. However, it remains difficult for researchers to gain "insider" information about the exclusionary practices of most clubs because they strictly maintain their privacy policies and make every effort to remain beyond the scope of inquiries by scholars, journalists, and other outsiders.

LIMITED INFORMATION AND ACTION WITHIN U.S. CLUBS

It is difficult to analyze discriminatory practices or efforts to bring about change in elite clubs because many private clubs are protected by law from having to divulge their membership rosters or to provide any details about their membership policies. As a result, accounts of the activities of exclusive clubs typically focus on national controversies such as the those involving the Augusta (Georgia) National Golf Club and the annual Professional Golfers' Association (PGA) Tournament held there. As we shall see, the Augusta National dispute is a prime example of how some members of Old Guard organizations zealously protect their club's privacy and their own privilege. This controversy also shows why it is difficult to engage in meaningful discussions about needed changes in membership policies with leaders of some prestigious clubs.

The Augusta National Country Club and the Issue of Privacy

The privacy rights of elite club members are clearly at issue when sports journalists seek to learn more about the membership practices of clubs such as the Augusta National Golf Club. This club is the owner and host of the annual Masters tournament—one of four major PGA men's championships and sponsored by major corporations such as General Motors, IBM, Citigroup, and Coca-Cola (Saporito 2002). During one controversy over the exclusion of women from membership at the all-male Augusta National, some sports journalists attempted to gain information about the club's membership, particularly its racial and gender composition, but they found out how resistant the leaders of prestigious clubs may be when it comes to providing information about their membership. Golf journalist Alan Shipnuck (2004:2) recalled a press conference, held on the eve of the 1999 Master's tournament, at which *USA Today* columnist Christine Brennan asked Augusta National chairman William Woodward (Hootie) Johnson about the club's membership:

Earlier in the week Brennan had read a clip about Augusta National's aversion to publicly discussing its membership; without identifying herself, Brennan said to Johnson, "We were talking yesterday"—reporters, that is—"trying to get the numbers straight. If you wouldn't mind telling us how many African Americans there are at Augusta National and how many women members? And if there are no women members, why aren't there?"

"Well, that's a club matter, ma'am, and all club matters are private," Johnson replied.

"Are there women members?" [asked Brennan].

"That's a club matter, ma'am, and all club matters are private" [Johnson replied].

Given that abrupt response, male reporters then shifted the interview with Johnson to questions about recent renovations that had been made to the club's golf course, and the press conference was over shortly thereafter (Shipnuck 2004).

But the storm was far from over. After Johnson's response to her questions, Brennan wrote the following in *USA Today*: "I made a right turn off the main drag in Augusta the other day and ended up in 1975. Or perhaps it was 1940. It was hard to tell" (quoted in Shipnuck 2004:3). Martha Burk, chair of the National Council of Women's Organizations (NCWO), read Brennan's column and sent a letter to Johnson expressing NCWO's concern about the club's exclusionary practices. According to Burk, since Augusta National was the host of the Masters, the most prestigious golf tournament in the country, the club was a "*symbol of business* as companies court investors and executives throughout that week, a *symbol of culture* [because] members include heads of state, charitable foundations, universities, and corporate life, and a *metaphor for why women are not seen as equals in these areas*" (Burk 2005, emphasis in original). However, when Johnson received the letter, he released a statement to the press indicating that neither he nor the club would engage in discussions with the NCWO or be threatened by such demands for "radical change."

In response, Burk proposed a boycott of corporate sponsors for the Master's tournament if the PGA did not relocate the tournament or if Augusta National did not change its exclusionary membership policies. Although a few major corporate sponsors did choose to not underwrite the PGA event for a year or two thereafter, they eventually returned or were replaced by other major sponsors. Burk (2005) criticized both the PGA and the tour's corporate sponsors for viewing gender-based exclusion as "acceptable discrimination" while considering race-based exclusion to be "unacceptable discrimination." Tiger Woods, a prominent African American golfer and a member of

Augusta National, stirred up his own controversy among women golfers and NCWO members by informing sports journalists that he believed the members of Augusta National were entitled to "set up their own rules the way they want them" (Greene 2002:SP9). Ultimately, the press coverage and boycotting of Augusta National and its corporate sponsors brought about neither a change in the location of this prestigious tournament nor any change in the club's membership policies. The so-called battle over Augusta National reveals how some elite clubs may be unwilling to make voluntary changes unless external intervention comes from state or federal courts or legislative bodies. This controversy also highlights how difficult it is to gain accurate information about the practices of private clubs.

Lack of Information: USA Today *Media Survey*

Lack of public information about the membership rosters and allegedly discriminatory practices of elite clubs is not limited to high-profile clubs like the Augusta National Golf Club: we know little about membership in private clubs throughout the United States. A 2003 *USA Today* survey of 129 private, semiprivate, public, and resort courses hosting golf tournaments, for example, found that most clubs would share very little, if any, information about their membership (Lieber 2003). Although 86 percent of the private clubs surveyed provided information regarding their total number of members, only 26 percent were willing to show a gender breakdown, and only 5 percent divulged the racial composition of their club. In response to a question about whether their club had a written nondiscrimination policy, less than half of the private, member-owned clubs stated that they had such a policy: about 20 percent of the clubs refused to answer the question (Lieber 2003). Similar surveys today would probably produce similar results, but none has been undertaken.

Club officials who refuse to answer questions regarding the racial and gender composition of their clubs argue that this information is confidential and that they are protected by First Amendment freedom of association rights. As previously discussed, constitutional protection of privacy interests is afforded to clubs that are have purely social, nonbusiness member usage. Or to put it in the down-to-earth language of the founder of one all-white men's golf club in Birmingham, Alabama, "This is our home, and we pick and choose who we want. We have the right to associate or not associate with whomever we choose" (Lieber 2003).

Limited Changes in Clubs

Because of the lack of available information, many people believe that elite clubs have been required to change their membership practices to comply with existing discrimination laws. However, change—to the extent that it has taken place—has left in its wake many unresolved issues regarding gender, racial/ethnic, religious, and class-based forms of discrimination. Although more affluent white women, people of color, and/or members of various racial, ethnic, and religious minorities have been invited to join certain prestigious city clubs, country clubs, or golf clubs, some of the most exclusive, Old Guard clubs remain bastions of affluent white men well into the twenty-first century.

When changes take place in a club's membership composition, these modifications typically occur as a result of strong external pressure brought on the group to change, not from the heartfelt desires of the club members themselves. As scholars have pointed out, the impetus for greater diversity in business, education, and other areas of social life did not come from *within* the U.S. power elite: change was the result of *external pressures*, and many elites have only reluctantly accepted greater diversity because they are required to do so (see Zweigenhaft and Domhoff 1998). According to a study by psychologist Richard L. Zweigenhaft and sociologist G. William Domhoff (1998), even when previously excluded categories of people are granted greater access to elite circles, profound "ironies of diversity" continue to exist. Among these ironies are the continuing significance that class, education, and light skin tone play in distinguishing between and among people. Zweigenhaft and Domhoff argue that a person's class origin is the most important factor in whether that individual will become fully integrated into the inner circle of the power elite or whether he or she will be marginalized. According to these scholars, the continuing exclusion of persons with darker skin, regardless of their class background or educational achievements, is one of the persistent ironies of diversity. Moreover, "outsiders" who gain admission to the power elite have an added burden in that they must continually "demonstrate their loyalty to those who dominate American institutions—straight white Christian males" (Zweigenhaft and Domhoff 1998:177). These observations appear to be true for those who gain access to our nation's elite private clubs as well.

Although elite clubs in some cities have declining memberships, their current members remain resistant to bringing in new members who do not fit the traditional mold of how a member of that club should look, think, or act. As one respondent stated, "Is anybody prejudiced in the membership selection process? Sure. Would they admit that they voted against someone because he was black or Jewish or [gay]? Probably not. They would just quietly vote against the guy."

The most prestigious clubs are still turning away prospective members at every turn and maintaining lengthy waiting lists even of "desirable" potential members. As a result, some very wealthy and/or newly rich individuals have decided not to apply for membership in "stodgy" Old Guard clubs and instead are starting their own clubs or joining existing ones that offer them the finest amenities and give members the opportunity to believe that they are members of "the best" private club in the nation.

OPULENT CLUBS FOR THE ULTRARICH

"Elegant. Imposing. Legendary." Although these terms are used to describe The Mar-a-Lago Club of Palm Beach, Florida, many clubs for the new rich and the ultrarich use similar adjectives to attract new members willing to pay initiation fees in the range of $150,000 to $300,000. The Mar-a-Lago Club was founded by billionaire real estate developer Donald J. Trump at the historic Marjorie Merriweather Post estate, the scene in past years of many high-society Palm Beach social events. Consider this description of the club's newly restored opulence:

> The Mar-a-Lago Club sits royally amid 20 valuable acres of manicured lawns, vibrant gardens and sweeping sea-to-lake vistas. A National Historic Landmark, the former Marjorie Merriweather Post estate maintains its position as a charter member on the VIP list of places and people that established Palm Beach as a winter haven for the elite many decades ago. With the creative genius of Donald J. Trump and a lot of tender, loving care, the 126 rooms have been fully renovated and restored to their original splendor. (Maralagoclub.com 2007)

By associating the "elite" nature of Mar-a-Lago in the past with the present state-of-the-art amenities—including but not limited to a "magnificent swimming pool, an award winning beauty salon, a world class spa, one grass and five red clay championship tennis courts, and a remarkable croquet court . . . two retail outlets: a tennis pro shop overlooking Lake Worth and a boutique adjacent to the Trump Spa"—the club seeks to attract self-made multimillionaires and billionaires who may not be invited to join Old Guard Palm Beach clubs such as the Everglades and the Bath & Tennis Club. To attract individuals who participate in the nouveau riche charity circuit and other free spenders from among the very wealthy, Trump modernized Mar-a-Lago's Gold & White Ballroom and built an all-new 20,000-square-foot Donald J. Trump Grand Ballroom, which was modeled after France's Versailles Palace and has "confectionary-white pillars and frosted molding" that give it the overall appearance of "a giant wedding cake" (Frank 2007:96).

According to the journalist Robert Frank (2007), the New Rich are attracted to clubs such as Mar-a-Lago because they are able to engage in a conspicuous display of wealth rather than being judged for membership purposes on their breeding and lineage. As Frank states, Palm Beach and numerous other cities have become the "land of dueling country clubs." When the new rich are shunned by members of Old Guard clubs, the ultrarich (the so-called Richistanis) create their own, more opulent clubs. Similarly, *New York Times* journalist James Traub (2007:21) stated that the Old Rich live with a "unique combination of luxury and dowdy," whereas the new superrich, who rise above the ranks of the merely well-to-do, are not worried about "old WASP clubs" that they are not invited to join: they can buy something much better. Traub (2007:22) also suggests that the New Rich may take perverse pleasure in making members of the Old Guard feel envious of their great wealth, even as the Old Rich "clump in a corner and talk about how over the top it all is." Trump's Mar-a-Lago Club appears to be a good example of some individuals' willingness to participate in this "new culture of display" (Traub 2007):

> The all-powerful country clubs, which divided the island by race and religion, are becoming less and less relevant. The rules may be the same—the Palm Beach Bath & Tennis Club and the Everglades Club still have few if any Jewish members, and the Palm Beach Country Club remains almost exclusively Jewish—yet the New Money prefers Mar-a-Lago, which takes anyone willing to pay the $150,000 membership fee, regardless of religion or last names. (Frank 2007:111)

Across the nation, clubs similar to Mar-a-Lago benefit from the snobbery of members of Old Guard clubs because those members of the New Rich who desire to hold membership in a "prestigious club" will pay whatever initiation fees are asked of them by the newer luxury clubs if they know that they will be excluded from the Old Guard/Old Money clubs. In the words of Donald Trump, "The fact that the other clubs are so restrictive has been great for me. It's one of the main reasons we're so successful" (quoted in Frank 2007:112). Throughout the United States, other clubs for self-made millionaires and billionaires have experienced similar popularity, and some of the newer clubs in Texas are no exception.

EVERYTHING IS BIGGER AND BETTER IN TEXAS: NEW-WEALTH CLUBS

Although Texas is typically known as a state with excesses, some clubs for the super rich in other states (including Trump's Mar-a-Lago and Tim Blixseth's Yellowstone Club in Big Sky, Montana) outdo some of the newer Texas country and golf clubs in their opulence and top-of-the-line facilities. Nonetheless, in this section, I describe member-owned clubs in Texas for the newer rich and the Texas-originated ClubCorp concept of holding membership in one club yet having access to numerous other clubs that are under the same club management structure.

Private, First Class: Only the Best Will Do!

"Who designed your golf course?" is the first question that some recently arrived wealthy individuals typically ask when they are discussing the possibility of joining one Texas's most expensive golf clubs, according to one respondent in my study. Apparently, there are only a few correct answers to this question from the perspective of rich club aspirants: Tom Fazio, Nelson Plummer, Pete Dye, and perhaps one or two other golf course architects. Among avid golfers, nothing is more important than how the club's course is designed and laid out. Consider, for example, this description of the course at Dallas National Golf Club, which has an initiation fee of more than $150,000 (but is currently sold out) and claims top golfers and celebrities such as Lee Trevino, Roger Staubach, entrepreneur Scott Ginsburg, financier Richard Rainwater, and former Pepsi chairman Roger Enrico as members:

> The topography of this enchanted landscape conjures thoughts of great golf courses in other parts of the country: Pristine fairways cutting through limestone canyons. Streams meandering through thickets of cedars, oaks and elms. Rolling hills stretching across 170-foot plateaus, with rich wood bridges spanning deep ravines, the dramatic changes in elevation provide stunning views. Truly a golf purists' Mecca. This may be Tom Fazio's finest project . . . all just ten miles from downtown Dallas. (Dallas National Golf Club 2007)

Golf course architect Tom Fazio apparently believes that the Dallas National course is one of his finest accomplishments, as he has stated on numerous occasions: "If Dallas National were the only course I ever designed, I feel I would have had a great career" (Dallas National Golf Club 2007).

Although Dallas National members have an avid interest in playing golf on the finest courses around the world, clubs such as this have a unique appeal to the newly wealthy because these facilities offer excellent amenities without the accompanying "snobbery and pretension" that are associated with Old Guard clubs such as the Dallas Country Club (DCC) or Brook Hollow Golf Club. According to Rob, an avid golfer who is member of multiple city, country, and golf clubs in the Dallas area,

> At first you could buy your way into Dallas National, and some retired en-
> trepreneurs who are golfing enthusiasts did just that to gain access to that
> incredible course, but it lacks a true connection to Dallas "high society,"
> and it doesn't have the kind of club house where you could throw your
> daughter's debutante party or wedding reception. Still, you can't join Dal-
> las National now because it's sold out and has a waiting list of golfers will-
> ing to pay over $100,000 to play Fazio's course. You can't join DCC, Brook
> Hollow, or Preston Trail either: it takes getting on a lengthy waiting list,
> but you'll still never get there, even if you're young when you get started,
> unless you know the "right people."

As this respondent's comments indicate, the most exclusive clubs, including
DCC, Brook Hollow, and Preston Trail in Dallas, maintain their panache and
can include (or exclude) whomever they choose. In the case of Preston Trail
Golf Club, for example, women are still excluded from membership, according to the same respondent:

> The focus [of women golfers' exclusion from elite clubs] has been on places
> like Augusta National because of the Master's tournament, but all of that
> happens much closer to home as well. Preston Trail has one of the top golf
> courses and a membership roster that reads like a "Who's Who" in the
> Dallas/Fort Worth area, but membership is strictly limited to men. DCC
> has some women members, particularly from Old Rich Highland Park
> families, but they still have a daily men's-only lunch even though women
> finally became voting members of the club in the 1990s.

Preston Trail Golf Club is an example of a well-to-do private club that was
founded several decades ago as a suburban golf or country club but that has
grown in stature to now be considered among the top clubs of the Old Guard.
This shift has occurred as numerous wealthy and influential residents of large
metropolitan areas such as the Dallas/Fort Worth metroplex have chosen to
move away from the old affluent enclaves such as Highland Park and University Park and instead reside in newer but equally wealthy and exclusive
suburban neighborhoods near newer but wealthy and exclusive country clubs.

When respondents in this study compared the Old Guard clubs with the
newer superrich clubs such as Dallas National, these individuals often pointed
out that the Old Guard clubs focus on questions such as "Who are you?"
"Who is your family?" and "Who do you know in the club?" By contrast, clubs
like Dallas National that cater primarily to New Money families are more
likely to focus on a person's self-made fortune and spending habits ("What is
your net worth?" and "How do you spend your money?") and on the quality
of their facilities ("Our golf course is better than your golf course."). Compe-
tition over which club has the "best" golf course is an example. Respondents

who are members of Dallas National emphasize that their course "plays tough" and measures 7,326 yards, which is appropriate for championship matches as well as ensuring "playability for members" (see also Dallas National Golf Club 2007). By contrast, DCC, which usually wins the most prestigious Old Guard club designation, loses out when it comes to some features of its golf club, which originally was built in 1896: "No longer do the major tournaments come to Dallas Country Club, partly because the members want it that way, and partly because the standard course today is 6,800 [yards], making the Club's championship tees at 6,280 a bit short" (see Galloway 1996:323). Some DCC leaders have suggested that the club should keep its clubhouse in the central, Highland Park location of Dallas but find "another outlet for our golfers, preferably in a more rustic setting in keeping with a country club environment" (Galloway 1996:329).

New Money club members who are avid golfers express interest in playing on the best golf courses and enjoy describing their favorite golf holes, and these individuals often note specific reasons for why they believe that their club's course is better than the ones found at Old Guard clubs. For example, one respondent explained how many yards should be in an eighteen-hole course, with par 70-72, for a player to really show his skill in using all his clubs and to demonstrate his shot-making abilities. When Dick Brooks, chief executive officer of a $5.5 billion Dallas utility holding company, described the seventh hole at Preston Trail Golf Club as his favorite hole, he stated, "It's the par-four seventh. The hole measures 422 yards from the back tees, and it's just such a challenge to play. You have to hit almost a perfect drive to get yourself in position to have a good shot to the green. And that green can be very tough to hit into" (quoted in Steinbreder 2000:1). For Brooks, the seventh hole is his favorite not simply because of its scenic location or the fact that something significant happened to him when he was playing that hole but rather because "I just like the design of the hole, and the challenge it presents. It really takes two good shots to be on in two. It's one of those holes where a good drive is absolutely essential to have a chance at the pin" (quoted in Steinbreder 2000:1). Devotion to the game of golf, such as Brooks expressed, is a central reason why many New Rich, as well as Old Guard, club members feel so strongly about their clubs and the traditions they represent, even if those traditions are just now being established.

ClubCorp, Inc.: From Up-and-Coming to Already Arrived?

Ads for ClubCorp, Inc., the world's largest owner and operator of golf courses, private clubs and resorts, state: "We're Not Just Your Father's Club. We're Your Son's and Daughter's Club Too." By emphasizing the age and family aspects of clubs that are affiliated with ClubCorp, Inc., these advertisements also suggest that membership privileges will be extended not only to upper-middle-class families but also to people of all ages and to females as well as male members. This type of open approach to membership sets apart the newer elite clubs from the Old Guard clubs, just as Robert H. Dedman Sr., ClubCorp's founder, intended. In 1957, Dedman, a Dallas insurance salesman, initiated plans for Brookhaven Country Club in Dallas (although the club did not officially open until two years later) and started Country Club, Inc. (later known as ClubCorp, Inc.), a corporation to own and/or manage golf courses, country clubs, and resorts worldwide. Brookhaven was marketed as an "affordable family club," and the developers wanted to appeal to individuals who were "on their way up" financially and socially rather than to people who already "had it made" because of Old Money or privileged family connections. Located in the Dallas suburb of Farmers Branch, Texas, Brookhaven's name was similar to that of the highly prestigious Brook Hollow Golf Club, causing some initial confusion, but it also provided prestige to Brookhaven during its early years because people mistook it for the more exclusive club. According to Dedman, traditional country clubs offered no opportunities for the young "up-and-coming family man" because they were for the Old Money set and "dominated by white male clientele" (Brookhaven Country Club 2007). Throughout Brookhaven's fifty-year history, the club has remained within the price range of some upper-middle-class families, with initiation fees of about $2,500 and lower monthly dues than Old Guard clubs such as DCC or the ultrarich clubs such as Dallas National.

Prior to his death in 2002, Dedman had become a self-made billionaire with a net worth of $1.2 billion. Some clubs in Club Corp's portfolio still focus on middle-class families, but many are now created for affluent individuals who would like a high profile in their community. Barton Creek Country Club in Austin is a case in point because its facilities appeal to avid golfers, well-known entertainers, and local celebrities such as Darrell Royal (the legendary Texas Longhorn football coach) and a host of New Rich entrepreneurs and financiers who may not have the "right connections" to join some of the city's top Old Guard clubs. The original idea for creation of the Barton Creek Country Club (and development of the high-end residential complex adjacent to it) came from the Ben Barnes–John Connally partnership, comprised of two individuals with vast state and national business and political ties. After the bankruptcy of the Barnes–Connally partnership in 1988, Jim Bob Moffett (chief executive officer of Freeport-McMoRan) bought the property to develop the club and a residential community and sold the country club to Robert H. Dedman and ClubCorp USA, Inc.

From this checkered past, Barton Creek rose, under the direction of ClubCorp, to be one of the top clubs for newly wealthy Austin-area residents who now enjoy two clubhouses and four outstanding golf courses—Fazio

Foothills, Fazio Canyons, [Arnold] Palmer Lakeside, and [Ben] Crenshaw Cliffside—designed by master golf architects or top players. The club also includes lighted tennis courts, multiple dining facilities that will "please even the most discriminating palate," a fitness center with an indoor jogging track, a complete health club with two aerobic studios, four swimming pools, a kids club, youth camps, access to the Austin Society, an organization that provides access to a number of other clubs within the Austin–San Antonio area, and associate club travel benefits where a member can visit any of the more than 200 other ClubCorp associate clubs and affiliates worldwide (Barton Creek Country Club 2007). As Barton Creek Country Club shows, corporations such as ClubCorp have found a unique opportunity, through the ownership of private clubs that appeal to individuals with large sums of money but few Old Guard social ties, to provide them with a social setting and amenities that give them the appearance of being in their community's social elite.

Clubs like Barton Creek that uniquely appeal to the newer rich and ultrarich are found in the suburbs of large urban areas. The clubs have excellent clubhouses for major social events and state-of-the-art facilities, including name-brand golf courses, tennis courts, swimming pools, and fitness centers. The clubs appear to be difficult to join. Outsiders are informed that the club has the same rigorous membership process as any other elite club (except that the club may offer nonmembers a chance to meet current members who can put them up for membership if they do not know any of them).

In Old Guard and New Rich clubs in Texas and throughout the nation, the battle continues between Old Money and the newly wealthy. Perhaps journalist Robert Frank (2007:112) best summed up this battle between Old Money and New Money when he wrote about the new rich in Palm Beach, "And for all the talk about rejecting the Old Guard, the new arrivals seem equally interested in re-creating their world." In this regard, private clubs in Texas and elsewhere are no different: exclusive clubs have had a unique appeal to people whether they were in nineteenth-century London or in twenty-first century Dallas or Austin. Those who are in the inner circle of social elites in the most exclusive clubs seek to remain there and to keep out anyone who might diminish the prestige of their group, while the "up-and-coming" (to whom Dedman wanted his clubs to appeal) are no longer "middle-class family men" but now are wealthy individuals who seek to convert their riches into a sense of personal affirmation by building strong ties with the "right people." For this reason, neither Congress, the courts, nor state legislatures will easily change the strong linkages that exist between the world of private clubs and exclusion that is based on class, race, gender, religion, or other social attributes that are deemed to be unworthy by those on the top rungs of current social, business, and political hierarchies.

· 7 ·

Beyond the Walls: The Wider Influence of Elite Clubs

$\mathcal{A}$s we look at the influence of elite clubs on the larger society and think about the future of these clubs in American life, consider the following statement (which I have summarized) from an older white male member's recollection of an earlier era at the Headliners Club of Austin:

> The 1970s brought not only fast growth to Austin, but also cultural changes that affected our state and nation. Men-only clubs were no longer the norm, as they were in the 1950s. The club's efforts to limit women's presence in the club created ill will among members' wives. The most cherished club tradition, the annual stag luncheon, slipped into the past tense along with the men-only membership requirement. The luncheon was a must-do event for all of the government, business and professional leaders in Austin in the 1960s. When [the] doors opened, hundreds of men poured through the doors, literally running to snag a good seat. The stag luncheon was the highlight of a 30-hour whirlwind of glamorous social events called the Awards Weekend that attracted not only Austin's social, political, professional and business leaders but also the leaders of Texas' major daily newspapers.
>
> After the final stag luncheon in 1977, the Awards Weekend never recovered. Various club presidents in future years tried to develop a stag luncheon-type event [but] they were frustrated by knowing they could not replicate the larger-than-life reputation of earlier decades. (Stromberg 2005:15–20)

Histories of exclusive clubs such as the Headliners are full of statements such as this describing how growth and change in urban and suburban areas brought about corresponding changes in many exclusive clubs. The changes at the Headliners Club are representative of similar changes that have occurred

157

at some other private clubs: Men-only rules have vanished, and traditional "stag" events, such as an annual luncheon featuring ribald political and social humor, have been banned. However, these changes have not occurred at all clubs. For each elite club that has made significant changes in its policies and daily practices, many other clubs remain virtually unchanged.

In this chapter, I examine the issue of why the exclusionary practices of elite clubs should matter to us when we are faced with many other pressing social problems. I discuss what is *gained* or *lost* by individuals and the larger community as a result of the presence of elite clubs. Then I describe the part that elite clubs play in perpetuating economic and social inequality and thereby exacerbating larger patterns of discrimination and inequality in society.

A REVIEW OF CLUB MEMBERS' BENEFITS

In *Members Only*, I have shown how membership in exclusive clubs is important to people who occupy the top tiers of economic and social hierarchies in the United States. Although many club members have vast and ever-growing amounts of economic capital, they find that members-only clubs provide them with something more: a unique sense of personal accomplishment and high-prestigious group identity ("I am even more important because I belong to this club!"). Findings from sociologist Peter Martin Phillips's (1994) study of California's Bohemian Club suggest, for example, that wealthy and influential individuals join elite clubs for personal friendship and bonding opportunities: Club membership offers a unique setting in which like-minded individuals meet on an intimate basis. Some members establish strong ties with each other that span decades, and many members come to possess "deeply-held feelings of comradeship and sentimentality" toward each other (Phillips 1994:141). Similarly, sociologist G. William Domhoff (2005) has found that social cohesion among club members is an asset for individual members both inside and outside the club. According to Domhoff, social cohesion is particularly strong among elite club members for several reasons. First, physical proximity helps produce group solidarity: elite clubs offer members physical proximity in the clubhouse, on the golf and tennis courts, and in other club facilities (or at meetings of the members of wall-less clubs) that are open only to members. Second, club members who frequently interact with one another develop a sense of togetherness and a strong feeling of trust. Third, groups (such as exclusive clubs) that are seen as high in status typically have members who are more cohesive: elite clubs have stringent membership requirements, long waiting lists, and high dues—all of which serve to heighten the value of a club in the eyes of its members. Consequently, members perceive of themselves as "special" people because they have been invited to join, and this perception heightens their attractiveness to one another. Fourth, the best atmosphere for increasing group cohesiveness is one that is relaxed and cooperative: private clubs typically operate on the principle that members should not be rushed as they drink, eat, and play at the club and that members should always receive luxury-level service. If Domhoff's assessment of social cohesion in private clubs is valid, then this level of social bonding among club members is useful within the club and beyond its walls. Although not all social networks formed in elite clubs constitute *strong ties*, even *weak ties* may be useful to members who need access to specific kinds of information or resources that only a "friend of a friend" (or, in this case, a "friend of a fellow member") may be able to provide.

Although club members enhance their social capital through interactions and tie building with other members, they also have numerous opportunities to accumulate cultural capital through involvement in planned social activities. The member may use what he or she has learned from a club-sponsored seminar taught by an art or antiques expert, for example, to negotiate a better deal when purchasing works of art or antiques, developing a private collection, or serving on the board of a prestigious museum. Members who avail themselves of club activities and programs gain information about many subjects, ranging from world travel to the latest medical facilities and procedures in their own community. This information may be extremely useful in everything from planning trips to making important health-related decisions or deciding to invest in a biotech start-up company.

In addition to social and cultural capital, club members gain political capital that may be useful both inside and outside the club. Members who attend special events—such as talks by political insiders, soft-sell political events where they meet up-and-coming politicians, or hard-sell political events where major contributors, lobbyists, and legislators come together—have a chance to build useful connections that they can call on when they need a political favor at the local, state, or national level.

To maintain the prestige of elite clubs and to make it possible for members to continue to accumulate social, cultural, and political capital, the most prestigious clubs in the United States and the United Kingdom have maintained and perpetuated exclusionary membership practices that are viewed by some people as overt patterns of discrimination. Throughout *Members Only*, I have examined how exclusive clubs attempt to justify these membership practices. We looked at the early gentlemen's clubs of London to see the strong influence these organizations had on shaping not only the physical structures of the top U.S. clubs but also many of these clubs' beliefs, values, and actions. By examining laws and court cases pertaining to private clubs, we have seen that these legal actions typically address a narrow principle or a single issue regarding elite clubs. As a result, laws and court cases often deal with issues such as what constitutes a private club or to what extent a voluntary organization should be required to admit persons who differ in some way from the "typical" member of that organization. For the most part, the decisions of legislative bodies, juries, and judges have had a limited effect in bringing about social change in our nation's most prestigious private clubs.

In the twenty-first century, membership in the most prestigious Old Guard clubs is treasured and carefully guarded by multiple generations of individuals whom I have somewhat arbitrarily classified as Old Money or Old Family Name club members. Meanwhile, many other wealthy, New Money individuals are joining New Rich luxury clubs in record numbers. Members of these New Rich clubs pay extremely high initiation fees and monthly dues for the privilege of using lavish club facilities and interacting with people who have been referred to in the media as Richistanis (Frank 2007). To join some New Rich clubs, individuals must purchase a luxury residence that ranges in price from several million to more than a billion dollars. Because of the popularity of New Rich clubs, we have every reason to believe that class-based exclusion in private clubs will remain strong in the future. Unlike some of the Old Guard clubs whose members may believe that they are upholding tradition, members of New Rich clubs have no compelling interest in excluding individuals on the basis of gender, race/ethnicity, religion, or sexual orientation. To them, membership may be all about the money. Or, in the words of classical social theorist Georg Simmel (1978), it all boils down to the question, "How much?" For some individuals, money becomes an end in itself, and everything (including social acceptance) has its price. In other words, the real value of membership in such a club is not found in the intrinsic nature of club life but rather in extrinsic factors such as how a top-dollar club may provide a venue in which individuals display their wealth and engage in conspicuous consumption (see Veblen 1953).

THE WIDE SHADOW CAST BY ELITE CLUBS

Elite private clubs across the United States continue to be a significant social factor in our society. Each club casts a wide shadow over the economic, political, and social landscape of the community in which it is located. City clubs, country clubs, and wall-less elite clubs typically operate as private worlds unto themselves, conducting business and engaging in pleasurable activities largely outside public scrutiny and beyond of the scope of media attention. Many private clubs are exempt from some discrimination laws that prohibit other types of groups and organizations from engaging in practices that categorically exclude or marginalize people on the basis of race, ethnicity, gender, religion, and/or sexual orientation.

Elite clubs have a physical presence in the cities and suburbs, whether they are situated atop a prestigious high-rise building or located in the suburbs where the passerby sees primarily the club's lush, rolling golf course and an ornate fence or gate bearing the ever-present sign "Members Only." But along with their physical presence in the community, elite clubs also have a social presence in the form of their members, who typically are among the more affluent and powerful individuals in the community. As a result, the influence of elite club members on the larger society is pervasive. Even if they are well known apart from their club memberships, these affiliations tend to enhance their overall prestige within the community. What else would explain the fact that most wealthy and influential community leaders, on their deaths, have their club memberships and leadership roles prominently listed in their obituaries?

To play on an overused slogan of the city of Las Vegas, Nevada, "What happens in a private club *does not* stay in the club." Members use their club connections to develop business, political, and social networks to gain advantages outside of the club. The U.S. Supreme Court has recognized that private clubs offer special business skills and advantages that typically are unavailable to excluded groups, such as white women and all people of color. Members possess an insider's advantage because they socialize with each other at the club, and their prior knowledge and trust carries over into important decisions that they make in the community and beyond. Nonmembers who do not possess similar high-grade business, political, and social ties are at a distinct disadvantage if they have to compete with club members who understand each other's game strategies. However, although members typically have the most to gain from the presence of elite clubs, nonmembers and the larger community may also be the beneficiaries of some aspects of club life.

HOW PRIVATE CLUBS BENEFIT THE LARGER COMMUNITY

Elite private clubs are not simply relics from a bygone era that exist solely for the benefit of their members. As we will see, many nonmembers enjoy activities at a club's facilities to which they are invited and may feel that they are hobnobbing with the top tiers of society when they attend such an event. Elite clubs also help the economy: they pay their employees, acquire goods and services that they provide to their members, and pay a variety of taxes. Likewise, many of these clubs have fund-raising procedures or events that support a variety of worthwhile causes.

Outsiders on the Inside (Even if Briefly)

Elite members frequently invite nonmembers (who typically possess similar socioeconomic and/or family backgrounds to their own) as guests at their club. These invitations are usually for lunch, dinner, a tennis match, a golf game, or some special family occasion. In addition, some individuals are invited to the club for a special event because the member believes that "it would not be proper" to leave out this person because he or she is "like a member of the family." People who are included in this category are individuals with whom the club member or another member of his or her immediate family come into frequent contact, such as the family minister, the children's teachers, or high-society service personnel, including real estate agents, masseuses, personal trainers, hairstylists, and nannies.

Club members typically invite guests to the club for an activity or event that fits the level of interaction the member has with the outsider. If a club member is interested in developing a new business or making a certain kind of social connection, for example, the nonmember will be invited for lunch or dinner. If the member wants to have a more informal, off-the-record social engagement, the nonmember is more likely to be invited to play a round of golf or enjoy a game of tennis.

A wide variety of nonmembers are invited to elite clubs for special family occasions, such as a milestone birthday, a wedding or anniversary, or a party honoring a daughter at the time of her formal debut to society. Do nonmembers enjoy attending an event at a club where they are not members? All evidence indicates that they do because of the lavishness of such occasions and the feelings of inclusion (even if only temporary) that are evoked by being invited to such an event. Like members of the club, nonmembers attending a special event can enjoy luxurious club facilities while feasting on an array of elaborately prepared food, consuming "call-brand liquors" (expensive, name-brand alcoholic beverages and wines), and enjoying fine entertainment, such as a top entertainer or musical group performing for the occasion. Some nonmembers leave the event with feelings of enhanced self-esteem: they believe that they have associated with some of the "best" people in the community. From their own observations, outsiders know that, for one evening, they have been part of an elaborate function that was highlighted by such elaborate displays as a tabletop ice sculpture of the bride and groom and a six-foot, ten-layer wedding cake. From the nonmember guest's visual observations alone, he or she knows that this event cost many thousands of dollars and that each guest's tab ran more than $100 for food and drinks alone.

How do we know that some nonmembers appreciate and—may be impressed by—their visit to an elite club? Although guests probably would enjoy a nice birthday party, anniversary celebration, or wedding reception in a variety of settings, including hotel or other rental facilities, it appears that having the event at an elite city, country, or golf club intensifies the pleasure of the experience. Guests feels that they are "members of the family"—if not members of the club—when they are invited to private club facilities for these events. According to Dee, a woman frequently invited to social events at local clubs but who held no memberships of her own,

> When you're invited to their club, it's almost like being invited to their home. The hosts greet you warmly and make sure that you know other people and have everything you need, just like they would at their own residence, but [the hosts] are able to visit with everybody because they don't actually have to do any work.

Some nonmembers accept an invitation to an event at a private club simply because they want to be a part of the special occasion that the invitation signifies; others come to the party or reception as a means of gaining their own temporary form of social capital that can be used as currency in conversations where they hope to show elites that they "belong" in their midst or to impress their friends and acquaintances who were not invited to the event. One prominent Texas hairstylist who is frequently invited to clients' parties and wedding receptions, for example, has a reputation in the community for describing to all the clients in the salon for the following week any event that this individual attends at an exclusive private club. Here is an example of a typical comment by the stylist (as reported by Betty, a regular client):

> When I went to Marla's reception at ——— [Country Club], I saw Charlene, and I can't believe she's pregnant again. Three kids should be enough for anybody! But, you also wouldn't believe how much that wedding and reception must have cost. I really think ——— [Country Club] is the best club in town for food, service, and general ambiance.

And the hairstylist's description continued from there about how lavish the wedding was and how pleasant the country club was as a setting for such an event. Betty stated that the hairstylist's comments really had nothing to do with having seen Charlene and everything to do with letting his clients know that he had been invited to Marla's wedding and to the reception at the private club. Although this is only one example, I do not believe that it is an isolated one: it appears that most nonmembers sometimes enjoy, even if briefly, their association with prestigious private clubs. Of course, some nonmembers may also leave a function at a private club feeling envy or disdain.

Employment Opportunities—Particularly for Part-Time and Seasonal Workers

Private clubs offer some nonmembers a variety of employment opportunities, ranging from full-time, professional positions such as club director, food and beverage service manager, and golf or tennis pro to part-time or seasonal positions such as lifeguard, caddy, housekeeping staff, and food service worker. There is both an upside and a downside to the kinds of employment that are typically available at elite clubs, but the economic impact of these jobs on a community may be significant, both in smaller towns where few employment opportunities exist and in major metropolitan areas where numerous private clubs in the central city and suburbs employ a large number of people.

It is difficult to gain accurate information as to how many people are employed by private clubs nationwide or to assess the economic impact of club operations on cities and states. We must rely on data gathered by organizations such as the Club Managers Association of America (CMAA). Although participants in CMAA manage only a small fraction of all the private clubs in the United States, the clubs it represents serve more than 1.8 million members and have a combined payroll of about $4 billion annually. CMAA reports that nearly 300,000 people are employed at the more than 3,000 clubs it represents, although it should be noted that more than half (about 58 percent) of those employees are either part-time or seasonal workers as compared to full-time, professional employees (CMAA 2007). Of the various types of clubs, city clubs typically have relatively higher payrolls than do golf or country clubs: while city clubs have fewer overall employees than other kinds of clubs, city clubs hire a higher percentage of full-time employees. If we think of the 300,000 full-time and part-time employees of CMAA-affiliated clubs and add to this number the thousands of other employees whose clubs are not represented by this association, we see that private clubs are major employers nationwide.

Some positions at private clubs are well-paid, year-round career-track positions that provide generous salaries and health and retirement benefits; others are slightly-above-minimum-wage positions with little job security and no benefits. Regardless of their position in the organization, however, elite club employees are expected to engage in emotional labor, meaning that they must display only certain carefully selected emotions while at work (Hochschild 1983).

For example, club service personnel must cater to the members and be helpful and friendly (but not too friendly) toward them at all times. As one study of luxury hotel service workers found, "Customized contacts with workers are a major part of what clients are playing for in many luxury sites, including high-end hotels, restaurants, spas, resorts, retail shops, and first-class airline cabins" (Sherman 2007:3). The same can be said for interactions between employees and members of an exclusive club. According to one private club manager, "We tell all employees that the member comes first, no matter what." In interactions with a club member, employees are advised to remember this slogan: "The Answer Is Yes, What Is Your Question?" (Private Club Associates 2007). Although a service-oriented philosophy such as this typically enhances the enjoyment of club members and provides them with feelings of importance and perhaps superiority, club employees who must abide by these *feeling rules* for their given role may have a deep sense of frustration or even alienation. However, club management associations emphasize that directors should ensure that their clubs are "employee friendly." According to one human relations consultant for elite clubs,

> Clubs put much emphasis on satisfying the needs of members without considering the fact that dissatisfied staff cannot produce satisfied members. Work to create a friendly, fun environment that makes staff want to return. . . . Maintain constant dialogue to be sure that your employees are pleased with their work and workplace. Just as satisfied customers serve as excellent public relations, so do satisfied employees. Both groups speak well of your club in circles that you may not be able to reach. (Smikle 2007:28)

Although some individuals may find that employment at a private club is not their preference, I heard many stories during my research of satisfied club staff who appreciated the employment opportunities they had found at an elite club. Some employees stated they liked their interactions with club members because most of the members were gracious and had "good manners." They also were pleased that they did not have to handle money or work for tips and that they were able to dress nicely and not have to wear a "silly uniform" or "a clown hat" like some places of employment. Other staff members said that part-time or seasonal work at the club made it possible for them to attend college during the school year and still have gainful employment. Others were parents who liked to work an alternate shift because they could remain with young children until a spouse or other relative relieved them of child care duties. Overall, most club personnel stated that they were "treated like family" or that they were treated "right" by the club.

Some clubs offer employees incentives for good work, including a year-end bonus or special recognition such as being named "outstanding employee of the month." Individuals receiving such an award typically have their picture posted on a club wall or their name on a plaque. They are also given a cash bonus and the use of a reserved parking space for the month. A number of staff members indicated that they appreciated being able to eat for free at the club before their shift started. According to one city club employee, "The food's sure better here than it was [at the fast-food chain] where I used to work. They'd give us free food if we wanted it, but it tasted so bad, I couldn't eat it."

Private clubs offer a wide range of employment opportunities for people with varying levels of formal education, on-the-job training, and experience in a community. Across the nation, private clubs spend billions of dollars in employee payrolls. In cities with a large number of elite clubs, these organizations are a significant component of the overall leisure industry in the region.

Spending and Taxes

In addition to spending billions on employee payrolls, private clubs in the United States spend billions of dollars on goods and services. Many purchases are made in their own communities, and these clubs also pay a variety of local, state, and national taxes. CMAA estimates, for example, that the average club spends approximately $3 million annually on goods and services, and a large percentage of this money is spent in the local community and home state where the club is located. According to CMAA data, the average club spends $1.05 million in the local community and about $1.2 million within the state as a whole (CMAA 2007). Around the country, CMAA clubs alone generate $6.21 billion (in addition to payroll) for state economics, and this does not include tens of thousands of other, non-CMAA clubs.

Private clubs generate business for architects, interior designers, furniture and kitchen appliance sales companies, insurance companies, attorneys and accountants, party and special events planners, pool and other maintenance services, real estate agents, and other individuals and corporations that offer goods and services that are integral to the daily operations of exclusive clubs. Although some of these businesses may be owned by club members, many of them are independent businesses that would be greatly disadvantaged if all the private clubs in their vicinity permanently closed their doors.

Along with paying for goods and services, private clubs pay property taxes, sales taxes, and other types of taxes across the nation. A typical CMAA club pays $150,773 annually in property taxes, and CMAA clubs across the nation generate more than $350 million annually in sales taxes, with city clubs averaging slightly more than $200,000 each in sales taxes. Other taxes also paid by some elite clubs include corporate taxes, liquor and alcoholic beverage taxes, and payroll taxes (CMAA 2007).

Giving Back to the Community through Charity Fund-Raising
Events and Scholarships

Private clubs and their professional associations are increasingly involved in raising funds to support a variety of worthwhile causes in their communities and beyond. The members of individual city, country, and wall-less clubs participate in group activities at their clubs that help them collectively give back to the community. Examples of these activities include participation by members and staff of the Edina (Minnesota) Country Club in "Sharing and Caring Hands; Store to Door," which delivers groceries to elderly and disabled persons in surrounding counties; VEAP (Volunteers Enlisted to Assist People); Toys for Tots; Hat and Mitten Tree for the underprivileged; and support for Edina Center for the Arts. In Texas, the prestigious Argyle Club of San Antonio (discussed in a previous chapter) states that it is "devoted exclusively to the support of the life-saving efforts of the Southwest Foundation for Biomedical Research." Members of the Argyle Club give time and money to support this independent research institution, and the Founder's Council holds regular luncheons, receptions, and holiday parties at the Argyle.

Although some fund-raising endeavors are a long-term commitment, others are short-term events, such as the one-day charity golf and dining event that ClubCorp held as part of its fiftieth anniversary celebration. This special event involved ClubCorp's ninety-four golf and country clubs around the nation as the clubs opened their courses to about 15,000 players for tournaments, dinners, and auctions designed to raise funds for charities. The proceeds from this event were donated to Susan G. Komen Foundation for the Cure, benefiting breast cancer research; the Muscular Dystrophy Association's "Augie's Quest," which is dedicated to finding a cure for ALS (Lou Gehrig's disease); the Professional Golfers' Association Foundation, for a special program that makes golf accessible to people of every ability, race, gender, and social and economic background; and the ClubCorp Employee Partners Care Foundation, which assists ClubCorp employees in time of need and creates a scholarship fund for employees and their children and grandchildren (clubcorpcharityclassic 2007).

Although ClubCorp does not publicly state how much money its charitable activities raises annually, CMAA reports that its member clubs raised a total of $367 million for charities in 2006, and an additional $6.4 million was raised for student scholarships. Clubs in the South tend to raise the most money in charity fund-raising, while clubs in the Northeast raise the least. However, the average amount raised by CMAA clubs that participated in charity fund-raising in 2006 was slightly over $350,000, with a median of about $55,000 (CMAA 2007).

Some private clubs fund scholarships for various types of recipients. Some clubs raise money for "special needs" and educational funds for the children of club employees, whereas other clubs establish college scholarship programs. The Headliners Foundation scholarship, established by Austin's Headliners Club, for example, is awarded to top journalism students in Texas universities. Since its inception, the Headliners Foundation has provided over a million dollars to more than 350 Texas college students. Scholarship winners are honored at a luncheon at the club and receive funds to help them complete their education and pursue a career in communications or journalism (*Headlines* 2006).

From all indications, more elite clubs will become involved in charitable and philanthropic endeavors in their communities in the future. Private clubs have long been the sites for fund-raisers hosted by club members who wanted to raise money for causes and organizations that are important to them; however, clubs and club management associations now are becoming more involved in their own philanthropic endeavors. Some of these activities take place quietly, while others are widely publicized to make outsiders aware that they are invited to participate in the events or perhaps to take the rough edges off of some outsiders' perceptions that exclusive clubs are bastions of elitism and snobbery.

POTENTIAL LOSSES FROM THE EXISTENCE OF ELITE PRIVATE CLUBS

Although I have documented a number of positive ways in which elite clubs may benefit the cities and states where they are located, such as by providing employment opportunities, spending large sums of money on goods and services, paying taxes, and giving back to the community through charitable fund-raising activities and college scholarships, my research and other sociological studies suggest that losses are also associated with the presence of exclusive private clubs.

Individual Losses: Lack of Access and Stigma Associated with "Outsider" Status

Members Only has highlighted ways in which the vast majority of people are categorically excluded from elite clubs. Members of private clubs have freedom to associate with whomever they so choose; however, club members also have license to reject altogether or to minimize the involvement of specific categories of people, including white women, people of color, members of non-dominant religious or racial/ethnic groups, and individuals who are not in the top socioeconomic tiers of society.

One of the central losses associated with private clubs at both individual and societal levels is outsiders' lack of access to scarce goods and resources that are readily available to members of our nation's most prestigious clubs. Among the scarce goods are having access to properties owned or controlled by city, country, and golf clubs that may include some of the finest golf, tennis, and entertainment facilities in the country. Scarce resources include the social, economic, and political connections that help people reach beyond their own spheres of influence and gain outside assistance in order to achieve some desirable goal or outcome. Elite clubs provide members with unique access to local, state, and national movers and shakers who can help them accomplish their goal regardless of what it may be.

In its examination of the issue of equal access, the U.S. Supreme Court developed an elaborate framework by which courts should weigh the associational freedoms of clubs against the compelling nature of a governmental interest in eliminating discrimination (Larsen 1999). In order to do this, the Court focused on ways in which private clubs provide certain kinds of assets to members. One of the most significant assets the Court identified was business connections, noting that these are tangible resources available to members but denied to outsiders. A concern about equal access to business contacts arises from the broader governmental interest in assuring all segments of society an unrestricted access to business opportunities (Larsen 1999). Although the past issues regarding equal access have been concerned primarily with public arenas such as education and housing, the issue of equal access may also be applied to private arenas such as elite clubs. In a private club it is possible for members to make important—and often far-reaching—business, political, and social contacts because of the members' affiliation with this prestigious organization. Intimate associations with other powerful members over an extended span of time in a cloistered environment provide an advantage to members that others simply do not possess. Efforts have been made in this country to remove barriers that may hinder disadvantaged groups' access to economic and political advancement, but economic inequality is rapidly increasing, and social segregation remains rampant across the nation (Larsen 1999). Today, many private clubs are as segregated as they were early in the twentieth century, before the passage of civil rights legislation and the implementation of affirmative action programs in education and employment. In elite golf and country clubs, for example, most club members are white, upper-middle and upper-class individuals, while lower-tier employees at these clubs are predominantly African American, Latino/a or first- or second-generation eastern European immigrants. Access to the club by subordinate-group individuals is as an employee or—at most—as a guest of the club or a member. Access to the social and cultural benefits of member-ship in the club is not available to any but a select few of such subordinate-group individuals, however.

Access is not the only loss that subordinate-group individuals sustain with regard to exclusion from private clubs. Stigma is another: "Exclusion from private clubs on the basis of race has the effect of perpetuating and lend-ing societal legitimacy to the stereotypes and perceptions of inferiority upon which such discriminatory policies are based" (Larsen 1999:401). Categoric exclusion suggests that an individual is in some way inferior and therefore un-worthy of club membership. Prominent author and attorney Lawrence Otis Graham (1995:2–3) eloquently described why he and other Ivy League–edu-cated, professional African Americans feel stigmatized when they are ex-cluded from elite clubs they easily can afford to join:

> Through my experiences as a young lawyer, I have come to realize that these clubs are where businesspeople network, where lawyers and invest-ment bankers meet potential clients and arrange deals. How many clients and deals am I going to line up on the asphalt parking lot of my local pub-lic tennis courts?
>
> I am not ashamed to admit that I one day want to be a partner and a part of this network. When I talk to my black lawyer or investment-banker friends or my wife, a brilliant black woman who has degrees from Harvard College, Harvard Law School, and Harvard Business School, I learn that our white counterparts are being accepted by dozens of these elite institu-tions. So why shouldn't we—especially when we have the same credentials, salaries, social graces, and ambitions?

A factor that compounds the stigma associated with exclusion is having the knowledge that a number of African Americans who have qualifications and achievements that far surpass those of the average white club member are also ignored or cautiously rejected when clubs select new members. Graham (1995:3) provides a specific example of this type of discussion among of his network of friends:

> My black Ivy League friends and I know of black company vice presidents who have to ask white subordinates to invite them out for golf or tennis. We talk about the club in Westchester that rejected black Scarsdale resi-dent and millionaire magazine publisher Earl Graves, who sits on *Fortune* 500 boards, [formerly owned] a Pepsi distribution franchise, raised three bright Ivy League children, and holds prestigious honorary degrees. We talk about all the clubs that face a scandal and then run out to sign up one quiet, deferential black man who will accept a special "limited status" membership, remove the taint, and deflect further scrutiny.

For up-and-coming African American professionals such as Graham when he wrote this statement, standing by and watching while prominent men of color are ignored or rejected by exclusive clubs further reveals the stigma associated with being a person of color, regardless of class, in the United States. According to Graham, this kind of exclusion contributes to a "racially polarized world," and it is obvious that patterns of physical and social segregation, whether in private clubs or in society as a whole, do not contribute to social or racial harmony but do have great psychological costs, particularly for those who are categorically excluded.

Community and Societal Losses: Physical and Social Segregation

In *Members Only*, I have shown how private clubs provide an arena for individuals in the upper classes to physically and socially segregate themselves from the masses. Being apart from outsiders makes it possible for elites to feel superior to nonelites and to ignore the needs and concerns of those who are not within their own inner circle of social, economic, and political elites. The political analyst Joel S. Hirschhorn (2007) refers to the physical and social segregation between elites and everyone else as a form of economic apartheid:

> The Upper Class has protected and gated mansions, private vacation spots and spas, special access shopping venues, private schools, lavish entertainment options, luxurious hospital accommodations, and private jets and stretch limos. The Upper Class does everything possible to PHYSICALLY separate itself from the poor, repugnant and uncouth members of the Lower Class. This physical separation is the hallmark of economic apartheid. The only contact the wealthy have and want with Lower Class people is when the latter serve, protect and pamper them.

Although Hirschhorn's analysis does not account for the presence of a middle class in the United States, his idea that elites' physical and social separation is harmful to society is based on a large body of elite theory that assumes that a few wealthy and powerful individuals control the political, economic, and social organizations of our society and have a major influence on people's quality of life across a wide variety of class, racial, and ethnic categories.

Community and Societal Losses: The High Cost of "Elite Think"

In prestigious private clubs, elites are provided with frequent opportunities to interact with one another. If elite theory is accurate, these interactions influence many elites to act out "narrow self-serving motives" and to be "subject to relatively little direct influence from the apathetic masses" (see Dye and Zeigler

2006:4). From this perspective, elites across various social institutions—including business, politics and government, the military, education, religion, and the media—act in their own self-interest when they make decisions about the allocation of scarce goods and services, and they typically pay little attention to—or even are completely unaware of—the wishes and needs of everyone else.

Since the American elite disproportionately represent the "well-educated, prestigiously employed, older, affluent, urban, white, Anglo-Saxon, upper- and upper-middle class male population" (Dye and Zeigler 2006:115), these privileged individuals control social policy and the public sphere through their "front-stage" and "backstage" performances (Goffman 1959). The front stage—the arena where a player performs a specific role before an audience—is where elites make formal decisions that are publicized to the outside world through the proper channels. Such front stages include but are not limited to corporate boardrooms, various levels of government and the courts, branches of the military service, prestigious colleges and universities, churches and other religious organizations, major medical centers, and any other settings in which the primary order givers and decision makers are members of the privileged upper classes. By contrast, the backstage—the arena where a player is not required to perform a specific role because it is out of view of a given audience—provides a private setting, obscured from the public eye and from members of the media, where elites are able to freely discuss issues and problems of concern and determine among themselves what course of action to take. Although private clubs are only one of many settings in which backstage interactions among elites take place (and not all elites are members of private clubs), evidence suggests that many elites use their club connections to further enhance their social power and create economic and political networks that are not available to ordinary middle-, working-, and lower-class people. Elites seek to maintain their top-tier positions in the social hierarchy, and spending most of their time with other elites in private clubs and other exclusive enclaves may make them oblivious to the needs and concerns that ordinary people face on a daily basis.

A classic example of how elites may not understand the real issues faced by nonelites in their everyday lives is the controversy that ensued following a speech given by President George W. Bush on July 10, 2007, in Cleveland, Ohio. Although this speech did not occur in a private club and President Bush has listed no private club affiliations while he has held public office (we do know that he and his father, President George Herbert Walker Bush, were avid club men while at Yale University and in their postcollege years), the kind of "elite think" that he demonstrated in this Ohio speech is representative of how elites may be out of touch with diverse populations, especially when they spend all of their time associating with other wealthy and powerful individuals. Here is the portion of the president's speech that represents "elite think" (whitehouse.gov 2007b, emphasis added).

> Let me talk about health care, since it's fresh on my mind. The objective has got to be to make sure America is the best place in the world to get health care, that we're the most innovative country, that we encourage doctors to stay in practice, that we are robust in the funding of research, and that patients get good, quality care at a reasonable cost.
>
> The immediate goal is to make sure there are more people on private insurance plans. *I mean, people have access to health care in America. After all, you just go to an emergency room.* The question is, will we be wise about how we pay for health care. I mean the best way to do so is to enable more people to have private insurance. And the reason I emphasize private insurance, the best health care plan—the best health care policy is one that emphasizes private health. In other words, the opposite of that would be government control of health care.

Although the president made a number of points in his Cleveland speech, the highlighted comment regarding people having access to health care by using a hospital's emergency room brought about resounding criticism of how his elitist perspective showed a lack of understanding about the needs of the uninsured and the underinsured as well as limited comprehension about how the health care system functions. As critics such as Donna Mason (2007), president of the Maryland's Emergency Nurses Association, have pointed out, emergency departments are intended to treat emergencies, not to provide primary care services or to treat chronic conditions such as diabetes, high blood pressure, or mental illness. According to Mason (2007), "Unfortunately, the President didn't offer insight into a solution; instead he demonstrated a complete lack of understanding as to how health care is delivered today and how near the breaking point our health care system has become."

Although the president's speech is only one example of what I have referred to as "elite think," his comments about use of the emergency room reflect a typical pattern of thinking among privileged individuals who themselves have no concerns about paying for health care or other needs. Since the president, his family, and closest friends and associates receive state-of-the-art health care and talk primarily only with others in the inner circle of elites, it is easy to overlook or minimize the true problems faced by our society in regard not only to health care but also to poverty, homelessness, and a myriad of other pressing social concerns.

Like the president of the United States, business and political elites make decisions that have a far-reaching effect on people. They also make choices that may either reduce or perpetuate inequalities based on race/ethnicity, gender, and social class. In *Members Only*, I have attempted to show how some members use elite clubs to physically and socially separate themselves from nonelites and to provide a setting from which they can view the world as they want it to be, not as it actually is. For the tiny percentage of privileged Americans who are part of this very small, highly selective world of exclusive private clubs, all may be well as they raise a glass of champagne to toast their latest social, business, or political accomplishment; however, for the vast majority of people in this country and throughout the world, the picture one sees as he or she looks up at the city club perched high atop a prestigious office building or at the country club's golf course, nestled in a beautiful, rolling suburban hillside, is a far different one from what is envisioned by those who suffer from "elite think." Perhaps the view from the bottom up is the one about which we all should be most concerned.

References

Allen, Mike. 2005. "Hard Cash Is Main Course for GOP Fundraiser." *Washington Post* (June 14):A1.

Allensworth, Kay. 2007. "Mark McKinnon—Delivering the Message." *Headlines* (Winter):8–10.

Amory, Cleveland. 1947. *The Proper Bostonians.* Orleans, MA: Parnassus Imprints.

Austin Country Club. 2007. "Our History." Retrieved July 21, 2007. Online: http://www.austincountryclub.com/club/scripts/section/section.asp?GRP=2966&NS=HIS

Baltimore City Paper. 2005. "Best Place to Hold a Political Fundraiser." Retrieved September 29, 2007. Online: http://www.citypaper.com/bob/story.asp?id=10554

Barton Creek Country Club. 2007. "About Barton Creek Country Club." Retrieved October 22, 2007. Online: http://www.bartoncreekmembers.com/about/index.htm

BBC Action Network. 2005. "Race Discrimination." Retrieved November 18, 2007. Online: http://www.bbc.co.uk/dna/actionnetwork/A1185473

Benoit-Smullyan, Emile. 1944. "Status, Status Types, and Status Interrelations." *American Sociological Review* (April):151–61.

Birmingham, Stephen. 1968. *The Right People.* Boston: Little, Brown.

Borne et al. vs. Haverhill Golf and Country Club, Inc. 2003. Social Law Library (Appeals Court Slip Opinions). Retrieved July 31, 2004. Online: http://www.social aw.com/appslip/appJune03g.html

Bourdieu, Pierre. 1984. *Distinction: A Social Critique of the Judgement of Taste.* Trans. by Richard Nice. Cambridge: Harvard University Press.

———. 1986. "The Forms of Capital." Pp. 241–58 in *Handbook of Theory and Research for the Sociology of Education,* edited by John G. Richardson. New York: Greenwood Press.

Bourdieu, Pierre, and Lois Wacquant. 1992. *An Invitation to Reflexive Sociology.* Chicago: University of Chicago Press.

Bragg, Roy. 2004. "Exclusive but Not Exclusionary." *San Antonio Express-News* (January 24):6H.

Brenner, Elsa. 1997. "Bias Still a Concern at Private Golf Clubs." *New York Times* (May 18). Retrieved November 3, 2007. Online: http://query.nytimes.com/gst/fullpage .html?res=9504E5DB1

Brook, Peter. 1985. *Reading for the Plot: Design and Intention in Narrative*. New York: Vintage.

Brookhaven Country Club. 2007. "A Big Idea." Brookhaven Country Club: Golden Anniversary 2007. Retrieved October 27, 2007. Online: http://www.celebrateour club.com/home.htm

Burk, Martha. 2005. *Cult of Power: Sex Discrimination in Corporate America and What Can Be Done about It*. New York: Scribner.

BusinessWeek. 1997. "Living It Up: The Elite Private Clubs." Retrieved December 13, 2004. Online: http://www.businessweek.com/1997/16/b3523139.htm

Cable, Mary. 1984. *Top Drawer: American High Society from the Gilded Age to the Roaring Twenties*. New York: Atheneum.

Capitolinside.com 2006. "Calendar—September, 2006." *Mike Hailey's Capitol Inside: The Ultimate Guide to Power in Texas Politics and Government*. Retrieved September 29, 2007. Online: http://www.capitolinside.com/calendar2-september2006.htm

CBS Broadcasting. 2007. "Caught on Tape: Bush Adviser Karl Rove Raps." Retrieved October 7, 2007. Online: http://cbs5.com/seenon/local_story_087232314.html

CBSSports.com 2007. "Proposed British Law Would Spell End of Restricted Golf Club Membership for Women." Retrieved October 11, 2007. Online: http://www .sportsline.com/golf/story/10222947

Chambers, Marcia. 2000. "The Changing Face of Private Clubs: The Integration of African Americans into Private Golf Clubs." *Golf Digest* (August):17, 18, 21.

———. 2004. "At Country Clubs, Gay Members Want All Privileges for Partners." *New York Times* (September 21):A31–A32.

City Club of Dallas. 2007. "Top of the City." The City Club: A Dallas Member-Owned Private Club. Retrieved June 13, 2007. Online: http://cityclubdallas.com

Clark-Madison, Mike. 1998. "Aqua Fest Goes Down." *Austin Chronicle* (July 17). Retrieved September 10, 2006. Online: http://www.austinchronicle.com/issues/vol17/ issue45/pols.aquafest.html

Clay, Bobby. 1996. "Breaking Par against Racism: Beyond Shoal Creek." *Black Enterprise* (September).

Club Management. 2003. "Borderline Call: In a Mexican Border Town, Harlingen Country Club Redefines Itself." (December 1):1.

clubcorpcharityclassic. 2007. "ClubCorp Charity Classic: Get Involved." Retrieved November 4, 2007. Online: http://www.clubcorpcharityclassic.com/main.htm

Club Managers Association of America. 2007. "Economic Impact Survey." ClubNet: The Official Website of the Club Managers Association of America. Retrieved November 10, 2007. Online: http://www.cmaa.org/who/index.html

Coleman, James S. 1988. "Social Capital in the Creation of Human Capital." *American Journal of Sociology* 94:S95–S121.

———. 1994. *Foundations of Social Theory*. Cambridge, MA: Belknap Press.

Colonial Country Club. 2007. "What Our Members Love about Us!" Cordova, TN: Colonial Country Club. Retrieved August 27, 2007. Online: http://www.colonial countryclub.org/view/176

Copp, Tara. 2006. "Headliners Club Takes Jabs at Rove." *Austin American-Statesman* (January 13):B1, B3.

Crouse, Karen. 2007. "New Day at the Old Course." *New York Times* (July 29):SP1, SP10.

D Magazine. 2005. "Fairways and Bankrolls." *D Magazine* (December):22.

Dallas Historical Society. 2006. "Idlewild Ball 1911." Dallas Historical Society. Retrieved November 7, 2006. Online: http://www.dallashistory.org/history/dallas/idlewild_ball.htm

Dallas National Golf Club. 2007. "Dallas National Golf Club Information." Retrieved October 18, 2007. Online: http://www.dallasnationalgolfclub.com

Dallas Petroleum Club. 2005. "About the Dallas Petroleum Club." Retrieved November 10, 2006. Online: http://www.thedallaspetroleumclub.com

Davis, Marcia. 2006. "The Press Club's Dinner of Ribs." Retrieved October 6, 2007. Online: http://www.washingtonpost.com/wp-dyn/content/article/2006/02/09/AR2006020900159.html

de la Rosa, Ysabel. 2007. "Art Appreciation." *Private Clubs Magazine* (March/April). Retrieved August 27, 2007. Online: http://www.privateclubs.com

Dee, James H. 2007. "Wrong for All the 'Right' Reasons." *Austin American-Statesman* (September 8):A17.

Department for Work and Pensions. 2004. "Disability Discrimination Bill: Consultation on Private Clubs; Premises; the Definition of Disability and the Questions Procedure." Retrieved July 7, 2007. Online: http://www.dwp.gov.uk/consultations/consult/2004/ddbl/private_clubs_premises.pdf

Dickens, Charles. 1888. *Dictionary of London.* Moretonhampstead: Old House Books.

Domhoff, G. William. 1974. *The Bohemian Grove and Other Retreats.* New York: Harper & Row.

———. 2005. "Social Cohesion and the Bohemian Grove: The Power Elite at Summer Camp." Retrieved September 18, 2005. Online: http://whorulesamerica.net/power/bohemian_grove.html

———. 2006. *Who Rules America? Power, Politics, and Social Change.* New York: McGraw-Hill.

Dunn, William J. 1971. *Knickerbocker Centennial: An Informal History of the Knickerbocker Club, 1871–1971.* New York: Knickerbocker Club.

Duquesne Club. 2006. "The Duquesne Club." Retrieved October 24, 2007. Online: http://www.duquesne.org

Dye, Thomas R., and Harmon Zeigler. 2006. *The Irony of Democracy: An Uncommon Introduction to American Politics* (13th ed.). Belmont, CA: Thomson/Wadsworth.

Edina Country Club. 2007. "Our Culture." Edina, Minnesota: Edina Country Club. Retrieved August 3, 2007. Online: http://www.edinacountryclub.org

Egelko, Bob. 2005. "Firms Must Treat Domestic Partners Like Married Pairs, Top State Court Says." *San Francisco Chronicle* (August 2). Retrieved December 18, 2006. Online: http://www.sfgate.com/cgibin/article.cgi?f=/c/a/2005/08/02/MNGFRE1IKQ1.DTL&hw=Birgit+Koebke&sn=003&sc=943

Epstein, Joseph. 2002. *Snobbery: The American Version.* Boston: Houghton Mifflin.

Ewing, Saul. 2004. "Newsletters/Updates: Anti-Discrimination Laws Applicable to Private Clubs or Not?" Retrieved September 19, 2004. Online: http://www.saul.com/articles/golf3.htm

Fairfield, Francis Gerry. [1873] 1975. *The Clubs of New York: New York Club-Life.* New York: Henry L. Hinton.

Feinstein, Edward. 2000. "City of Angels: Rosh Hashana, 2000." Rabbi Edward Feinstein Archives, Valley Beth Shalom, Encino, California. Retrieved February 6, 2006. Online: http://www.vbs.org/rabbi/rabfeins/city_bot.htm

Fenton, Ben. 1998. "MCC Lifts 211-Year-Old Ban on Women." Telegraph.co.uk (September 29). Retrieved July 7, 2007. Online: http://www.telegraph.co.uk/html Content.jhtml?html=/archive/1998/09/29/ncric29.html

Field, John. 2003. *Social Capital.* New York: Routledge.

Flynn, Eileen E. 2000. "Headliners' Manager Was at Club From Start: In Years behind Bar, Brieger Made Mark with Warmth, Loyalty." *Austin-American Statesman* (August 20):B1, B6.

Foxnews.com. 2005. "Ehrlich Brushes Off Country Club Dust-Up." (July 6). Retrieved September 8, 2007. Online: http://www.foxnews.com/story/0,3566,161710,00.html

———. 2007. "Bushes Attend Secretive Alfalfa Club Dinner." Retrieved October 6, 2007. Online: http://www.foxnews.com/story/0,2933,247820,00.html

Frank, Robert L. 2007. *Richistan: A Journey through the American Wealth Boom and the Lives of the New Rich.* New York: Crown.

Futterman, Matthew. 2005. "For Baltusrol Members, Hassle Is Well Worth It." *The Star Ledger.* Retrieved July 26, 2007. Online: http://www.nj.com/sopranos/ledger/index.ssf?/golf/ledger/index.ssf?/golf/stories/072705.html

Galloway, Diane Caylor. 1996. *Dallas Country Club: The First 100 Years.* Dallas, TX: Dallas Country Club.

Gerth, Hans H., and C. Wright Mills. 1946. *From Max Weber: Essays in Sociology.* New York: Oxford University Press.

Giddens, Anthony. 1975. *The Class Structure of the Advanced Societies.* New York: Harper Torchbooks.

Gilbert, Dennis. 2003. *The American Class Structure in an Age of Growing Inequality* (6th ed.). Belmont, CA: Wadsworth.

Gillman, Todd J. 2007. "AG Alberto Gonzales Resigns." *Dallas Morning News* (August 27). Retrieved August 27, 2007. Online: http://www.dallasnews.com/shared-content/dws/dn/latestnews/stories/082807dnnatgonzales.7541271e.html

Goffman, Erving. 1959. *The Presentation of Self in Everyday Life.* Garden City, NY: Doubleday.

Graham, Lawrence Otis. 1995. *Member of the Club: Reflections on Life in a Racially Polarized World.* New York: HarperPerennial.

Granger, Tom, and Jane Greig. 2006. "Headliners Celebrate 50th Anniversary with Star Studded Gala." *Headlines* (Spring):1, 4, 7–9.

Granger, Tom, and Joan Talley. 2006. "Politics Past and Future." *Headlines* (Fall):4–6. Austin, TX: Headliners Club.

Granovetter, Mark S. 1973. "The Strength of Weak Ties." *American Journal of Sociology* 78:1360–80.

———. 1983. "The Strength of the Weak Tie: Revisited." *Sociological Theory* 1:201–33.

Graves, Charles. 1963. *Leather Armchairs: The Chevas Regal Book of London Clubs.* London: Cassell.

Greene, Linda S. 2002. "At Augusta, It's Symbols That Mean Most." *New York Times* (August 4):SP9.

Gronow, Jukka. 1997. *The Sociology of Taste.* New York: Routledge.

Hart, Elizabeth Kirby. 2007. "Private Clubs: Equal Access Issues and Public Status." Hospitality Financial and Technology Professionals. Retrieved October 9, 2007. Online: http://www.hftp.org/members/bottomline/backissues/2000/aprmay00/priv clubs.htm

Haynes, Michaele Thurgood. 1998. *Dressing Up Debutantes: Pageantry and Glitz in Texas.* New York: Berg/Oxford University Press.

Headliners Club. 1992. *The Headliners Club of Austin.* Austin, TX: The Headliners Club.

———. 2006. *Headliners Club Membership Directory.* Austin, TX: Headliners Club.

Headlines. 2006. "Headliners Foundation Launches Fundraising and Awareness Campaign." *Headlines* (Fall):26.

———. 2007. "Looking for the Headliners Club New President, Hector De Leon?" *Headlines.* Austin: The Headliners Club (Spring):1.

Heap, Kristiana. 2006. "Party of the Week: Idlewild Club Ball." (November 30). Retrieved from *Park Cities People* on July 29, 2007. Online: http://www.peoplenews papers.com

Henry, William A., III. 1991. "The Last Bastions of Bigotry." *Time* (July 22). Retrieved July 24, 2007. Online: http://www.time.com/time/magazine.article/0,9171, 973453,00.html

Herman, Andrew. 1999. *The "Better Angels" of Capitalism: Rhetoric, Narrative, and Moral Identity among Men of the American Upper Class.* Boulder, CO: Westview.

Hirschhorn, Joel S. 2007. "From Economic Apartheid to Political Revolution." Retrieved October 31, 2007. Online: http://www.silverbearcafe.com/private/apartheid .html

Hochschild, Arlie Russell. 1983. *The Managed Heart: Commercialization of Human Feelings.* Berkeley: University of California Press.

Hoppe, Christy, and George Kuempel. 2004. "Files Linked to DeLay's Daughter among Others Sought in PAC Inquiry." Texans for Public Justice. Retrieved September 7, 2007. Online: http://www.tpj.org/page_view.jsp?pageid=449&pubid=275

Hornblower, Samuel. 2000. "Fifteen Minutes: The Old Boys' Clubs." *Harvard Crimson Magazine* (April 27). Retrieved November 3, 2007. Online: http://www.thecrimson .com/article.aspx?ref=100719

Jeffreys, Daniel. 1999. "No Jews on Their Golf Courses: Country Clubs in the U.S. That Still Exclude Jewish People from Their Membership." *New Statesman* (August 23).

Jolly-Ryan, Jennifer. 2006. "Teed Off about Private Club Discrimination on the Taxpayers' Dime: Tax Exemptions and Other Government Privileges to Discriminatory Private Clubs." *Social Science Research Network* (March 20). Retrieved October 9, 2007. Online: http://ssrn.com/abstract=894335

Kendall, Diana. 2002. *The Power of Good Deeds: Privileged Women and the Social Reproduction of the Upper Class.* Lanham, MD: Rowman & Littlefield.

———. 2005. *Framing Class: Media Representations of Wealth and Poverty in America.* Lanham, MD: Rowman & Littlefield.

Kleiner, Diana J. 2002. "River Oaks, Houston." *The Handbook of Texas Online.* Retrieved July 29, 2004. Online: http://www.tsha.utexas.edu/handbook/online/articles/view/RR/hpr1.html

Knights of the Symphony. 2006. Knights of the Symphony: Roster. Unpublished document.

Lacayo, Richard. 1988. "Storming the Last Male Bastion." *Time* (July 4):43.

Lamont, Michele, and Annette Lareau. 1988. "Cultural Capital: Allusions, Gaps and Glissandos in Recent Theoretical Developments." *Sociological Theory* (Autumn):153–68.

Lara, Adair. 2004. "The Chosen Few: San Francisco's Exclusive Clubs Carry on Traditions of Fellowship, Culture—and Discrimination." *San Francisco Chronicle* (July 18):A1, A18.

Larsen, Shawn M. 1999. "For Blacks Only: The Associational Freedoms of Private Minority Clubs." *Case Western Reserve Law Review* 49 (Winter):359–405.

Lazarsfeld, Paul F., and Robert K. Merton. 1954. "Friendship as a Social Process: A Substantive and Methodological Analysis." Pp. 18–66 in *Freedom and Control in Modern Society*, edited by Morroe Berger. New York: Van Nostrand.

Lejeune, Anthony, and Malcolm Lewis. 1984. *The Gentlemen's Clubs of London.* London: Dorset Press.

Lester, Will. 2003. "Bush Brings Fund-Raisers to Barbecue." Associated Press. Retrieved August 9, 2003. Online: http://news.yahoo.com/news?tmpl=story2&cid=544&u=/ap/20030810

Lieber, Jill. 2003. "Golf's Host Clubs Have Open-and-Shut Policies on Discrimination." *USA Today* (April 9). Retrieved September 19, 2004. Online: http://www.usatoday.com/sports/golf/2003-04-09-clubs-policies_x.htm

Lin, Nan. 2001. *Social Capital: A Theory of Social Structure and Action.* Cambridge: Cambridge University Press.

Lopez, Edward J. 2002. "The Legislator as Political Entrepreneur: Investment in Political Capital." *The Review of Austrian Economics* 15:2/3:211–28.

Maguire, Jack. 1990. *A Century of Fiesta in San Antonio.* Austin, TX: Eakin Press.

Maralagoclub.com. 2007. "The Mar-a-Lago Club." Retrieved November 24, 2007. Online: http://www.maralagoclub.com

Masello, Robert. 1989. "The Knickerbocker Club." *Town & Country* (September): 218–19, 259, 270, 272.

Mason, Donna. 2007. "ENA President Responds to President George Bush regarding Health Care." Maryland Emergency Nurses Association, Press Release (August 20). Retrieved November 18, 2007. Online: http://www.mdeena.org/news/07%20Aug%20Bush.htm

Mason, Jackie. 1997. "Didya hear da one about da Pope and da Jew who walk intah dis country club. . . ?" *Jewish World Review* (December 31). Retrieved July 4, 2007. Online: http://www.jewishworldreview.com/121097/mason1.html

Mayo, James M. 1998. *The American Country Club: Its Origins and Development.* New Brunswick, NJ: Rutgers University Press.

McConnell, Bill. 2005. "Washington's Hidden Persuaders." *Broadcast and Cable* (June 27). Retrieved September 17, 2007. Online: http://www.broadcastingcable.com/article/CA621494.html?display=Feature&q=Hidden+Persuaders

McKinnon, Mark. 2003. "How to Sell a Candidate." *Texas Monthly* (July). Retrieved September 17, 2007. Online: http://www.texasmonthly.com/20030701/howto2.php

McLean, Stewart. 2005. "The Elkridge Club: A Brief History." Retrieved September 8, 2007. Online: http://www.elkridgeclub.org

McPherson, Miller, Lynn Smith-Lovin, and James M. Cook. 2001. "Birds of a Feather: Homophily in Social Networks." *Annual Review of Sociology* 27:415–44.

Miller, Richard. 1987. "The Tees of Texas Are upon You." *Town & Country* (July): 122–25.

Mills, C. Wright. 1956. *The Power Elite*. New York: Oxford University Press.

Molesworth, James. 2006. "Editors Picks." *WineSpectatorOnline* (August 26). Retrieved September 3, 2007. Online: http://www.winespectator.com/Wine/Daily_Wine/0,1142,3561.00.html

Moore, Gwen. 1979. "The Structure of a National Elite Network." *American Sociological Review* (October):673–92.

Nagourney, Adam. 2004. "The 2004 Elections: The Presidency—The Overview: Bush Celebrates Victory." *New York Times* (November 4):A1.

New York Times. 1886. "Harmonie Club Reception: Good Paintings Which Are on Exhibition in the Clubhouse." *New York Times* (November 25):8.

———. 1987. "Women, Too, Have Exclusive Clubs." *New York Times* (February 1):E7.

Novak, Shonda. 2006. "Austin Company, Partner Buy Downtown High-Rise." *Austin American-Statesman* (June 21):D1–D2.

Nowlan, James D. 2004. *Glory, Darkness, Light: A History of the Union League Club of Chicago*. Evanston, IL: Northwestern University Press.

Old Colony Club. 2007. "The Founding of the Club." Old Colony Club, Plymouth, MA. Retrieved July 25, 2007. Online: http://www.oldcolonyclub.org

Order of the Alamo. 1925. *Courts of the Order of the Alamo, 1909–1925*. San Antonio: Order of the Alamo.

Orman, Shelley. 2007. "Headliners Club Tops the List for City's Movers and Shakers." *Austin Business Journal* (August 24):1.

Peppard, Alan. 2003. "Idlewild Debs Take Their Bows." *Dallas Morning News* (November 24). Retrieved January 7, 2005. Online: http://www.DallasNews.com

Petroleum Club of Houston. 2007. "Membership Benefits." Petroleum Club of Houston. Retrieved February 9, 2006. Online: http://www.pcoh.com

Phillips, Michael. 2006. *White Metropolis: Race, Ethnicity, and Religion in Dallas, 1841-2001*. Austin, TX: University of Texas Press.

Phillips, Peter Martin. 1994. "A Relative Advantage: Sociology of the San Francisco Bohemian Club." Unpublished doctoral dissertation, University of California, Davis. Online: http://libweb.sonoma.edu/regional/faculty/phillips/bohemianindex.html

———. 2001. "San Francisco Bohemian Club: Power, Prestige and Globalism." *Sonoma County Free Press* (June 8). Retrieved July 26, 2004. Online: http://www.sonomacountyfreepress.com/bohos/San_Francisco_Bohemian_Club_Power_Prestige_Globalism. html

Portes, Alejandro. 1998. "Social Capital: Its Origins and Applications in Modern Sociology." *Annual Review of Sociology* 24:1–24.

Porzelt, Paul. 1982. *The Metropolitan Club of New York*. New York: Rizzoli.

Powell, Frances. 2004. "Artillery Club Holds Anniversary Ball." *Galveston Daily News*. Retrieved November 5, 2006. Online: http://news.galvestondailynews.com/story .lasso?wcd=66274

Powers, Kay. 1992. "The Headliners Club of Austin." Austin: The Headliners Club.

———. 2000. "Arnold Garcia, Jr. Is Club's New President." *Headlines* (Spring):1, 11.

Private Club Associates. 2007. "Private Club Associates: About Us." Retrieved November 4, 2007. Online: http://www.privateclubassociates.com

Public Strategies Inc. 2007. "Mark McKinnon." Retrieved September 17, 2007. Online: http://www.publicstrategiesinc.com/personprofile.php?eid=160

Putnam, Robert. 2000. *Bowling Alone: The Collapse and Revival of American Community*. New York: Simon & Schuster.

Ranshaw, Emily. 2007. "Is Race Keeping Exec Out of Club? *Dallas Morning News* (February 1). Retrieved July 4, 2007. Online: http://www.dallasnews.com/sharedcontent/ dws/spt/golf/stories/020107dntexcountryclub.1d05f5b.html

Rennie, David. 2006. "Europe Blasts Away Traditional Sex Discrimination at Golf Clubs." *Telegraph* (June 1). Retrieved July 7, 2007. Online: http://www.telegraph.co .uk/core?Content/news/2006/01/05.html

Rich, Frank. 2007. "He Got Out while the Getting Was Good." *New York Times* (August 19): WK10.

Robbins, Alexandra. 2002. *Secrets of the Tomb*. Boston: Little, Brown.

Roberts v. United States Jaycees. 1984. 468 U.S. 609.

Robinson, Clay. 2006. "Gift Giving Comes Early for Lobbyists." *Houston Chronicle* (November 26). Retrieved September 7, 2007. Online: http://www.chron.com/ disp/story.mpl/editorial/robison/4361327.html

Rogers, Barbara. 1988. *Men Only: An Investigation into Men's Organisations*. London: Pandora.

Sandberg, Lisa. 2006. "Politicians' Cash Hunt is on Now." *San Antonio Express* (December 1). Retrieved September 29, 2007. Online: http://www.mysanantonio.com/ news/politics/stories/MYSA120206.01B.lobbygiving.303de88.html

Saporito, Bill. 2002. "Getting Teed Off." *Time* (September 16):50.

Seal, Mark. 1987. "Members Only: The Best Clubs in Texas." *Ultra Magazine* (May): 44–45, 76.

Sherman, Rachel. 2007. *Class Acts: Service and Inequality in Luxury Hotels*. Berkeley: University of California Press.

Shipnuck, Alan. 2004. *The Battle for Augusta National: Hootie, Martha, and the Masters of the Universe*. New York: Simon & Schuster.

Simmel, Georg. [1907] 1978. *The Philosophy of Money*. Ed. and trans. by Tom Bottomore and David Frisby. London: Routledge and Kegan Paul.

Simnacher, Joe. 2006. "John Rauscher, Jr.: Built Dallas Investment Firm." *Dallas Morning News* (November 16).

———. 2007. "Hanna Frank Howell: '32 Debutante Gave Time to Arts, Charities." *Dallas Morning News* (January 19).

Smikle, Joanne L. 2007. "Human & Professional Resources: The Search for Seasonal Staff." *Club Management* (September/October):27–28.

Smith, R. Jeffrey. 2005. "DeLay PAC Is Indicted for Illegal Donations." *Washington Post* (September 9):A3.

Somers, Fred L. 2003. "Reduce New-Member Sponsors? Not So Fast!" *Private Club Advisor* (April). Retrieved September 8, 2007. Online: http://www.privateclubadvisor .com/focus-newmbrsponsors.htm

Steinbreder, John. 2000. "A Perfect Drive—Dick Brooks, Head of Central and South West Recommends the Preston Trail Golf Club." *The Chief Executive* (September):1.

Stolberg, Sheryl Gay. 2007. "Former Chairman of G.O.P. Will Join Bush's Inner Circle." *New York Times* (June 14):A22.

Stromberg, Ernie. 2005. "Headliners History: 1970s." *Headlines* (Winter):14–19. Austin, TX: Headliners Club.

Suellentrop, Chris. 2004. "America's New Political Capital: President Bush Infects Washington with His Favorite Buzzword." Retrieved August 17, 2007. Online: http://www.slate.com/toolbar.aspx?action=print&id=2110256

Texans for Public Justice. 2007. "Austin's Oldest Profession: Texas' Top Lobby Clients and Those Who Serve Them." Retrieved September 7, 2007. Online: http://www .tpj.org/reports/austinsoldest06/clients.html

Traub, James. 2007. "The Measures of Wealth." *New York Times Magazine* (October 14, 2007):21–22.

Tuten, James H. 2005. "Liquid Asset: Madeira Wine and Cultural Capital among Lowcountry Planters, 1735–1900." *American Nineteenth Century History* (June): 173–88.

United Kingdom Parliament. 2004. Joint Committee on the Draft Disability Discrimination Bill. "Chapter 7: Private Clubs and Membership Associations (Clause 5)." Retrieved November 18, 2007. Online: http://www.publications.parliament .uk/pa/jt200304/jtselect/jtdisab/82/8210.htm

Useem, Michael. 1984. *The Inner Circle.* New York: Oxford University Press.

Vachon, Dana. 2005. "The Tao of Skinny-Dipping: Two Private Clubs Keep the Faith of Men Swimming Nude." *New York Times* (April 28):E1, E4.

Veblen, Thorstein. [1899] 1953. *The Theory of the Leisure Class.* New York: New American Library.

Warfield v. The Peninsula Golf and Country Club. 1995. 10 Cal. 4th 594; 896 P.2d 776.

Warner, W. Lloyd, and Paul S. Lunt. 1941. *The Social Life of a Modern Community.* New Haven, CT: Yale University Press.

Wecter, Dixon. 1937. *The Saga of American Society.* New York: Charles Scribner's Sons.

Weinman, Sam. 2003. "Private Clubs Are in the Public Eye." *TheJournalNews.com* (Westchester, NY). Retrieved July 1, 2007. Online: http://www.TheJournalNews.com

Weiss, Phillip. 1989. "Masters of the Universe Go to Camp: Inside the Bohemian Grove." *Spy Magazine* (November):59–78. Retrieved September 23, 2007. Online: http://sociology.ucsc.edu/whorulesamerica/power/bohemian_grove_spy.html

whitehouse.gov. 2007a. "Alberto Gonzales, Attorney General." Retrieved July 27, 2007. Online: http://www.whitehouse.gov/government/gonzales-bio.html

———. 2007b. "President Bush Visits Cleveland, Ohio." White House News Release (July 10). Retrieved November 18, 2007. Online: http://www.whitehouse.gov/news/ release/2007/07/20070710-6.html

Winfrey, Carey. 1978. "In New York, Private Clubs Change with Times." *New York Times* (January 5):B1, B5.

Wolff, Kurt H. 1964. *The Sociology of Georg Simmel.* Trans., ed., and intro. by Kurt H. Wolff. New York: Free Press.

Woolcock, Michael. 2001. "The Place of Social Capital in Understanding Social and Economic Outcomes." *Isuma: Canadian Journal of Policy Research* 2(1):1–17.

Zweigenhaft, Richard L., and G. William Domhoff. 1998. *Diversity in the Power Elite: Have Women and Minorities Reached the Top?* New Haven, CT: Yale University Press.

Index

About the Author

Diana Kendall is professor of sociology at Baylor University where she has been named an Outstanding Professor. She is the author of *The Power of Good Deeds: Privileged Women and the Social Reproduction of the Upper Class* and *Framing Class: Media Representations of Wealth and Poverty*, which was selected as one of the Outstanding Academic Titles in Sociology by the American Library Association. Dr. Kendall is also the author of numerous journal articles and several widely used textbooks, including *Sociology in Our Times* and *Social Problems in a Diverse Society*.